The Law Student's Handbook

THIRD EDITION

Elizabeth Cassell

OLD BAILEY PRESS

OLD BAILEY PRESS
at Holborn College, Woolwich Road,
Charlton, London SE7 8LN

First published 1998
Third edition 2003

ISBN 1 85836 513 9

British Library Cataloguing-in-Publication.

A CIP Catalogue record for this book is available from the British
Library.

Printed and bound in Great Britain.

Contents

Section III: EU Law and Human Rights Law

Historical background – British membership of the European Union – Community legislation – Direct effect – The institutions of the European Community – Websites – Reading a European case

Historical background – The European Convention on Human Rights and the scope of its articles – The Human Rights Act 1998 – Future applications to the European Court of Human Rights

Section IV: Academic Study Skills

Preparation – Understanding – Researching your subject – Constructing your answer – Reflection – Reasoning – Structure – The need to write – Reviewing your structure – Evaluation – Plagiarism

Developing your own style – Gender-free language – Structure – Presentation – Footnotes and bibliography – Citing academic sources – Editing – Thinking like a lawyer – Writing skills self-assessment exercise – Self-assessment checklist – Postscript

Presentation skills generally – Choosing your language – Know your audience – Personal delivery skills – Rehearse and refine – Presentation skills in tutorials and seminars – Presentation skills for interview

Preparation – What do you need to know? – The examination – Exam stress

Section V: The Legal Professions

Solicitors – Barristers – The judiciary

Professional values and conduct

Preface

This book is primarily intended for students who are new to the study of law or new to an LLB programme. Many students are intimidated when taking their first steps in law – the language of the subject can be obscure. Different rules apply to its assessment. This is an attempt to dispel the mystique which surrounds the study and practice of law and to enable the student to make a confident start.

Traditionally, law students came from families with close connections to the law and the law degree was almost an automatic passage into the branch of the legal profession of the student's choice. However, the backgrounds of today's students are more diverse and their future is less certain. Many are first-generation lawyers; if they are mature students, they may have had little formal education before their access course but, at the same time, will bring a wealth of life experience to enhance their perception of law; a high percentage of students in our law faculties come from overseas. I have tried to provide answers to the questions they may be too shy to ask, and which lecturers may treat as assumed knowledge. Students should be active consumers of education, with the confidence to ask for the help they need in order to take responsibility for their own learning, and to learn to appreciate the subject for its own sake.

In recent years, our first year students have responded to a questionnaire which asks *them* what are their perceived study needs – it is hoped that most of these have been addressed in this book.

The proposed changes to the criminal justice system reflected in the second edition are covered in greater detail in the third edition.

The book is divided into five parts. So that students know where to begin when everyone else around them seems to be making a confident start, Part I offers an introduction to the law department, the scheme of study of law and to basic study skills, including use of the law library. Part II includes a *brief* introduction to the legal process – the common law and equity, the court system, doctrine of precedent and principles of statutory interpretation – and Part III is an introduction to European law and a chapter on human rights law. Part IV gives some guidance on the *academic* skills of research, the writing and presentation to be applied to all aspects of the course, including examinations, and Part V covers an introduction to the legal professions, an enlarged chapter on the professional ethic and a career in law and alternative careers to law.

The book includes full case reports for three cases – two English cases and a European case – together with the Queen's Printer's Copy of the Treasure Act 1996. The cases and statute have been printed in full in Appendices A–D so that the student can gain practice and confidence in using source materials. The material has been kept to a minimum to ensure that the student looks deeply into a limited selection of primary sources rather than superficially into more.

The text is designed to be used by the students working alone, perhaps in the summer vacation before they embark on their law course, as well as for use as a text for an introductory skills course, either on an LLB programme or where law is a component course in a programme in another discipline.

Elizabeth Cassell
Department of Law
University of Essex

Acknowledgements

I am truly grateful to Professor Avrom Sherr and to Professor Jonathan Hyman of Rutgers University, New Jersey, for their encouragement and advice in setting up the legal skills programme in the Department of Law at Essex University, to Professors Maurice Sunkin and Geoff Gilbert and to Peter Luther for their unfailing support and encouragement.

Joanna Symons, Senior Adviser in the Essex University Careers Advisory Service, and Caroline Checkley, our Law Librarian, supplied much practical information, as did the law students at Essex.

Professor Brigid Hadfield and Jane Wright helped with the chapter on Human Rights.

David Cassell and Miranda, Mark, Beth and Holly Andras were willing guinea pigs when I needed to test the intelligibility of the text and also supplied much helpful advice and reasons for a break!

Thanks are also due to the many specialists in legal education whose papers I heard at conferences and seminars, in particular to Julian Webb, Graham Gibbs, Philip Jones, Hugh Brayne, Nigel Duncan and Nigel Savage. I was introduced to the dimensions of knowledge (in Chapter 2, section 2.7) at a conference run by the Oxford Centre for Staff Development, in a presentation by Carol Bond of Griffiths University, Australia.

Figures 1 and 2 – from *Preparing to Teach* by Graham Gibbs and Trevor Habeshaw, reprinted by permission of Trevor Habeshaw.

Figure 7 – from *Improving the Quality of Student Learning* by Graham Gibbs, reproduced by permission of Trevor Habeshaw.

The publishers and I would like to thank the Incorporated Council of Law Reporting for England and Wales for its kind permission to reproduce extracts from the Weekly Law Reports, as well as the Council of Europe for its kind permission to include extracts from the European Convention on Human Rights.

UK statutory material in this publication is acknowledged as Crown copyright, and is reproduced with the permission of the Controller of Her Majesty's Stationery Office.

Extracts from the European Court Reports are also reproduced by permission.

Section I
How to Begin

1

The Law Course

1.1 Introduction

1.2 Law department personnel

1.3 The structure of the law course

1.1 Introduction

The law degree has a dual function. First, it is a purely academic course of study which is an end in itself, developing critical and analytical skills in the student which may have a variety of applications in later life. Second, degrees recognised by the Law Society and the Bar Council form the first stage of training for practising lawyers. There is a tension between these two purposes and the need to concentrate on practical legal issues from an early stage, or indeed at all, is disapproved by many academic lawyers who believe that students should be free to pursue their university life without career considerations getting in the way. Yet the law develops through practice and many fine academics are also practitioners so the distinction is perhaps artificial. In any event, practitioners favour a broad liberal education on degree courses. Practical legal skills are usually developed at the next stage of training.

Perhaps it can be said that the best law degree enables students to think like lawyers and lawyers to think like human beings! The best education for any career is a broad one which develops the reasoning powers of the student and prepares them for a full and happy life. This is sometimes overlooked by the students themselves under the pressures of the course in pursuit of a 2:1 degree.

There is now a much greater diversity of students whose needs must be catered for. Twenty years ago the vast majority of law students came up to university straight from the sixth form with recent A Levels. Now the student intake is much more wide-ranging. Many institutions have a high proportion of overseas students and a large number of mature students.

Most law departments do not expect the new intake of students to have any prior knowledge of law. Until quite recently, it was unusual for students to have studied law at GCSE, or at A Level or on a law access course, although many had family connections with legal practice. Yet your choice of a law course is almost certainly an informed choice. Take time now to consider what attracted you to law in the first place. It could be:

- a passion for justice;
- a passion for order;
- the human interest;
- the social implications of legislation;
- a well paid job at the end of the course;
- other considerations to do with your personal history.

Consider where you stand on the debate on membership of the European Union and other political issues with legal implicatons, and try to understand the reasons for thinking the way you do. You should get into the habit of reading a broadsheet newspaper and listening to the news programmes on radio and television – the *Today* programme at breakfast time on Radio 4 has particularly good news coverage giving the background to many issues of importance to lawyers.

Consider your own educational history and how you are influenced by it. Think through the stages by which you decided to study law: what encouraged you and what held you back; which events were turning points in your education and which teachers were most influential in your development and why. There are no right answers to these questions other than the honest ones. The purpose of this self analysis is to give you a degree of self-knowledge which will enable you to respond effectively to all the demands which will be made on you in your new environment. If you know where you are coming from, it will be easier for you to start the course with confidence and to take charge of your learning.

When you enter the law department, you must be ready to claim it as your territory. It is very easy to skirt round its edges wondering what is expected of you, never quite knowing how or whom to ask for directions. The study of law must be tackled thoroughly and systematically but, as with any other degree courses, it is the responsibility of the **student** to devise an effective system of study. For every hour of classroom contact the student should put in three additional hours of effective private study. This amounts to a 40-hour week, with yet more time for the preparation of assignments and examination revision.

The great temptation is always to concentrate on the subjects in which there are pressing time-sensitive deadlines for coursework, but at the end of the course you will probably be required to take a rigorous examination in each of your subjects when your performance will suffer if you have not worked consistently on all subjects throughout the year. The assessment of nearly all law courses presents both long-term and short-term goals and being able to perform effectively to all these requirements is a fundamental part of your legal education.

1.2 Law department personnel

The law department has both administrative and teaching staff. Increasingly lecturers have heavy administrative duties and academic research requirements as well as a teaching load. Nevertheless, they will place a high priority on student needs outside the lecture theatre and the tutorial room. They have three primary functions in relation to students – as lecturers, tutors and personal tutors.

In most institutions, academic and administrative staff reserve time during which they are available to see students. As far as possible, these hours should be respected so that staff are available as promised and students do not make unnecessary demands on staff time outside the advertised times except by appointment or in an emergency.

Lecturers

In their role as lecturers, university teachers set the pattern of the course, emphasising the points they consider important. Very often they are instrumental in setting the examination papers. They deliver the lectures which are the keynote of the course to be undertaken. As course lecturer, they have a general responsibility rather than a responsibility for individual students. There will usually be a team of lecturers covering the syllabus throughout the year.

Tutors

Tutors have responsibility for small group teaching. The lecturer nearly always acts as tutor to some of the groups. The tutor sets the tutorial work and leads the tutorial group. The tutor's principal role is to ensure that everyone in the group understands the subject or can ask questions to clear up points of difficulty, and to make sure that the discussion in class is not monopolised by a small group of students. If you need help with the subject outside the tutorial group, you should arrange to see your tutor – but you should first try to work things out for yourself.

Your personal tutor (personal adviser)

This is the member of staff who is responsible for your pastoral care, so that if you have personal, family or accommodation problems, the personal tutor may be able to help. Some of these matters may be sufficiently serious to count as extenuating circumstances when your performance is assessed, so it is always advisable to inform your personal tutor in writing, supported by medical evidence if appropriate, when there is a real danger that your work will be adversely affected.

Personal tutors may also be able to help in the event of a dispute between you and one of your tutors or with student members of your tutorial group. If disciplinary proceedings are ever taken against you, your personal tutor will help you to defend yourself and may act as your advocate.

One further important function of the personal tutor is to provide references after you leave. So it is advisable for you to maintain regular contact during your university career even if it is a relatively uneventful one.

With increasing constraints on staff time, some universities are reducing the number of personal tutors or replacing the system with a central counselling service. This is a policy which is deeply regretted by many university teachers and by their students. If you ever need help and do not know where to turn, there is almost always a sympathetic teacher to whom you can turn for assistance in finding proper help. Consult a member of staff whom you trust.

The dean

The dean of faculty is a senior member of the academic staff, responsible for maintaining academic standards within the law department, for disciplinary proceedings and for matters relating to the award of degrees and prizes.

The head of department

The head of department is often elected from among the academic staff and is responsible for setting and co-ordinating the policy of the department including the implementation of new courses. The head of department usually chairs the staff/student liaison committee when representatives from each year meet with staff representatives to put forward new ideas and to air student grievances.

The senior tutor (senior adviser)

The senior tutor has overall responsibility for the pastoral care of students in the Department and can be contacted in emergencies when your personal tutor is not available.

The year co-ordinator

The year co-ordinator has responsibility for the academic work of students in each year of study and may be responsible for granting or refusing extensions if essay deadlines are not met. The year co-ordinator is also responsible for monitoring the progress of individual students in all subjects so that if necessary assistance can be offered. Student attendance records are kept for this purpose.

The departmental secretaries

The departmental secretaries are responsible for the administration of the department. They give out handouts, take in essays, often give out the essay marks and generally are a mine of information about the department, including staff availability. They have a very heavy workload in addition to answering student queries, etc. Please respect their office hours.

You

If there were no students, there would be no department. You must be prepared to contribute to the running of the department by being punctual and well prepared. There will be opportunities for you to stand for office as a student representative and for the student law society which runs many entertaining and informative activities providing an invaluable background to your course of study.

Your main duty is to be a good student and a considerate colleague of other students. The requirements for private study are described in the next chapter.

1.3 The structure of the law course

On most English law degree courses, four or five subjects are studied in each year. On a modular course, there will be a greater choice of subjects, some studied for a term rather than for the whole year. The Law Society and the Bar Council require that seven core subjects are studied by all students who intend to qualify as solicitors or barristers. Furthermore, the university may make additional subjects compulsory for all students – for example, the study of jurisprudence (the philosophy of law).

There is much more law to be studied now than in previous generations. In order to demonstrate this point, Professor Len Sealy weighed his volumes of the 1948 Companies legislation and their 1984 equivalents (LS Sealy, *Company Law and Commercial Reality*, Sweet & Maxwell, 1984). In 1948 they weighed one-and-a-half pounds and in 1984 over seven pounds! There is much more law to be fitted into the same courses. Moreover, much of the law you study at university will be obsolete by the time you begin to practice. The Criminal Justice and Public Order Act 1994 and the Family Law Act 1996 have transformed their fields of legislation. The law degree must prepare students to cope with these changes.

Because of the size of student year groups, and because of the nature of the material to be studied, most first year courses and many subsequent courses consist of two lectures per week delivered to the whole year group and one tutorial per fortnight for which work is set. Tutorial groups consist of up to twenty students and are principally intended to test the effectiveness of the student's private study. Staff/student contact is thus very much less than on an A Level course or access course.

Lectures

Lectures are intended to be a guide for your private study. It is impossible for the lecturer to cover the subject in sufficient depth in a mere two hours a week, and if you rely entirely on your lecture notes in preparation for the examination you will barely have enough material to pass.

The lecture is the way in which new, complex material is introduced to the student. Explanations therefore are intentionally simplistic to enable the student to grasp the essential elements of the subject and then to go away and read widely to extend and deepen the knowledge acquired in the lecture.   The lecturer may have written and researched extensively in the field of the lecture, but it is important to remember that, although this work may lead to a clear authoritative delivery of the lecture, a thorough study of the subject demands a great deal more information gathering on the part of the student. The lecture is only the tip of the iceberg.

Lectures should not be missed. The lecturer will emphasise the aspects of the course that he/she considers important and interesting, together with background information which will help your overworked memory to retain the highly technical material.   In addition, the lectures will keep you abreast of important changes in the law. The law is in a state of constant change and development. Even in these days of desktop publishing and frequent new editions, the prescribed textbooks cannot contain the most recent legislation and decided cases. These will be more extensively covered in the lectures as the new material may be of the utmost significance. Important announcements are given out at lectures, including information as to the examiner's expectations for assessed work.

Lectures are usually heard in silence, often with little interaction between lecturer and students – it is for the lecturer to set the style of the lecture. It is considered extremely discourteous both to the lecturer and to fellow students to talk or to make any disturbance in lectures (you should take careful note of this if you have been educated in places where such disruptions are accepted). Yet, in order to make the best use of the lecture, the student must find some way of interacting with the lecture so as to maintain concentration and to retain the information.

Many students take notes of everything that is said in the lecture. In order to do so, they ruin their handwriting, yet produce barely legible scripts of data which has had little chance to pass through the brain on the way from the ear to the paper. The very act of listening to the lecture rather than reading the subject in a book or on the internet processes the information in a different way and will help you to recall it later. Most lecturers use OHP transparencies or Powerpoint as visual aids to help your concentration. It is more important to look up and follow the lecture rather than to note down the contents of these visual aids. The lecturer may well use mannerisms, tone of voice, catchphrases or anecdotes precisely in order that the student will be enabled to recall important, but not necessarily riveting, information.

Fifteen to twenty minutes into the lecture, student concentration falls away so that, unless steps are taken to recapture the students' attention, much of what is said will be missed – until the final five minutes when the audience wakes up again, knowing release is nigh. If you are aware of this concentration curve (see *Figure 1*), you can combat it for yourself – although experienced lecturers will pause for questions to be asked or a specific point to be discussed to break the pattern so that the concentration curve is renewed at intervals (see *Figure 2*).

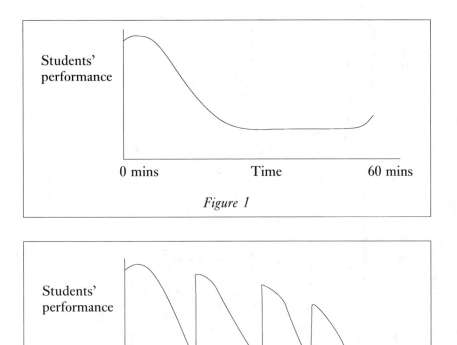

Figure 1

Figure 2

One useful technique which assists concentration and interaction is known as mindmapping – drawing a map of the lecture, starting at the centre of a blank page with the main idea of the lecture and then developing a design to incorporate all the essential information as the theme is developed by the lecturer. A mind map of this chapter will be found at *Figure 3*. As you draw your map, your mind sorts and grades the information, selecting the most important points so that you make the subject matter your own rather than the lecturer's. This is much more effective than taking down the lecture word for word and unselectively by linear note-taking. As with every other form of lecture note-taking, however, the result must be expanded and developed through your own private study.   Your note-taking will be vastly improved if you develop for yourself a set of abbreviations – 'P' for Plaintiff, 'C' for Claimant, 'D' for Defendant, 'H' for husband, 'W' for wife and so on. Devise similar abbreviations for frequently used legal phrases – '3p' for third party, 'b/a' for bank account, for example.

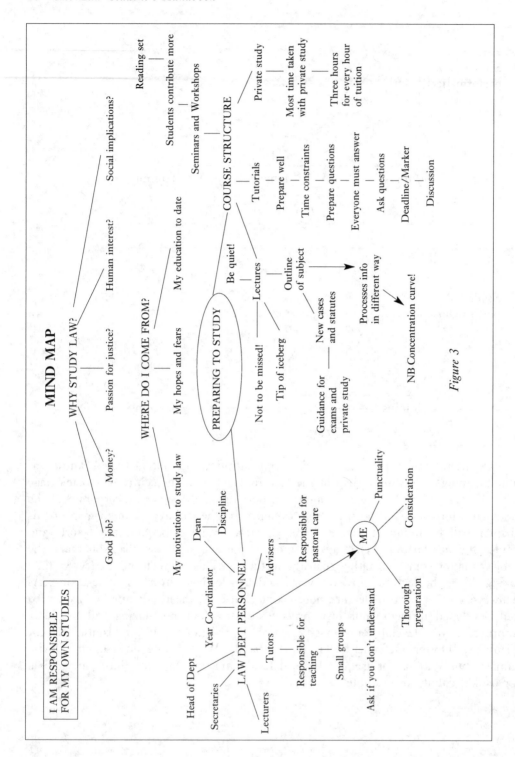

Figure 3

Some – but by no means all – lecturers permit students to tape record lectures and this may be useful if English is not your first language or if a number of lectures must be missed through illness. However, listening to a tape is not nearly as satisfactory as listening to a live lecture. There is a real danger that much time will be wasted in transcription of the lecture – or indeed in transcription of lecture notes. Whether taped or noted, the resulting material should be used in its original form – copying out lecture material is a timewasting, counterproductive exercise.

Most lecturers will give out handouts to enable you to follow the lecture with an accurate reference list to cases and statutes. Useful quotations may also be included together with a reading list. This information is invaluable and it may well be that, if you have to miss a lecture, you can catch up by following the recommended reading rather than by borrowing lecture notes from another student or having the lecture taped. Some lecturers provide a complete set of notes for each lecture to free the student to participate in discussion, problem-solving or critical analysis of the material under discussion. Handouts and lecturers' materials are often available online.

No one will force you to attend lectures, but if you choose not to do so your studies will be impoverished and your confidence will be diminished. You will also be in danger of creating the impression that you have a careless attitude to study which will not be helpful when staff are asked for a reference for you. Law is a social science requiring social contact with lecturer and fellow students. Study in isolation is much more difficult for most students. The discipline of regular attendance at lectures develops good habits of work for the rest of your life.

If you do not understand the subject matter of the lecture, try to clear up the difficulty by your own reading (or by asking fellow students). If you are still unsure at the time of your tutorial, be sure to make a note of the point so that you can ask the lecturer or tutor. If you let the misunderstandings go unresolved, you will lose confidence and may fall behind in your studies.

Tutorials

In most subjects, you will be allocated to a small group which will meet at weekly or fortnightly intervals to review recent work. Often work will be set for the tutorial, usually based on past examination questions and this is tested orally in the tutorial. Ideally, the tutorial is also a forum in which students can test their own ideas and discuss the concepts in depth, but with the dramatic increase in recent years in the student:staff ratio, and the volume of material which has to be covered, this is simply not feasible in the fifty minutes or so allocated to the tutorial. It is therefore essential to ensure that the time is put to the best possible use. This entails thorough preparation on the part of *every* student in the group. The group simply cannot afford to carry passengers. Yet this is a problem which groups appear to be reluctant to tackle for themselves.

Your primary duty is to take responsibility for your own work – to make sure you are as thoroughly prepared as possible. If others persistently arrive unprepared, relying on you to do the work for them, it is difficult for the tutorial to progress beyond the basic material of the lecture and you may feel embarassed to discuss your exciting new ideas on the subject. If you are one of the shy ones and don't speak up, or if you persistently come to tutorials underprepared, you must take steps to understand why you have adopted this pattern of behaviour – it can serve no purpose. Most student groups are very supportive of people whom they know have difficulty in overcoming shyness.

While the tutor should not allow such a situation to persist, very often peer group pressure is much more effective in getting wayward students to toe the line. It is a matter of preference whether the tutor asks each student to contribute to the discussion in turn or allows a free discussion with students contributing voluntarily. If you wish to contribute to the discussion in tutorials, it is up to you to make sure you do – even if other students seem to be more articulate and better informed.

In a recent student survey, there were an equal number of complaints from the articulate and the shy students that participation in tutorials was not shared. This highlights one of the most important skills derived from the tutorial system – being aware of the needs of the group so that the work is properly shared. This is particularly important when student groups are of mixed nationalities and mixed educational backgrounds.

One student in the survey observed: 'I go to the tutorials with more questions than answers and I've found that tutorials are the most productive way which helps me to understand the subject.' No-one expects students to have all the answers when they come to tutorials but they are expected to try to understand as much of the material as possible, and to make a genuine attempt to answer the questions set. If you ask for clarification of points which you do not understand, you may well be helping the entire group. Some will not even have considered the point you raise, while others are too timid to ask. Good tutors will invite queries at the beginning and at the end of the tutorial.

Tutorials are good examination practice. You will get a feel for the necessary depth of answer that is required of you and you will have a chance to construct and deliver your own answers. The tutorial group is a safe place to try out ideas without fear of failure. The very fact that you are prepared to advance your ideas is all that is required at this stage, provided that you have taken time to structure your argument.

The tutorial sets a deadline – by the time your tutorial comes round, you should have a working knowledge of the topics set on the tutorial sheet. The sheets are invaluable for revision purposes. With time constraints and larger classes it is not always possible to cover the full range of work set in the time. This raises a dilemma for the student and for the tutor – is it better to cover some of the work in the appropriate depth rather than all the work set superficially? Inevitably this depends on the subject matter. Sometimes it may be even better to abandon the tutorial sheet altogether and to allow a free ranging discussion of some related topic of interest to the group. A balance must be struck between all these preferences and this can only be done effectively if every student prepares and participates. The tutorial sheet can in any event be used as a private study guide and the tutor is then available to answer questions and resolve difficulties in time set aside for private consultation.

At the end of the tutorial cycle, the student will have approached the subject matter in a number of different ways – through attending lectures, through private study and through small group discussion. This initial work is vital to success on the course and the more effort that is made at this stage the greater the likelihood of success in the course assessments. If for any reason you must miss your own tutorial group, it is almost always possible to join another and keep up with the course. If, however, this is not possible, you can still work through the tutorial sheet on your own and ask your tutor to mark your answers.

Seminars and workshops

In recent years, there has been a preference for seminar teaching. Seminar groups tend to be somewhat larger than tutorial groups. Instead of being given a lecture, the students are set reading from textbooks, cases and statutes, articles on the point of law or on the social, political or economic background to the subject. Points are then raised for discussion so that there is much more interaction between lecturer and students. Sometimes students are selected to lead the seminar. This method has the great advantage of putting the student more in charge of their own learning so that the lecturer is a facilitator rather than an expert controlling access to all the knowledge.

Workshops follow the same format and are used for skills training on options such as client interviewing and advocacy.

2

Effective Private Study

At university, the whole emphasis of your work is shifted on to private study. Lectures give the student direction and tutorials provide markers along the way by which time particular subject areas should have been covered. Participating in tutorials also gives the student an indication of what remains to be done in order to perform well in assessments and examinations. The more efficiently you manage your private study time, the better your performance will be.

2.1 Study materials

Reading lists for all your courses will be supplied by the lecturer or tutor at or shortly before the beginning of the course. If a choice of books is given, look at them all carefully in the library or the bookshop before making your choice. Usually the teacher will have a stated preference and you should, of course, pay heed to this. Where the choice is left to you, however, ask for recommendations from students in other years. Don't rush into a choice – it may be better to borrow from the library or photocopy the reading for the first tutorial than to buy a book which doesn't suit you.

A textbook is essential and a casebook is highly desirable. (Some lecturers may choose a cases and materials book instead of a textbook as their main text.) The casebook will contain extracts from the judgments of key cases. Some also include

15

extracts from learned articles, statutes and contextual materials such as the Law Commission reports. Some give a commentary on the materials and questions for the student to answer. It is very useful to be able to refer to the words of key judgments and to see what was actually said by the judges rather than what textbook writers said they said!

In some courses, a statute book is essential. These give the key sections of Acts of Parliament to be studied on the course. Usually the approved statute book can be taken into the examination room for reference. Therefore the text should not be marked except by underlining and highlighting, and you should choose a student edition with no annotation. If you take your statute book to all lectures and tutorials and have the text open before you, this will help you to understand the legislation much better than trying to mark up your copy at the very end of the course when you are preparing for examinations.

You may also find it useful to have a shorter, simpler introductory text to help you to grasp the essentials of a subject you find difficult. This should be bought in addition to the set books, certainly not instead of them.

Law books are very expensive and, with today's extreme pressures on student budgets, it is important that any books you buy will be of value to you. There are usually plenty of secondhand copies available which can be bought from students in other years, at a book sale or at the campus shop. But beware – out of date copies are worse than useless because they will omit key changes in the law. Check with your tutors which editions can be bought safely. If you have to buy a new textbook, you can sell it next year and recover some of the cost. One way of cutting the expense of textbooks is to share with other students so that between you a good selection can be obtained.

You may also find a small law dictionary of use to you. This will enable you to look up the terms used in lectures which you don't understand. There will be dictionaries available for use in the reference section of the law library if you can't afford your own.

2.2 An introduction to the law library

By far the most important source of study materials is the law library. In the first weeks of term there will be guided tours for students. Be sure you take advantage of these and familiarise yourself with the library catalogue and the location of the essential law reports and journals (see Chapter 3). If it is now too late for you to take one of the official visits, don't be afraid to ask the law librarian to show you round – it may be as well to check whether any other students would like to join you. You must make yourself feel comfortable and confident about using the library at a very early stage. If all your reading is from textbooks and casebooks, you will miss one of the essential elements of your legal education – ie, working with source materials – and you will never attain the required standard in your assessments and examinations. Reading the full case, rather than the extract in the casebook, deepens your understanding of how law is made and how and why the law has changed.

2.3 Study methods

In our recent survey of student study methods, the students were asked how many hours they devoted to each subject and how much of their study time was used productively. Nearly everyone responded that all the time was productive! If you are to have enough time for all the other aspects of university life, you must make sure that this is in fact the case.

Reading the responses, we wondered whether this particular cohort of students was never bored or demotivated by the reading matter, never distracted by their love life or money worries, never too tired to study after a late night or unsure of what was expected of them – or simply desperate for a cup of coffee or distracted by the view from the window. These are the normal hazards of any course of private study and they can be overcome.

There are two objectives of all work that is set on the law degree: first, to gain a good general knowledge of the subject area together with the skill to apply that knowledge. The second objective is to enable you to answer specific questions raised on the tutorial sheet and in examinations. This may entail solving a legal problem or understanding set reading which may include a case report or a statute.

The work set for tutorials should provide a focus for your study. Although you will have to read more widely than is strictly necessary to answer the questions set, you can search for the answers while you are working through the materials. With this focus, you will notice other aspects of the subject which have not previously been obvious. Your concentration will be improved because you are reading for a specific purpose rather than generally.

You should develop a system of study. First, you should read your lecture notes as soon as you can after the lecture while it is fresh in your mind. You should fill in any points you missed and mark any points which you do not fully understand so that you can cover these in your reading and, if necessary, ask the lecturer or tutor for help. Then you should read the notes through again when you are preparing for the tutorial to see what is relevant to the work set and also for your general information. The lecturer may have given further information as to what is expected of you in tutorial.

Look at the lecture handouts to ensure you read what is set and to note down any key cases which should be studied from the law reports. It is certainly not necessary to read every case on the handout. You may wish to photocopy the major cases so that you have them with you for writing essays and for revision. Alternatively, you can record them in a card index – key facts, main issues, ratio decidendi, useful quotations, etc. (See Chapter 6.)

Then you must tackle the set reading. There may be several chapters of text to read. Stop at intervals to make sure you have read and understood what you are reading. Keep looking for points to help you with the tutorial work. Keeping up with the reading is one of the more difficult aspects of private study. It is all too easy to lose concentration. If your eyes glaze over and slip down the pages, stop. You are not studying effectively and you are wasting time. Take a short break and then go over what you have missed – or if you have been reading for more than an hour, take a longer break. If you vary your reading between notes, textbooks and cases, you will maintain concentration for longer. Once you have finished the reading, make brief notes for later reference when revising and make other notes specifically for the tutorial.

This thorough preparation is the essence of good study and good performance in assessment and tutorial. Look at the source materials – see Chapter 6 on how to read a case and Chapter 7 on how to read a statute.

It may be that you have been told to read an article from one of the law journals so make sure you have a copy to hand in good time. Note the main points made in the article and consider whether they are valid – much legal writing is open to challenge and you must form a reasoned opinion on the writer's views (including mine!). If you have difficulty in finding cases and articles recommended for reading, inform the tutor or the librarian. If you do find the materials, make sure you replace them promptly for the use of other students.

2.4 Study diary and record keeping

You may find it helpful to keep a study diary, noting the work you have done and when and how long it has taken you. In particular, over the course of a month or so, notice when it is easy for you to study and when it is difficult and why – for example, it is rarely easy to study immediately after lunch. If you can work out a pattern, make sure you tackle the tasks you find most difficult at a time when you are most alert.

Make a note of how long each assignment takes you. Although this will probably be less as you get further into the course, it will help you to be realistic when you are planning your time. Similarly, you may find it useful to keep a reading log – either as a diary or in a card index system – giving references to material you have found particularly helpful so that you can find it easily for essay preparation or revision.

Remember that all these techniques should save you time, not create more work. If you can devise a systematic scheme of study which works for you, you will build you confidence and free your time for more leisure pursuits and a more interesting, less stressful, life generally.

2.5 Time management

Your work will consist of the study of four or five subjects, in all of which you will be set deadlines. At the same time, you are having to cope with a new environment. If you can learn to manage your time effectively now, this will help you throughout your degree course and into your professional life. Once you have established your best work pattern, you can work out your study timetable for the day, the week, the term, the year – and when you have to work outside term time, for the vacations. The timetable must be as realistic as possible and should take account of your need to look after yourself, to eat, to get some fresh air and exercise and a social life.

Not only do you have to cover the ground in one subject and do well in that – to do really well on the degree you must do well in all subjects and you must resist the temptation to neglect some subjects for others – regardless of personal preference, the greater demands of some lecturers or conflicting priorities and deadlines. More than anything else learnt on any degree course, this ability to balance priorities and perform tasks on time will stand you in good stead in professional life.

As you are set the work, allocate a priority to it, taking into account the deadline and the nature of the work. It helps to keep an up-to-date list of all you have to do – assessed coursework, going to the bank or the launderette, attending Law Society functions or family gatherings or going out with friends. Consider keeping a priority grid (see *Figure 4*).

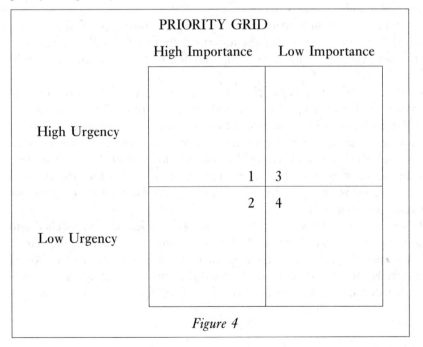

Figure 4

Note: The tasks should be rated according to their importance to *you*.

How would you balance the following priorities?

* essay to be handed in in two days;
* tutorial preparation for next day;
* tutorial preparation for three days' time;
* assemble scarce library materials for next essay – deadline three weeks;
* out of cash – must get to bank;
* must buy present for grandmother's 80th birthday at weekend;
* lecture attendance;
* owe letter to best friend at home;
* meeting to set up joint study project to be handed in next term;
* Law Society commitee meeting.

If the essay is part of your assessed coursework, this must be given a very high priority but is this as important/urgent as getting to the bank or sending off the present so that it arrives on time?

If you neglect your tutorial preparation and attendance, two more courses may suffer and you may not be able to keep up in them. The same can be said for lecture attendance.

If you don't get to the library early, it may take you much longer to assemble all the materials or you may miss some altogether.

If you skip the Law Society meeting, you may miss the chance of an interesting job which would look good on your CV.

You could offend your fellow students if you don't turn up to the project meeting and you may be allocated one of the less rewarding parts of the project.

The letter to your friend may have been on your list of things to do for months now.

If you review your priorities regularly, it is much more likely that you can foresee the conflicts and take steps to deal with them in time. The grid can be reviewed every day and the tasks moved to different boxes – or completed to time. Simply listing and numbering the tasks for the day increases the motivation to get through them all. Another way of keeping the backlog down is to have a rule that every day you do the most urgent thing and then one thing from the list that you really want to do, one thing that you have been putting off for a long time and one thing that you really don't want to do.

If you find unexpectedly that you have free time – say a lecture is cancelled and you have an hour to spare – use it to tackle the list. Using the example, you could go to the bank and buy the birthday present in an hour, or you could go the library for the essay materials, or you could bring forward the project meeting. Think now of your own circumstances – what could you take off your own list if you had an hour to spare?

Remember the top ten time wasters:

* procrastination;
* inability to say no;
* lack of self discipline;
* personal disorganisation;
* attempting to do too much;
* interruptions;
* peer pressure;
* not knowing what is expected of you;
* no priorities, no planning ahead;
* crisis management.

We all succumb to some or all of these at some time in the term, but if you are aware of how damaging they are, you are more likely to keep them at bay.

2.6 Your working environment

If you can create a pleasant working environment where you can work comfortably without distractions, your life will be much easier. In fact, you need two working environments – one where you live and one where you work – probably the common room or library.

You need to assemble the tools for the work so that no time is wasted in searching for pens, paper, etc. Organise a good filing system for your notes, handouts and photocopies – one big lever arch file for each subject is a good simple way to do this, with a smaller day file to keep your current papers for the work that you need to keep with you. Be sure to choose a good pen which makes your handwriting as legible as possible. Ball point pens should be avoided if possible. A highlighter for marking-up photocopies and handouts will save you time. All work that is handed in for marking should be securely stapled and word processed, so make sure your working environment includes access to a computer or word processor. Make sure you know what computer facilities are made available to students and how long in advance you must allow before an essay deadline to be able to have your work printed to hand in.

If you have university accommodation, you will almost certainly have a suitable desk and bookshelves and a comfortable chair. If the chair is uncomfortable, it may be an investment to buy one that suits you better. The height of the chair should enable you to rest your arms on the table at the height of your elbow and with your feet squarely on the floor and your back well supported by the chair, so that neither your back nor your arms are strained by long periods of sitting in the same position. Your desk should be big enough for you to have your writing materials in front of you and reference books around you – again without having to strain any parts of your anatomy with long periods of sitting. Even when you have achieved this you should get up and walk around at regular intervals. Ideally, you should work in good natural daylight supplemented by an anglepoise lamp when light levels are low.

It is best to work at a desk or table rather than in an easy chair but if you have a lot of reading to do, you may find it easier to concentrate if you can change your posture and work from an easy chair which supports your back properly but not one that is so comfortable that you are likely to fall asleep! Be aware of possible distractions – don't work where it is easy for you to look out of the window or where you are distracted by possible temptations or by the pile of washing up!

When you are planning your working day, try to avoid times when your living quarters are noisy – around teatime, for example, or at half term when the children are at home. If you need to work at these times, it may be best to work in the library or well away from other members of the household if the noise levels or demands on your time are likely to be too distracting. Another useful tool might be a large 'DO NOT DISTURB' notice – as long as you show that you mean exactly that.

Library facilities in most universities are usually over-subscribed nowadays and you may be disturbed by chatter or queries from other students. Check on the library opening times – if the library is open over the weekend, you may find it quieter then. Often the library is less busy first thing in the morning and last thing before closing. This may also be the best time to track down source materials. If you want to work away from your fellow students on the course, try a floor of the library where books on other subjects are kept.

2.7 The goals of effective study

The main goals must be to acquire, understand, retain and be able to apply knowledge. Consider the following dimensions of knowledge:

- Knowledge as a complete picture, a jigsaw – seeing the surface;
- Knowledge as a big bank of everything you know – seeing beyond the surface;
- Knowledge as a mass, it accumulates – seeing behind what they say;
- Knowledge is how things work, why they are like that and the relations betweeen things – turning it around;
- Knowledge is ideas joining together and forming a whole body – a visual picture which you can move all round and come back to the beginning, a three-dimensional maze of interconnected pathways;
- Knowledge can be modified and changed – seeing the problem in relation to what one knows, seeing the key issues and the supporting material;
- Knowledge can be viewed from different perspectives – seeing different ways of looking at it;
- Knowledge is the insight behind the concept in relation to other things – drawing connections, seeing what determines it, makes it stand out;

- Knowledge is a whole rather than parts – putting it all together and looking at the bigger picture of things that are around you;
- Knowledge is applying new material to experience – putting meaning to experience;
- Knowledge is building on what you have – turning the knowledge around, changing it in your head;
- Knowledge is the building blocks of understanding and meaning – it is constructed on the basis of what you get which in turn changes that construction; and, finally,
- KNOWLEDGE IS THE SUM TOTAL OF WHAT YOU ARE.

You can see from these definitions that the more complex the material you study, the deeper and more complete your knowledge. Some of the definitions talk of building blocks, and in some subjects you need to acquire a number of blocks of material before you can see the complete picture.

If you study only from your lecture notes and the most basic introductory textbook, you will acquire only a superficial knowledge with little understanding. If you apply yourself to more difficult reading, you may have some initial difficulty in grasping the subject matter, but once you have done so you will have a deeper understanding of the subject and will be working towards the required depth of knowledge to do well in your assignments and to develop the instincts necessary for the practice of law. If you go on to study the cases themselves, to look at the exact words of the judgments and the statutes and to read the commentaries of academic lawyers, your knowledge will be yet deeper and you then have plenty of material on which to base your own analysis of the subject matter.

When it comes to applying this knowledge, to essay questions or problems, you must be selective and critical. As the pressures mount during the term, there may be a strong temptation to abandon this deep approach to learning – if this happens, go back over your material during the vacation and catch up with your studies.

2.8 Answering problem questions

There is a simple formula for answering problem questions – ISAC:

- Identify the Issues;
- State the law;
- Apply the law;
- Draw a Conclusion.

This formula will be further elaborated in Chapter 10.

A problem question will give you a set of facts and ask you to apply the law to them. Sometimes you are asked to discuss the question generally, sometimes to advise one party. So first you identify the issues which the problem raises. Needless to say, there will be some complications since the object of the exercise is to test your legal reasoning skills. There may be additional factors which do not feature in the cases you have studied. Analysing the problem and pointing out the difficulties and discrepancies is one of the main points of the exercise.

Once you have identified the issues, you must state the law applicable. This means you must cite the **relevant** cases and statute law. This is not an invitation to restate the whole of the lecture notes or the set reading but to be selective. The statement of the law should include all the law – not just the law which will assist A if you are asked to advise A, but also any arguments which can be used against her. You must give the good news and the bad news if you are to do your job properly.

Then you must apply the law to the facts. There may be cases where similar facts have differing outcomes. There may be a definition in statute law which is not quite met by the facts of the problem. Again, the object of the exercise is for the student to note the differences. This may mean that on the basis of the law as it stands, there is no clear-cut outcome to the problem – a real hazard of real litigation.

However, the final part of the exercise is to put yourself in the judge's seat and to give a reasoned decision based on the facts and the law. Think of the scales of justice and balance the points at issue and reach a **reasoned** conclusion. You may at this point wish to make your own comment on the state of the law and the outcome of the case. Avoid the temptation to be emotive – the aim is to display the skill of objective reasoning and the common law places a high emphasis on certainty which should deliver a just result for all by laying down clear rules.

2.9 Working in groups

Sometimes assignments and projects are set for groups of students. This gives you valuable training in working as a team with people whom you would not necessarily choose. You might also consider forming discussion groups offering mutual support and assistance. These can be particularly helpful in the period before examinations when each member of the group takes it in turn to teach the others a particular topic for revision. Groups can be helpful for the collection of study materials and the sharing of textbooks.

The one danger, though, is that there must be no co-operation or collaboration in the preparation of any assessed coursework and this work must be kept entirely separate. Collusion and plagiarism are serious disciplinary matters so beware. (see Chapter 11).

If you can be disciplined in your study methods now, you will develop good practice for your working life and your organisational skills will lead to greater clarity of thinking and expression.

3

The Law Library

The best way to use this chapter is to take it to the library so that you can find and inspect the volumes referred to.

3.1 Using the library

The quality of the law library should be one of the reasons for choosing to study at a particular university – the extent of its collection of law reports and learned journals, the availability of the most up-to-date textbooks and access for students to the principal electronic retrieval systems should all be key factors.

Yet often the library can be an intimidating environment for new students. If you miss the library tour at the beginning of your first term, this feeling may persist. If, for any reason, you have to miss the official tours, it may be worth asking the law librarian to give you a brief tour of the main facilities. In any event, the staff at the help desk will help you track down your immediate needs if you cannot work the system out for yourself.

Catalogues for books and journals received by the library from the 1980s onwards will almost certainly be computerised. Earlier acquisitions may still be catalogued manually on an index system. Each book is given a reference – usually a collection of letters and numbers according to subject and author. There should be a booklet available to students explaining the cataloguing system which can be kept for reference. You should familiarise yourself with the numbering system for the law library.

It should be possible to access the computerised catalogue by author, by title or by both or by key words in the subject area. The more clearly you define the book you are looking for, the shorter your search will be. The catalogue will also tell you whether the book is available for loan. It may be part of the short-term loan collection, only available for use in the library during a short period at a time, or it may be on loan to another borrower. The publication may not be displayed on the library shelves – it may be stored in an archive and available only after the librarian has had time to retrieve it. Some publications will not be available in the library's collection but the library may be able to find a copy for you through the inter-library loan service. This service is normally only available to students with the permission of a lecturer or tutor.

At the beginning of your law course you should locate in the library the main source materials that you require. Although the full library collection may be very comprehensive, the materials you actually require for your course of study will probably be confined to a much more manageable area.

3.2 The law reports

The main series of law reports will be arranged together in alphabetical order according to title. The earliest law reports are known as the *Yearbooks* and go back to the thirteenth century. It is unlikely that you will need to refer to these in the early part of your law degree. Sometimes the collection begins with the *English Reports*, a reprint of the nominate reports, the series of law reports compiled between the sixteenth and nineteenth centuries which were usually known by the name of the law reporter who compiled them – *Coke's Reports*, etc. The series has an index listing (in alphabetical order) cases heard before 1865.

The principal series of modern law reports is the General Series produced by the Incorporated Council for Law Reporting – known collectively as the *Law Reports*. These are regarded as the most authoritative case reports. There are four current series: Appeal Cases (AC) which reports cases heard in the Court of Appeal, House of Lords and by the Privy Council; Chancery Division (Ch) which reports cases heard in the Chancery Division and appeals from the Chancery Division to the Court of Appeal; Queen's Bench (QB) which reports cases heard in the Queen's Bench Division and appeals from the Queen's Bench Division to the Court of Appeal; and Family Division (Fam) reporting cases heard in the Family Division and appeals from the Family Division to the Court of Appeal. Until 1972 the Family Division was known as the Probate, Divorce and Admiralty Division and the volumes of reports were known under this title and cited as 'P'.

The Incorporated Council of Law Reporting also produces *Weekly Law Reports* – produced weekly so that the volume for the current year will be in unbound weekly sections. The *Weekly Law Reports* are available more quickly and they tend to be preferred by practitioners who subscribe either to the *Weekly Law Reports* or to the

All England Law Reports, a similar commercially produced series. You will find guidance on how to read the law reports in Chapter 6.

Short reports of cases can be found in *The Times*, *The Independent* and other broadsheet newspapers. Volumes of the *Times Law Reports* are available in most libraries and online. The *Financial Times* often contains extensive coverage of major changes in the law and is a useful source of material on current issues in European Law. Professional journals such as the *New Law Journal* and the *Solicitors' Journal* contain brief reports of recent cases. The library will also have a collection of specialist law reports covering a specific subject area.

The most commonly found series of case reports are cited as follows:

Weekly Law Reports	WLR
All England Law Reports	All ER
Times Law Reports	TLR
British Tax Reports	BTR
Building Law Reports	BLR
Butterworths Company Law Cases	BCLC
Commercial Law Reports	Com LR
Cox's Criminal Law Cases	Cox CC
Criminal Appeal Reports	Cr App R
Criminal Appeal Reports (Sentencing)	Cr App R (S)
Estates Gazette Law Reports	EGLR
European Human Rights Reports	EHRR
Family Law Reports	FLR
Housing Law Reports	HLR
Industrial Relations Law Reports	IRLR
Lloyd's List Law Reports	Ll LR (1919–1950); Lloyd's Rep (1951 on)
Local Government Law Reports	LGR also known as
Knight's Local Government Law Reports	KLGR
Property, Planning & Compensation Reports	P & CR
Reports of Patent Cases	RPC
Road Traffic Reports	RTR

Finding reports of cases

The first place to look for the citation of a case is in the list at the front of your textbook. Otherwise, for cases reported from 1947 onwards, consult the *Current Law Case Citator* which will give you all the references to the reports of a case. This is in two volumes with a cumulative supplement which is issued annually. It will also tell you whether the case you are looking for has been referred to in subsequent cases.

Cases heard before 1947 and after 1865 can be traced through *The Digest* and pre-1865 cases through the index to *The English Reports*.

3.3 Statutes

The most authoritative volumes of statutes are the *Public General Acts*, which are duplicated in the *Law Reports Statutes* published by the Incorporated Council of Law Reporting. *Current Law Statutes Annotated* is a third series which is updated by looseleaf supplements. These volumes are arranged chronologically. There are two series which are arranged by subject: *Halsbury's Statutes of England* which is updated by looseleaf supplements, and *Statutes in Force* published by HM Stationery Office and which is also constantly updated.

Finding statutes

You can either look in *Halsbury's Statutes* under the appropriate subject heading or in the *Index to the Statutes* which covers all legislation from 1235 onwards which is currently in force. To find out whether a statute is yet in force, consult the *Chronological Table of the Statutes* which comprises two volumes listing all statutes passed since 1235, whether or not in force, but which lists those which are wholly or partly in force in bold type. *Halsbury's Statutes* has an annual supplement called *Is It in Force?* which lists all acts passed in the last 25 years.

3.4 Statutory instruments

Statutory instruments contain legislation which is created, usually by a member of the government or a statutory body under powers given to them in an Act of Parliament. This is a useful device when there are matters covered by the legislation which can better be decided in the future, and/or which are of minor importance so that they do not warrant the expenditure of parliamentary time in debating the fine detail. These are listed in *Statutory Instruments*, in annual volumes, in *Halsbury's Statutory Instruments* in order of subject. Statutory instruments can be traced and checked in the *Index to Government Orders* and the *Table of Government Orders*, which lists those in force in bold type.

3.5 Periodicals and articles

Bound volumes of periodicals and articles are usually arranged in alphabetical sequence according to title. For greater security, the most recent unbound editions and parts are usually kept under the supervision of the library staff elsewhere in the library, or on display, so that the attention of library users is drawn to the new materials. You will probably find a selection of the following journals in your law library and you will see references to them in the footnotes in your textbooks:

Business Law Review	Bus LR or BLR
Cambridge Law Journal	Camb LJ or CLJ
Company Lawyer	Co Law or CL
Conveyancer	Conv
Criminal Law Review	Crim LR or CLR
Current Legal Problems	CLP
Estates Gazette	EG
Family Law	Fam L or LF
Industrial Law Journal	ILJ
Journal of Business Law	JBL
Journal of Legal History	JLH
Journal of Planning and Environment Law	JPL or JPEL
Journal of Social Welfare Law	JSWL
Law Quarterly Review	LQR
Legal Studies	LS or Leg Stud
Lloyd's Maritime & Commercial Law Quarterly	LMCLQ
Modern Law Review	MLR
New Law Journal	NLJ
Oxford Journal of Legal Studies	OJLS
Public Law	PL
Solicitors' Journal	SJ

The monthly issues of *Current Law* contain lists of recent articles. These form a separate section in the *Current Law Yearbook* and are arranged under subject headings.

The Index to Legal Periodicals is an American publication which covers most English language law journals, with quarterly cumulative supplements. There is a subject and author index.

3.6 British government publications

Your library should keep the *Parliamentary Debates* (Hansard) containing reports of the parliamentary proceedings of the House of Lords and the House of Commons and *Parliamentary Debates, House of Commons Standing Committees*, together with the government papers known as Command Papers – those prepared at the command of the government, sometimes by outside organisations. These include Royal Commission reports and Law Commission reports, major government reports and reports of tribunals of enquiry. The Command Papers also comprise government White Papers for proposed legislation. They are an invaluable source of background material for your research. The Law Commission reports are particularly valuable since they contain a statement of the existing law as well as recommendations for change.

Different series of command papers are indicated by different abbreviations for the word 'command' in the reference. The current abbreviation, since 1979, is Cm. The papers are not necessarily numbered in chronological order. It may be necessary to consult the annual *Catalogue of Government Publications*. Libraries have varying ways of storing these and your law librarian should be consulted if you have difficulty in finding them.

3.7 Reference books and encyclopaedias

Halsbury's Laws of England is the most complete encyclopaedia of English Law. It is a practitioner's reference book and it may be a good idea for you to know how to use it in case you are set a practical exercise as part of a job interview. It is also useful on the law degree because it gives a comprehensive statement of the law on a particular subject, provided that you make sure that you consult the supplements which update the encyclopaedia regularly.

Your library should keep a range of legal dictionaries and you will find your own dictionary useful.

Another useful work is *Raistrick's Index to Legal Citations and Abbreviations* which contains a list of abbreviations in common use. If you are referred to a law report of journal with an unfamiliar citation, you can look it up to discover the full name of the work.

A more comprehensive guide to use of the law library is given in *Using the Law Library* by Peter Clinch, published by Blackstone Press.

3.8 Electronic retrieval systems

Most libraries depend on electronic systems and the amount of access to these which is afforded to students varies according to university policy. Nevertheless, you should be aware of the main databases.

- *WESTLAW* is the West Group's online source of legal and business information offering full-text legislation, case law, law reviews, texts and newspapers from across the world.

   The first screen to appear when you have logged on to WESTLAW is the UK search screen. This screen is divided into three parts:

   a) case locator;

   b) UK legislation;

   c) legal journal index – a bibliographic search tool containing selected full-text journals published by Sweet & Maxwell. It also covers (as an index only) approximately 400 academic law journals including EU-related journals.

- *LEXIS-NEXIS Professional* is an online database containing full reports of virtually all English cases reported since 1945 and also some unreported cases. It also contains all public general acts and statutory instruments in force, decisions of the European Court of Justice, Australian and New Zealand and some French law reports and some articles from journals.

    It contains over two billion documents gathered from 28,000 sources, including: UK reported and unreported cases; English legislation; legal journals; a UK current awareness library; EU law; Commonwealth law; worldwide legal sources; and international law.

    When first searching for information on English law, you should first consider what type of material you wish to search for: case law, legislation or journal articles. You can select the file you wish to search in one of the following ways:

    a) Using *Assisted Search* you can choose to search either UK cases or legislation, or EU cases or legislation.

    b) Using the *Source Directory* you can choose the file legal (excluding US), choose United Kingdom, choose case law, legislation or journals.

    LEXIS-NEXIS has only a limited number of UK journals, including *The New Law Journal, Estates Gazette, The Lawyer, The Law Society's Gazette* and *The Journal of the Law Society of Scotland.*
- *LAWTEL* offers a daily updated index to a wide range of unreported cases with summaries going back 20 years and links to other case law and legislation, an index of articles from major UK legal publications, a legislation and case citator, statute summaries, a legislation tracking service (commencement and repeals, Bills and Command Papers) and jobs in law.
- *Current Legal Information* consists of seven interlinked databases which are updated daily, the most useful of which are: *Current Law Cases*, a summary of all reported cases going back to 1947; *Case Citator*, a guide to case law giving the full judicial history of each case and details of whether they are referred to in subsequent decisions.
- *The Electronic Law Reports* comprises the full text of the law reports from 1865 which can be searched according to court, parties or free text.
- *The Current Law Case Citator* contains references to all the reports of a case and whether it has been cited judicially since it was decided.
- *Casebase* is a free internet service from Smith Bernal (official shorthand writer to the court) which provides full access to all Court of Appeal and Crown Office cases from April 1996. Cases are indexed by name, date, case number and court.
- *Court Service website*: http://www.courtservice.gov.uk/index.htm. This comprises a full-text database of recent judgments from UK courts and tribunals. Also includes court guides and notices, practice directions, etc.

- *The Incorporated Council of Law Reporting for England & Wales website*: http://www.lawreports.co.uk/. This lists recent judgments published in the Law Reports, and provides the Daily Law Notes Service, a 24-hour service providing updates from the House of Lords, the Privy Council, the Court of Appeal and all divisions of the High Court.
- *HMSO online*: http://www.hmso.gov.uk/acts.htm. A searchable website containing the full text of acts from 1996. Also includes the Criminal Appeal Act 1995 and the Disability Discrimination Act 1995.
- *BOPCAS* is based on the Ford Collection of British Official Publications at Southampton University. It covers UK parliamentary and departmental publications.
- *UKOP* indexes all official publications including both HMSO and departmental or non-HMSO publications from 1980 onwards. Enables the user to search or browse by subject.
- *UNCOVER* is a database of periodical articles in all subjects published since 1988. It indexes a number of major English legal journals and is a useful source for bibliographical references. It is also possible to pay be credit card to have a copy of a relevant article faxed to you.
- *PERIODICALS CONTENTS INDEX* is an index of over 3000 periodicals in the humanities and social sciences from their date of issue to 1993. This index covers over 100 law journals.
- *UK PARLIAMENT website*: httm://www.parliament.uk/. This contains information about the House of Commons and the House of Lords and their procedures and members. It also includes the full text of selected parliamentary papers; parliamentary debates (Hansard) from approximately 1996 onwards; standing committee debates from session 1997–98 onwards; Bills; the weekly information bulletin; and judgments of the House of Lords from November 1996 onwards.
- *BRITISH AND IRISH LEGAL INFORMATION INSTITUTE website*: http://www.bailli.org/. Includes cases and legislation from the UK and Ireland.
- *IGENTA* is a database of periodical articles in all subjects published since 1988. It indexes a number of major English legal journals and is a useful source for bibliographical references. It is also possible to pay by credit card and to have a coy of a relevant article faxed to you.
- *PCI FULL TEXT* is an index of over 3,000 periodicals in the humanities and social sciences from their date of issue until 1995. PCI covers over 100 law journals. In addition, the full text of 165 journals has been made available.
- *JUSTIS* is a CD-ROM containing the texts of the *Weekly Law Reports* from January 1985 onwards, *The Times* and *The Independent* law reports from October 1987 and December 1989 respectively.
- *CELEX* is the database of European Community law, which is updated every six months. JUSTIS-CELEX is the CD-ROM version and CELEX is the online

version which can be used for updating information from the CD-ROM. It is available on the World Wide Web.

In addition, your library will have its own page in the university's web pages.

Section II
How Law is Made

4

Equity and the Common Law

4.1 Historical background

4.2 The development of equity

4.3 The equitable remedies

4.1 Historical background

It is often said that the English legal system began with the Norman Conquest in 1066 but William the Conqueror was the duke of a small dukedom which had no developed legal system of its own. By contrast, England at the time of the conquest had been united for a hundred years, since the time of Alfred the Great, and so what in fact happened was that William adopted the existing English legal system which by that time was highly developed. In any case, William refused the description of conqueror. He claimed to be entitled to the English Crown by a promise made to him by the former king. He claimed that King Harold, whom he defeated at the Battle of Hastings in 1066, was not the true king. He also decreed that all land belonged to the Crown (and indeed it still does) so that interests in land were held under him. William's contribution to the growth of the common law, which was so called because it was practised in, and therefore common to, the whole of England, was very effective administration and enforcement.

The King's court operated by a writ system in many respects similar to the one operated by the courts today, but in the eleventh-century claimants could only bring a claim to a court if their case fell strictly within one of a very few standard forms of action available. In particular, if they wished to bring a claim in respect of property, they had to show that they owned the legal title to the property. Yet often there would be interests in the property which fell short of a legal title and which it would be unjust to deny, especially when the legal title to property was conveyed to one person with the intention that it was to be held for the benefit of others. Today this arrangement is known as a trust.

In addition to the jurisdiction of his courts, the king had an overriding duty to his subjects to ensure that justice was done and so, if no redress was available to the injured parties through the courts because they did not hold the legal title to the property, they could petition the king as the fount of all justice and ask him to resolve the dispute. Naturally, the king did not deal with all these petitions

37

personally – there were far too many – and the Lord Chancellor dealt with them on the king's behalf. In the middle ages, the Lord Chancellor was always a senior member of the clergy and so he was considered suitable to judge on moral issues and matters of justice. He was also the Keeper of the Royal Seal, which was stamped on to documents to endorse the king's authority. By the end of the fourteenth century, petitions were addressed direct to the Lord Chancellor rather than to the king. In this way, two separate court systems grew up – the common law court and the Court of Chancery.

Up until the late nineteenth century, women could not own land. If the husband was unable to manage his own affairs – for example, when he was abroad fighting for the king – he would transfer the legal title to his family property into the name of a trusted friend or relative so that they could manage the property 'for the use of' the owner's wife and children. This early form of trust was known as a 'use'. If the knight made an unwise choice, and chose someone who abused his position as trustee, the beneficiaries could not sue in the king's common law court because they were not legal owners of the property, but they could petition the Lord Chancellor for justice. The Lord Chancellor could not interfere with the legal ownership of the property, but he could make orders directing the use of the property for the benefit of the beneficiaries (the owner's wife and family). Failure to comply with such an order was punishable by imprisonment. The Lord Chancellor's court, or Court of Chancery, could dispense equity to do justice in the individual case, while the common law of the King's court preserved a uniform system of law for the whole country.

The two entirely separate court systems developed for the administration of the common law and equity caused many problems. For example, it was often necessary to use both the common law court and the court of equity in the same dispute. There were some improvements but the court's administration had become very inefficient, resulting in long delays in the settlement of disputes, and often the trust fund was used up by high legal costs rather than for the benefit of the beneficiaries. This was very well illustrated by Charles Dickens in his novel *Bleak House*.

So, in 1873 and 1875, the Judicature Acts were passed. These provided for the creation of one Supreme Court to replace the separate courts which had existed previously. The Supreme Court was divided for convenience only into three divisions of the High Court: the Queen's Bench Division; the Chancery Division; and the Probate and Admiralty Division (renamed the Family Division in 1970). In practice cases are sent to the most appropriate division, but in fact any case can be heard by any division and all divisions can award both common law and equitable remedies.

It was specifically provided by s25(11) Judicature Act 1875 (now s49 Supreme Court Act 1981) that, where there is a conflict between the common law and equity, the rules of equity shall prevail. Even after these reforms, the common law and equity survive as two separate systems of law. They are not fused into one.

4.2 The development of equity

In the early days the equitable jurisdiction of the Lord Chancellor developed on an ad hoc basis – equity was said to be 'as long as the Chancellor's foot', ie Chancery cases were judged entirely at the discretion of the Lord Chancellor. But by the seventeenth century, Lord Chancellors tended to be lawyers rather than clergymen and a system of precedent had begun to develop. A set of principles or maxims emerged which form the rules of equity. These are not rules to be construed like a statute and indeed the wording of the maxims varies in different source materials. Many of the maxims emerged as part of the reasoning in judgments of individual cases. They form the general basis for the law of equity and in order to invoke the court's equitable jurisdiction, one of these rules must apply to the case. Equity does not provide an automatic remedy. Its rules are applied entirely at the discretion of the court. The equitable maxims are:

Equity will not suffer a wrong to be without a remedy

Perhaps the most obvious example is the trust itself. The enforcement of the strict rights of the trustee as legal owner against the person for whose benefit he has agreed to hold the property would lead to gross injustice. So the beneficiaries will have their rights recognised by the court in equity despite the fact that the beneficiaries have no rights in common law.

Equity follows the law

The traditional role of equity was to 'temper and mitigate the rigour of the law'. Equity will intervene and overrule the common law if justice requires it. But equity does not overrule common law judgments. The court simply refuses to apply the previous judgment in this particular case. The common law rules stand but the defendant in the individual case is prevented from relying on his or her strict legal rights.

He who seeks equity must do equity

Even if the claimant can establish an equitable right or interest, the court will not grant a remedy if it holds that the claimant is unworthy. The person seeking an equitable remedy must act equitably. For example, one possible equitable remedy is an injunction – an order of the court which stops a proposed course of action. If an injunction is sought to prevent a breach of contract, the court will not grant this equitable remedy if the claimant is not prepared to fulfil his or her side of the bargain.

He who comes to equity must come with clean hands

This is the 'clean hands doctrine'. The person seeking equity must not be guilty of unconscionable conduct. If you ask the court for an equitable remedy, your own conduct must be beyond reproach. The unconscionable conduct must relate directly to the matter before the court – the court cannot deny a claimant an equitable remedy simply because they are of bad character.

Where equities are equal the law prevails; where equities are equal the first in time prevails

These two maxims are concerned with priorities when there are grounds for both parties to seek the court's equitable jurisdiction. In the event of a conflict, the interests take effect in the order in which they were created. If the parties are equally entitled to an equitable remedy, the court will apply the common law. If one equitable right arises before the other, the first takes priority over the second. If there is a conflict between a number of equitable interests, they will have priority in the order of their creation, but this is subject to the 'equities being equal' – ie there being no unconscionable conduct on the part of any claimant.

Equitable interests will not prevail against equity's darling – the bona fide purchaser of a legal estate for value without notice

If an innocent party acquires legal title to property having paid for it or exchanged other property for it and has no knowledge of the equitable claim to the property and should not have known about it, the third party will own the property free of any equitable claim.

Equity imputes the intention to fulfil the obligation or *equity looks on as done that which ought to be done*

When someone undertakes to perform an obligation, his or her later conduct will be construed as if they intended to fulfil that commitment. BUT

Equity will not perfect an imperfect gift

At common law, a promise is unenforceable unless something is given in return. This is known as the doctrine of consideration. So unless a gift is handed over voluntarily, nothing can be done to enforce it. An exception to this is the **doctrine of promissory estoppel** (see Chapter 6, section 6.1): where a person spends money on property or acts to his or her detriment in another way, for example by carrying out repairs, and has done so in reliance on a promise made by another party, then equity will intervene to prevent the other party from acting on their strict legal rights and hold them to their promise because it would be unconscionable to allow the other party to profit from their actions. Equity will only compensate the person relying on the promise to the minimum extent that will give them what they could expect. As Lord Templeman said in *Winkworth* v *Edward Baron Development Co* [1987] 1 All ER 114 at p118 'Equity is not a computer. Equity operates on conscience but is not influenced by sentimentality'.

Equity will not assist a volunteer

A volunteer in this context is someone who has not given consideration (has given nothing in return for the promise). In particular, equity will not enforce a promise to create a trust in favour of a volunteer. If someone promises to leave property in trust for a beneficiary at some future date, the beneficiary cannot enforce the promise unless he has given consideration for it. See, for example, the case of *Tweddle* v *Atkinson* (1861) 1 B & S 393 in your contract textbook.

Equality is equity

In the absence of any express intention as to what is to happen to property, the court will divide any fund equally when several people are entitled to it, for example the court will divide a joint bank account equally between the holders. This rule will not be applied when it is clearly *not* the intention of the parties that an equal division should be made.

Equity will look to the substance rather than the form

The court will look at the true nature of the arrangement between the parties, rather than what they say it is in any documents. For example, a mortgage deed contains a legal date for the redemption of the mortgage (the date when the deed says all the money has to be repaid). This date is usually six months or so into the term of the mortgage. Most mortgages are agreed to be repaid over a period of twenty years or more. If the lender seeks repayment on the legal date, the court will only allow this if the borrower is in breach of his or her obligations under the terms of the mortgage. If the borrower has performed his or her part of the agreement, equity will look to the substance of the agreement rather than the form and allow repayment over the agreed period – the equitable right to redeem the mortgage rather than the legal right provided in the mortgage deed.

Delay defeats equities

This is also known as the equitable doctrine of **laches**. If you know you have a claim against someone and you do nothing about it, this could be an indication to the other party that you do not intend to exercise your rights. For example, if you own land and the title deeds contain a covenant which prevents your neighbour from building on his adjoining land and you stand back and allow building to proceed without raising any objection, it would be inequitable for the court to order the demolition of the building when you could have intervened before the work was started. So if you wish to enforce your rights you must give the other party notice of your intention to do so at the earliest opportunity or the court may not grant you a remedy.

Equity acts in personam

This is another way of saying that the common law binds the whole world and equity cannot alter the common law but only prevent its application in the individual case so that the defendant is prevented from exercising his or her legal rights.

Another aspect of this rule is that equity acts against the person of the defendant so that the remedy does not lie in damages. The sanction for refusing to obey any order of the court made under its equitable jurisdiction is imprisonment for contempt of court.

Equity will not suffer a trust to fail for want of a trustee

If an otherwise valid trust is created but no trustees are appointed, or if the trustees die and there is no one else who can appoint trustees, the court will step in to do so either by its statutory powers or within its inherent jurisdiction.

Equity will not permit a statute to be used as an instrument of fraud

Statutory rules which impose procedural requirements can be used to defraud innocent but ignorant people. For example, contracts relating to interests in land must be made in writing. In *Bannister* v *Bannister* [1948] 2 All ER 133, a woman conveyed her house to another who, in return agreed orally to allow her to live there as long as she wished. This agreement was unenforceable at law because it was oral, but when the new owner tried to evict the woman, the Court of Appeal upheld the oral contract in equity applying this equitable maxim.

Equity is not a panacea for all the wrongs inflicted by application of the common law – injustice will not automatically be prevented by equity. The court must apply the rules given above which provide a degree of certainty for the parties to litigation.

4.3 The equitable remedies

At common law the only available remedy is damages – a financial sum in compensation for any loss suffered. Equitable remedies are only granted when damages are considered inappropriate or inadequate. To be granted an equitable remedy, the claimant has to prove not only that there has been an infringement of a right but also that the case is one in which equity should provide an alternative remedy to damages. Today, s49 Supreme Court Act 1981 gives the right to administer equitable remedies to all courts exercising jurisdiction in civil cases. There are a number of rules which govern the granting of equitable remedies:

1. Equitable remedies are **discretionary** whereas common law remedies are available as of right. At common law the successful claimant is automatically entitled to damages and, if necessary, enforcement of the remedy by the court's officers. In equity, the court can decide not to grant a remedy if the conduct of the claimant is questionable.
2. The court decides whether an equitable remedy is appropriate by **applying the equitable maxims.**
3. Generally an equitable remedy is given **only if there is no common law remedy.**
4. A court will not grant an equitable remedy unless it can ensure enforcement of that remedy. If enforcement is likely to require the constant supervision of the court it would be impractical for the court to order the remedy. For example, the court will not order specific performance of a contract of employment. If the relationship between employer and employee has broken down, there is a danger that the order will require enforcement and it would be impracticable to force the parties to work together, so it is appropriate to make an award of damages to compensate the employee for loss of earnings.

The equitable remedies which are available are as follows:

Specific performance

A decree of specific performance is an order of the court which compels the person to perform their obligations either under a contract or under a trust. The court will apply the equitable maxim 'equity looks on as done that which ought to be done'. The remedy is not available as of right but is discretionary. The court decides whether in the circumstances damages will not give a full remedy. The court cannot decide this simply according to what would be fair but must apply the equitable rules. The order is issued against a specific defendant and refusal to comply will be a contempt of court punishable by imprisonment. For example, let us take a situation where the sale of a house has been agreed and contracts have been exchanged. The sellers are a couple in the process of divorce and one of the couple refuses to move out of the property so that the sale cannot be completed. If the purchaser is ready, willing and able to complete the purchase (the clean hands doctrine), the court may order specific performance of the contract of sale – that the sellers must sell the house to the purchaser in accordance with the terms of the contract. If the spouse still refuses to move out and complete the sale, they will be in contempt of court and can be sent to prison.

An order for specific performance is more likely to be granted when the property which is the subject of the contract has a unique quality or a special value which will not be covered by damages. This will include property such as:

1. **Land**. Because traditionally family wealth is tied up in land, the court is always ready to declare the unique character of a piece of land and will grant specific performance, either to the seller or to the purchaser under the principle of **mutuality** (it would be inequitable to grant such a remedy to one without granting it to the other). Specific performance can even be granted in relation to property which is situated abroad because the right is enforceable against the person of the defendant and can be enforced when the defendant returns to the jurisdiction of the English court. The effect of the availability of specific performance of contracts relating to land is to make the purchaser the beneficial owner of the land from the time of exchange of contracts, although legal title to the property is held by the seller until registration of the title to the property at HM Land Registry after completion. After exchange of contracts the seller holds the property as a constructive trustee.

2. **Personal property**. Contracts relating to personal property (sometimes called chattels – objects which do not form part of land) will be specifically enforceable only when the goods are unique or possess a character which makes them special to the purchaser. A contract to buy back a family heirloom would be specifically enforceable, as would a contract to buy a Van Gogh painting. If goods have been set aside for a particular customer, the sale contract would be specifically enforceable. Contracts for the sale of goods which are readily available and can be bought elsewhere or resold are not specifically enforceable. The injured party can be compensated adequately for damages in lieu of the profit which would have been made on the sale or the higher cost of buying the same item elsewhere.

Contracts which are not specifically enforceable include:

1. Voluntary contracts (contracts for which no consideration is given) even if these are made in the more solemn form of a deed for which consideration is not normally required.
2. Contracts relating to personal property where the subject matter is not unique.
3. Contracts requiring constant supervision.
4. Contracts for a specific person to do work or perform services.
5. Contracts lacking mutuality – for example, people under the age of 18 cannot be contractually bound in most situations so, under the rule of mutuality, they will not be given the right to enforce a contract against someone who is of full age and therefore contractually bound to them.
6. Contracts tainted with illegality or immorality.
7. Contracts which in the light of subsequent circumstances can only be partially performed. The order must be for performance of the contract in its entirety.
8. Partnership agreements – because they are contracts for personal services.

9. Contracts for the sale of the goodwill of a business (the good name and right to deal with the customers of the business) where this is sold separately from the business premises.

An order for specific performance is not available against the Crown.

Injunctions

An injunction is an order of the court directing a person or persons to stop doing something (a prohibitory or restrictive injunction) or, in rare cases, to do some particular thing (a mandatory injunction). The court exercises its discretion in the same way as for orders of specific performance. An injunction might be granted in the following circumstances:

1. To prevent a breach of contract.
2. To protect property rights and to prevent a tort (civil wrong) – to stop someone going on to your land, to prevent a nuisance such as excessive noise, to protect easements such as rights of way, to enforce restrictive covenants such as a covenant not to build, to stop the publication of a libel, and so on.
3. To prevent breaches of confidence by employees – to stop them giving away your trade secrets, for example.
4. To prevent a breach of copyright, patent or trade mark rights.
5. To prevent a breach of trust.
6. In family and matrimonial matters – for example to prevent one parent taking a child abroad.
7. An injunction can be granted before a case comes to full trial so that the status quo is preserved pending trial. This is known as an **interim injunction** (formerly an interlocutory injunction). Sometimes the result of granting an injunction before trial is to resolve the matter once and for all.

If the injunction is imposed after a full hearing, it is known as a **perpetual injunction**, although this does not necessarily mean that the injunction is imposed for all time – it will be imposed for the minimum period necessary to do justice between the parties. A perpetual injunction will only be granted if damages do not give a sufficient remedy and only if the injury suffered is likely to be of a continuing nature. The court will consider the rights of the parties and of all others who may be affected by the granting of an injunction.

Normally, a perpetual injunction will only be granted if notice has been given to the defendant so that he or she has enough time to prepare a defence to the application. But in genuine cases of emergency an injunction may be granted without notice (formerly known as an *ex parte* injunction) – in the absence of the person who is likely to be affected by the injunction. This could lead to a very serious infringement of that person's civil liberties so the claimant in an ex parte injunction is under a strict duty to disclose to the court all material facts that would influence its decision whether or not to grant the injunction. The other factors which the court will take into consideration when deciding whether or not to proceed are:

1. The clean hands doctrine – if the claimant is also in default, an interim injunction will be refused.
2. The balance of convenience – if the court is in any doubt as to the consequences of granting an interim injunction, the burden of proof is on the claimant to show that the refusal of the injunction would, on balance, cause greater inconvenience to him/her than to the defendant.
3. The damage which the claimant wishes to avoid must be substantial and irreparable, for example, if the defendant were proposing to demolish a building, an interim injunction might be granted pending a full hearing.
4. The equitable doctrine of laches – delay defeats equity. Standing by and letting the defendant do what you are now complaining of may be construed as acquiescence and result in an award of damages rather than an injunction.

In exceptional circumstances the court will grant a **freezing order** (formerly a Mareva injunction) and/or a **search order** (formerly an Anton Piller order). These are ex parte interlocutory injunctions (renamed interim injunctions without notice under the Civil Procedure Rules 1998).

A freezing order is granted when it is feared that the defendant will remove all his/her assets out of the jurisdiction of the English courts so that, if a judgment is given in favour of the claimant, there will be nothing left which the court can take in order to satisfy the amount of damages. At first, such injunctions were used to ensure that ships did not leave port but they can also be used to freeze bank accounts and secure other property.

A search order is granted if it is feared that evidence essential to establish a case will be destroyed unless it is seized. Initially these orders were used against makers of pirate audio and video tapes in order to prevent them from destroying the materials when a writ was served on them. The use has been extended to cover many other types of evidence.

The court is extremely cautious when granting such draconian rights over the defendant's property and the injunctions are only granted with stringent conditions attached, including the opportunity for the defendant to protect his/her interests and to seek legal advice at the earliest opportunity. There are heavy sanctions against the abuse of these procedures.

The court can grant a *quia timet* **injunction** ('quia timet' means 'because he fears') in order to restrain a threatened action before an infringement of the claimant's rights has occurred. The claimant must show that such proposed action will inevitably lead to a violation of his/her rights and that there is a strong possibility that the threatened action will in fact be taken.

Rescission

In certain circumstances one party to a contract will have behaved in such a way in the creation or the performance of the contract as to allow the innocent party to have the contract set aside in equity (rescinded) rather than having to rely on damages at common law. The claimant will be restored to his/her position as if the contract had never been made. This must still be possible when rescission is claimed. The remedy is discretionary.

Rescission will be granted for:

1. Fraudulent misrepresentation – when one party makes a statement with the intention that the other party should act on it and the other party in fact acted upon it.
2. Innocent misrepresentation – when one party makes an incorrect statement believing that it is true if that statement is a condition of the contract. Under the Misrepresentation Act 1967 the court can award damages in lieu of rescission if in its opinion it would be just and equitable to do so.
3. Mistake as to a fundamental term of the contract which is made by both parties so that the meaning of the contract is destroyed.
4. Constructive fraud – if the contract has been entered into because of undue influence, the contract may be rescinded in equity.
5. Substantial misdescription of the subject matter of the contract.
6. An express term of the contract that, in given circumstances, the parties will have the right to rescind.

The right to rescind will be *lost* when:

1. When the contract is affirmed either expressly in writing or where affirmation can be implied from the claimant's conduct.
2. Where it is no longer possible to restore the parties to their pre-contractual positions. The property must be capable of being restored to the original owner in its original condition. There may be a right to compensation if the other party has made improvements to property which now must be returned.
3. Where an innocent and bona fide party has acquired for consideration rights in the property.

Rectification of documents

If a written document, as a result of a mistake by both parties, does not accurately express an agreement between those parties, equity may rectify the document so that it corresponds with what was actually agreed. The remedy is intended to correct the agreement, not to improve it. A complete agreement must have been recorded by the document. The parties' intentions must have continued unchanged. The mistake must be a mistake of fact which is common to both parties and there must be no alternative remedy.

Four other remedies
1. The court can order the **delivery up and cancellation of documents** which are no longer valid but which give the appearance of being valid from the face of the document – for example, a contract which, from its date, appears to be still in force but which the parties have agreed is no longer subsisting.
2. **A receiver** may be appointed either to hold property which is vulnerable or to enable a person to obtain his/her rights over the property or to obtain the payment of debts when legal remedies are inadequate for this purpose.
3. **Account** – an order is granted so that sums due from one party to the other in certain specific transactions may be impartially investigated.
4. **Tracing** – the equitable right to trace is a proprietary remedy, where the claimant has a right to recover the property itself rather than compensation for the loss of it, which entitles the true owner to recover the property or its equivalent from whoever now has possession of it. The rationale for the remedy is the doctrine of unjust enrichment, a concept which does not have full recognition in English law. Nevertheless, if, for example, trust funds have been embezzled by a trustee, and the trustee has bought, say, a painting with the money, the painting can be recovered as trust property since it represents the money which was taken from the trust. As long as there is a fiduciary relationship (a relationship in which one of the parties is in a special position of trust towards the other) somewhere in the chain of possession, the property can be traced into the hands of whoever now has possession of it and can be recovered by the true owner. There are special rules relating to the tracing of property in and out of bank accounts.

5

The Court System

There are, in effect, two court systems, one for civil law and one for criminal law, with some overlap between the courts which deal with the two systems.

5.1 Civil law

The civil law system deals with disputes between individuals or organisations. If one individual suffers a wrong at the hands of another, s/he may be able to claim compensation from the other party. In order to do so, it may be necessary to bring a civil court action The case will be known by the names of the parties (*Smith* v *Jones*).

If you are involved in a car crash, this may well lead to criminal proceedings, but the parties may also have an action in the tort of negligence to recover damages for loss or injury. This will be a civil action in which one individual claims against the other.

If a trustee runs off with the trust money, there may be a criminal case for theft or fraud and also civil proceedings for breach of trust.

5.2 Criminal law

Most crimes give rise to loss or injury inflicted against another, but criminal behaviour is behaviour which is abhorrent to society as a whole. It is a breach of the code by which the community has agreed to live, a code which can be traced back to ancient times. The state, therefore, takes action on behalf of society against the offender. The prosecution is carried out in the name of the Crown (*R* v *Smith*).

Individuals can also bring private prosecutions for crimes against them but these actions are rare and are still dealt with within the criminal system.

5.3 The court system

The court system has a hierarchical structure. The courts at the very bottom of the hierarchy – the magistrates' courts and the county courts – deal with the vast majority of cases in England and Wales. Yet they are known as **inferior courts** – their jurisdiction is limited by value and/or geographically. These courts are intended to serve the local area. Their decisions are not recorded and are not binding on other courts.

More important cases are heard in the **superior courts** – the High Court for civil matters and the Crown Court for criminal matters. The Court of Appeal and the House of Lords, as appeal courts, are also superior courts. All superior courts are *courts of record*: an official record is kept of their proceedings, and the decisions of the court are binding on other courts at the same level or below them in the hierarchy. It is important to understand the hierarchy because the higher the level at which the case is heard, the more significant is the judgment.

5.4 The criminal court system

The diagram opposite (*Figure 5*) illustrates the criminal court system.

The magistrates' court

Most magistrates are not trained lawyers, although they undergo a thorough training before they are allowed to sit as magistrates. They are chosen by the Lord Chancellor's Department often on the recommendation of members of the local community. They are also known as Justices of the Peace and can use the letters JP after their name. There are approximately 30,000 **lay magistrates** (non-lawyers) in England and Wales. They are local people and the court serves a very limited community. Lay magistrates are assisted by a **justices' clerk** who takes no part in deciding on the outcome of the case but who is a trained lawyer providing advice to the magistrates on points of law.

In some magistrates' courts in the big cities, paid professional lawyers sit as **stipendiary magistrates**. Where lay magistrates usually sit as a bench of three, stipendiaries sit alone. The government plans to extend the use of stipendiary magistrates.

All criminal cases are heard initially in the magistrates' court. This is the process by which defendants charged with an offence can be brought to court speedily to enter a plea of guilty or not guilty. Depending on the nature of the crime, the court

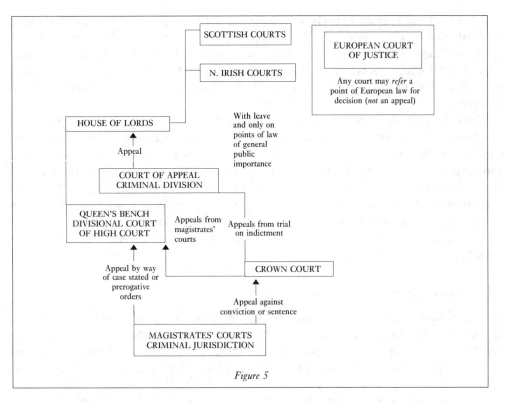

Figure 5

then decides how to proceed. If it is a minor offence, the magistrates will deal with it immediately at a **summary trial**.

For some offences, the defendant can choose whether to have the case heard by the magistrates or to elect for trial by jury in the Crown Court. These offences are **triable either way**. The defendant may be advised that s/he has a better chance of being acquitted by a jury, or the crime may be one committed for a cause (for example, by someone protesting about a new road scheme) and the defendant may wish to seek greater publicity through a Crown Court trial. The Home Office is proposing to introduce the Criminal Justice (Mode of Trial) (No 2) Bill which will limit a defendant's freedom to elect for Crown Court trial (jury trial) in either way offences.

The most serious crimes, **indictable offences**, can only be tried in the Crown Court but the initial hearing takes place in the magistrates' court. The proceedings in the magistrates' court are known as **committal proceedings**. The magistrates hear the prosecution evidence only, which is usually submitted in writing, although the defence can ask for the prosecution evidence to be presented orally in order to test the strength of the prosecution's evidence and, more particularly, the credibility of their witnesses.

Magistrates also try cases relating to defendants under 17 years of age in the

youth court. This is an entirely separate system from the system which deals with adult offenders. The court is held in a separate courtroom, often in a different part of the building with a separate waiting area so that the juveniles do not come into contact with adult offenders. Magistrates who sit in the youth court have special training in dealing with young offenders. At least one member of the bench must be a woman.

Appeals from the magistrates' court against conviction or sentence are heard by the Crown Court when magistrates will sit with the judge who hears the appeal. Appeals are by way of case stated: any person who was a party to the proceedings, and who is aggrieved by the decision of the magistrates, can appeal to the Queen's Bench Division of the High Court on a written statement of the facts found by the magistrates and ask the High Court to rule on any question of law or jurisdiction (ie whether the magistrates have powers to try the particular case).

The magistrates also have a civil jurisdiction, discussed under the civil court system.

The Crown Court

This is almost exclusively a criminal court, the only civil jurisdiction being to hear appeals from the magistrates on licensing matters. All the Crown Courts in England and Wales comprise a single court, although there are approximately ninety courts in England and Wales. The Crown Court is part of the Supreme Court and a court of record but it also operates under the supervision of the High Court.

As a concession to the City of London, the Central Criminal Court – the Old Bailey – maintains certain ancient privileges. All serious crimes committed in London are tried there. The Lord Mayor and Aldermen of the City of London are entitled to sit as judges – but never do – and two of its judges are appointed in consultation with the City.

Four different kinds of judges sit in the Crown Court, namely: High Court judges who hear the most serious cases – murder, manslaughter and rape; circuit judges who hear less serious cases, but can in some circumstances hear rape cases; and recorders and assistant recorders who are barristers or solicitors being tried out for judicial office.

There are special rules for allocating the place of trial for serious crimes. Often they are sent to a larger court in the region rather than being heard in the local Crown Court. These are also special courts to hear serious fraud cases.

The Queen's Bench Division of the High Court

The Queen's Bench Division hears appeals in criminal matters from the magistrates' court and the Crown Court. The President of the Court is the Lord Chief Justice. As we have seen, High Court judges of the Queen's Bench Division also hear serious criminal cases in the Crown Court.

The Court of Appeal

This court only hears appeals on points **of law** from the lower courts. If new facts emerge, the case is sent to a lower court for retrial.

The Lord Chancellor is President of the Supreme Court – the Court of Appeal, the High Court and the Crown Court together. The Lord Chief Justice is President of the Criminal Division of the Court of Appeal. Normally a bench of three judges considers the appeal.

The House of Lords

Appeals are heard by at least five, and normally seven judges who are members of the House of Lords. These are the Lords of Appeal in Ordinary who are appointed from the most eminent judges. The Lord Chancellor is a Lord of Appeal. Appeals are usually heard in a committee room at the House of Lords. The judges do not wear robes. They deliver an *opinion* giving their reasons for allowing or dismissing the appeal.

The House of Lords is *not* part of the Supreme Court system because, when this was set up in the 1870s, it was intended that the House of Lords should be abolished.

The European Court of Justice

The European Court of Justice is **not** an appellate court. Any court or tribunal can apply to it direct for a ruling on the interpretation of a point of European Law. This is necessary to ensure that the same interpretation is applied in all Member States of the European Union. It means that interpretations given in all cases from the courts of other Member States are binding on and must be applied in the courts of the United Kingdom.

Requests can be made for:

1. the interpretation of the EC Treaty and other treaties;
2. interpretation and validity of acts of the Community institutions; and
3. interpretations of statutes of bodies established by the Council (delegated legislation).

The function of the European Court of Justice is to 'ensure that in the interpretation of the Treaty the law is obeyed'.

Modernisation of the criminal court system

Because of the pressures on the criminal court system, a number of measures are being taken to reduce the delays, to reduce sums spent on legal aid, to reform the jury system and generally to refocus the criminal justice system to the advantage of the victim and of the community as a whole.

The Criminal Justice Bill makes the following proposals:

1. Changes are proposed to the jury service to the effect that all except the mentally ill are eligible for jury service and no one will be exempt. The purpose of this change is to widen the representation on juries. Some classes of potential jurors will be able to defer their jury service but not to avoid it altogether as at present. Further, the Bill proposes that trial by judge alone should be used in cases concerning complex commercial matters.
2. The Bill extends the powers of the Crown Prosecution Service to appeal against the granting of bail by the magistrates' court so that appeal is available regarding all imprisonable offences. There will be a new presumption that those who are charged with imprisonable offences and who, having been tested positive for Class A drugs, refuse treatment, will not be entitled to bail.
3. The decision to charge a suspect will now lie with the Crown Prosecution Service rather than the police. The Crown Prosecution Service will also have a right of appeal against a Crown Court judge's decision to end the trial early.
4. The current rule that a suspect cannot be tried more than once for the same offence – the double jeopardy rule – is to be subject to exceptions for very serious offences.
5. The trial judge will be able to disclose to the jury evidence of the defendant's previous convictions and bad character where this is relevant to the case or where the defendant has tried to mislead the court as to his character.

Since April 2000, the legal aid system is now administered by the Community Legal Service. Under the auspices of the Legal Services Commission, the system also oversees the work of legal aid solicitors who now work under licence. This has led to a significant reduction in the amounts overclaimed by legal aid practices. Funding is also available for training of students who wish to become legal aid solicitors.

5.5 The civil court system

The diagram opposite (*Figure 6*) illustrates the civil court system.

The county court

This is the lowest tier of the civil court system. The rules for bringing a case in the county court are set out in *The County Court Practice*, usually referred to as *The Green Book*. This gives all the rules of procedure and evidence and, most importantly, the time limits for each stage of the case.

There are approximately 280 county courts in England and Wales. Some of these are designated to deal with divorce matters. Whereas, generally, the county court jurisdiction is limited geographically, so that only cases which arise in the immediate locality can be heard, there is no such limit on the county court's jurisdiction in

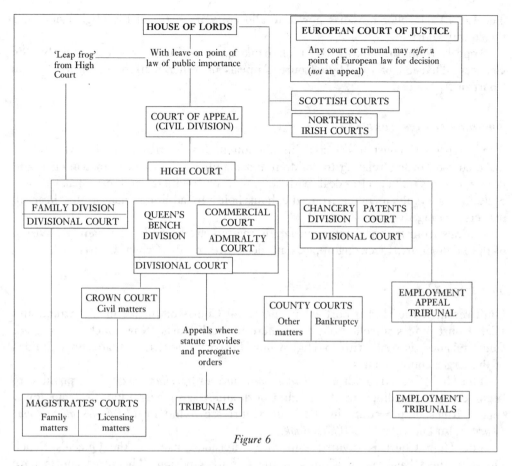

Figure 6

divorce matters, so that the parties can choose to have their divorce petition heard in another locality.

England and Wales is divided into six circuits for administration purposes. In practice, each county court has its own **circuit judge** and this is the least senior judicial appointment. Each court also has a number of **district judges**. These are full time posts, occupied by very experienced solicitors and barristers who hear the procedural cases which arise as the case is prepared for trial. Both circuit judges and district judges can hear cases in the **small claims court** – an informal tribunal to settle small claims at which the parties appear in person without legal representation. District Judges also have a wide jurisdiction in the financial matters which are related to divorce and judicial separation.

In recent years, the High Court has become overloaded and therefore subject to very long delays. The financial limit on the county court's jurisdiction has therefore been raised substantially in order for more cases to be dealt with at this level which is more cost effective both to the parties to litigation and to the public exchequer.

The Lord Chancellor now has power to allocate work between the High Court and the county court.

Appeals from the county court on bankruptcy petitions are dealt with by the Chancery Division of the High Court. Appeals on other matters are heard by the Court of Appeal.

The magistrates' court

The magistrates' court has a civil jurisdiction in family matters under which they make custody orders relating to children and maintenance orders in matrimonial and domestic cases. They also deal with adoption proceedings, and can make orders excluding a family member from the household. In addition, magistrates hear all matters relating to liquor licensing.

Appeals from the magistrates on family matters are heard by the Family Division of the High Court. Licensing appeals are dealt with by the Crown Court.

The High Court

Until recently, the High Court sat in the Royal Courts of Justice in the Strand and High Court judges travelled out from there to local courts. Now much of the High Court business is dealt with in High Court District Registries situated in buildings of the larger county courts.

The High Court is both an *original court* and an *appellate court*. It is possible to begin court proceedings in the High Court and it also hears appeals from lower courts. Rules of procedure in the High Court are found in *The Rules of Supreme Court* – also known as *The White Book*.

The High Court is divided into three divisions, namely: the Queen's Bench Division; the Chancery Division; and the Family Division. The three courts have separate jurisdictions. No limit is set on the jurisdiction of the High Court. It serves the whole of England and Wales.

The Queen's Bench Division

The President of the Queen's Bench Division is the Lord Chief Justice. In addition to its criminal jurisdiction, the QBD hears tort and contract cases. The QBD also has judges who specialise in hearing commercial cases and admiralty cases in the Commercial Court and the Admiralty Court which have different procedures from the other QBD courts. In civil matters, the QBD hears appeals for district judges in the county courts and from some tribunals.

The Chancery Division

The President of the Division is the Lord Chancellor, but in practice he never sits. The effective head of the court is the Vice Chancellor.

Most chancery actions are heard in London. The Chancery Division tries matters concerned with trusts, company matters, insolvency, cases relating to land and patent and trademark actions which are heard in a special court. If there is a dispute over a will or the possessions of someone who has died, this will be heard by the Chancery Division, as will bankruptcy cases. The Court of Protection, which oversees the property and affairs of mental patients is also part of the Chancery Division.

The Chancery Division hears appeals from the county court on bankruptcy matters. It hears appeals relating to land registration (the system by which ownership of land is recorded) and income tax appeals from the Commissioners of Inland Revenue.

The Family Division
The head of the court is the President of the Family Division. The court hears *all* defended matrimonial cases, which are rare nowadays. The Family Division makes declarations of legitimacy and of the validity or invalidity of marriages. It hears proceedings for the presumption of death, wardship, adoption, guardianship and some matrimonial property matters.

The Family Division hears appeals on matrimonial and family matters from the county court and the magistrates' court.

The Court of Appeal

In both criminal and civil matters, the Court of Appeal has its own judges known as the Lords Justices of Appeal. Cases are also heard by *ex officio* judges (judges who sit by reason of the office they hold): the Lord Chancellor, the Master of the Rolls, the President of the Family Division, the Lord Chief Justice, the Vice Chancellor, the judges from the House of Lords and former Lord Chancellors.

Usually three judges sit together, but where they are hearing a very difficult or significant point of law, five judges will hear the case.

The Civil Division of the Court of Appeal hears appeals from lower civil courts. If a party is given leave to appeal to the Court of Appeal, there may be very considerable delays before the appeal comes to trial. The Court of Appeal hears a greater number and variety of appeals than any other court including the House of Lords. The complexity of the appeals heard is also increasing, as can be seen from the number of reserved judgments, ie instances where the Court deliberates on its finding and delivers a written judgment at a later date rather than delivering an immediate oral judgment at the end of the hearing.

The House of Lords

The House of Lords hears appeals from:

1. the Court of Appeal (when leave to appeal is granted either by the Court of Appeal or on application for leave to the House of Lords);

2. the High Court (with the permission of the House of Lords Appeals Committee)
    – where there is a point of law of general public importance, the case can
    leapfrog from the High Court direct to the House of Lords;
3. the Scottish Courts;
4. the Northern Irish Courts; and
5. some Commonwealth courts, where the same judges sit as the Privy Council.

It is currently proposed to replace the Judicial Committee of the House of Lords
with a new Supreme Court.

Tribunals

Tribunals are judicial bodies which meet to hear disputes in specialised matters such
as employment, social security, mental health, special educational needs and so on.
The tribunal usually consists of a chairperson who is a lawyer and two lay members
who have expertise in the matters which are to be dealt with. The most developed
system is probably the Employment Tribunal which has a chairperson and two lay
people, usually one representing the employers and the other representing the
employees, so that you might have one member who was a member of the Institute
of Directors and the other a trade union official. The Employment Tribunal has its
own offices. The rules of procedure and evidence are more relaxed than those of a
formal court hearing. When the system was set up, it was envisaged that the parties
to a dispute would not have legal representation but this is by no means certain.
Appeals from the Employment Tribunal are heard by the Employment Appeal
Tribunal which is a court of record, with the possibility of a further appeal to the
Court of Appeal and the House of Lords.

The European Court of Justice

As noted above, the European Court of Justice is **not** an appellate court. Any court
or tribunal can apply to it direct under art 234 EC Treaty (formerly art 177) for a
ruling on the interpretation of a point of European law. See section 5.4 for further
details.

5.6 The Woolf reforms

New Civil Procedure Rules were introduced in the civil court system in April 1999
with the aim of conducting court business more speedily and encouraging the
settlement of cases without recourse to litigation. As a result of these reforms there
has been a reduction of 11 per cent in cases coming before the county court and a
37 per cent reduction in claims before the High Court.

The court takes a more active role in case management. Responsibility for this rests with the judge, who is given wide powers to set a timetable for disposing of preliminary issues. If there is undue delay, the court can issue an 'unless' order or strike out a case if there is a failure to comply with a rule, practice direction or court order.

The case can be adjourned for up to one month to allow the parties to pursue alternative dispute resolution methods, which are encouraged by the court under the new procedure. The court is under a duty to apply a cost/benefit analysis to the chosen method of hearing and can redirect the matter to a more appropriate forum (from High Court to county court, for example). The court is under an obligation to weed out claims and defences which have no real merit and can strike out claims or defences which disclose no reasonable grounds or which are an abuse of the court process or if they obstruct the just disposal of the proceedings. Appeals from these decisions are to the next level of judge in the hierarchy.

Personal injury and clinical negligence cases are subject to a new pre-action protocol under which there is an expectation that the parties will act reasonably over the exchange of information and documents and will try to avoid litigation. They must agree on a single joint expert witness whose overriding duty is to the court.

The sanction for non-co-operation over the new procedures lies in the award of costs. The old rule that costs follow the event (the party who loses has to pay the costs of the other side) is now only a starting point and, in making the award of costs, the court must now take into consideration the conduct of the parties, whether or not the party is successful in all or part of the case and whether any payment into court by way of settlement has been made.

Under the old system, it was possible for a claimant to issue proceedings as a threat, never intending to act on them. Now the claimant has a time limit of four months in which to serve the claim form (six months if the defendant is living abroad). This discourages vexatious claims. The defendant can now serve notice requiring issue of the claim form in order to bring the matter before the court. This might be appropriate if there were a counterclaim, for example.

The Civil Procedure Rules brought in new terminology. Now the plaintiff is referred to as the claimant and other changes have been made to simplify the terminology of the court system.

5.7 Alternative Dispute Resolution

One of the proposals from the Woolf reforms was the greater use of alternative means of settling disputes without resort to the civil courts. The skills of negotiation and mediation have always played a significant role in the working life of a solicitor or a barrister, but in recent years they have been formalised into techniques which can be applied successfully to international disputes (such as those in the Middle East and Northern Ireland) and to domestic issues on the breakdown of relationships or in commercial contexts.

Negotiation takes place when the parties to a dispute are able to meet (with or without their professional advisers in attendance) to reach an agreement and to preserve their ongoing working relationship.

However, there are times when the situation is so delicate that the parties find it impossible to resolve their own dispute without an intermediary to prepare the ground for a face-to-face meeting where all the issues can be discussed in a controlled environment. The mediator must be completely impartial and able to offer a neutral forum so that the issues between the parties can be addressed in a climate of equality between the parties. The advantages of ADR are confidentiality, time and cost saving and that the parties enjoy a much greater degree of control over the process of mediation and its outcome. The parties are urged to put the past relationship behind them and to seek workable solutions for the future. These may not be in accordance with their strict legal rights since it may be to everyone's advantage that some of these are waived in order to find a workable solution. This, of course, raises points of conflict for lawyers involved in the process who are under a duty to their clients to protect such rights. This is usually resolved by very clear advice on the significance of relinquishing their legal position.

The Civil Procedure Rules provide that ADR should be considered before proceedings are commenced and at every stage throughout the litigation.

In the recent case of *Dunnett* v *Railtrack plc* [2002] EWCA Civ 302 permission was granted to Mrs Dunnett to appeal against the dismissal of her negligence case against Railtrack. This permission was subject to a recommendation that the parties first tried to settle their dispute by mediation or arbitration. Knowing that the appeal was unlikely to succeed, Railtrack refused to submit the dispute to mediation. When they were successful in the Court of Appeal their claim for the costs of the appeal was dismissed because of their failure to comply with the court's recommendation.

6

The Doctrine of Precedent

6.1 Introduction

The common law develops through its case law, and this development is dependent upon the cases which are brought before the courts day by day. In formulating their judgments the judges review the existing body of cases and apply them to similar situations. Many of the principles which are applied are derived from ancient customary law and from Roman law. It is often said that judges do not make law but merely declare the existing law. This concept requires an efficient system of law reporting so that the existing law is accessible to litigants who need to be able to predict their likely chances of success.

The court rarely has to decide on cases which are based on identical facts. If a similar case has been decided, this is likely to be conclusive in subsequent cases. But no two cases are exactly alike – the law applied in previous cases must be extended to meet new situations and so the law moves on. Some judges are very ready to extend the existing principle of law to meet the developing social values of society. Others are much more cautious.

Lord Denning developed a new equitable doctrine by extending the principle established in the nineteenth-century case of *Hughes* v *Metropolitan Railway* (1877) 2 App Cas 439 to meet the needs of the housing market in war-time London. The case in question was *Central London Property Trust* v *High Trees House Ltd* [1947] KB 130, usually referred to as the *High Trees* case, in which at the beginning of World War II, the owners leased a whole block of flats to a company who let them out individually. After war broke out, many people moved out of London and very few people wanted the flats. The owners and the company came to an agreement that the rent for the building should be reduced by half so that lower rents could be charged for the flats. No time limit was put on this reduction in rent. At the end of the war, when there was a shortage of property in London, and the flats were once more fully occupied, the owners sued the company for the full rent for the period after the war had ended. The court held that the owner was entitled to the full rent for that period. Now that the war was over, the full rent must be paid because the reduction was only intended to meet the war-time conditions.

The judge who heard the case was Denning J (as he then was), sitting in the High Court. He knew that, if the owners were successful in recovering the full post-war rent, they intended to sue for the full rent for the period during the war as well on the grounds that both parties had signed a lease which entitled them to the full rent. Denning J therefore went on to say that, if they had done so, the owners would have failed. In order to reach this conclusion, he applied a rule derived from *Hughes* v *Metropolitan Railway*, a case in which a landlord's strict legal rights were **suspended**. In the *High Trees* case, however, Denning J said that the owner's agreement to accept a lower rent, an agreement on which the company relied, **extinguished** the owner's strict contractual rights under the original lease of the block of flats. This new doctrine is known as the **doctrine of promissory estoppel**: if a party makes a promise and the other party relies on it and acts to his own detriment, the first party is bound by his promise. It is an equitable doctrine which overrides common law rights. Denning J took the underlying principle from a case where the landlord and tenant were in negotiation for the tenant to buy the landlord's freehold interest in the property. Before the negotiations began, the landlord had a served a notice requiring the tenant to repair the property. It was appropriate to the facts of *Hughes* v *Metropolitan Railway* that the notice should be suspended and should only begin to run again when the negotiations had broken down when once more the landlord had an interest in ensuring that the repairs were carried out. In the *High Trees* case, it was appropriate to the facts that the owner should lose his right to the unpaid war-time rent altogether but should be entitled to the full rent when the property market revived. Denning J did more than simply apply an existing principle of law – he extended it to meet the new situation.

Most judges are considerably more cautious than Lord Denning, however. Judges are aware that, in order to be fair to all, the law must be certain and the outcome of any case must be reasonably predictable. If judges were not bound by the previously decided cases, no one could predict the likely outcome of a case and the risks of litigation would be unacceptable. If the law has a degree of certainty, the parties will be more likely to negotiate a fair settlement of their differences out of court. Much of your time as a law student will be spent in analysing given facts and applying the rules from the case law so that you can predict the likely outcome of a case.

Judges must also be very careful to avoid making new law. Under the doctrine of separation of powers, this is the function of Parliament through legislation.

6.2 Stare decisis

The fundamental principle on which the doctrine of precedent is based is known as **stare decisis** – let the decision stand. Any previous decision of a higher court of record is binding on judges in lower courts, unless there are reasonable grounds for distinguishing the case on its facts.

The statement of law which is essential to the decision in the case is binding on future courts. This is known as the **ratio decidendi** – the reason for the decision – the legal principle to be derived from the decision based on the material facts. Each judge who gives a full judgment will provide a ratio decidendi and these may vary. Sometimes it will be difficult to find any clear ratio at all. There may be conflicting rationes (plural), especially when the decision of the court is not unanimous and there are dissenting judgments.

6.3 Obiter dicta

Any statement of law which is not essential to the decision in the case is **not** binding on future courts but it may be influential, especially if the dicta were delivered by a distinguished judge. Such statements are known as **obiter dicta** – statements made aside from the main issue in the case. Denning J's doctrine of promissory estoppel in *High Trees* was given obiter. The court was only required to decide the level of rent applicable after the war had ended. Although it was a matter of common sense for Denning J to give his opinion on the rent payable during the war, it was not material to the outcome of this particular case. This part of the judgment was therefore not binding in subsequent cases.

Nevertheless, Lord Denning was able to apply his doctrine in subsequent cases where it **was** material to the outcome of the new case and so the doctrine of promissory estoppel became binding in subsequent cases of a similar nature. Lord Denning was 'persuaded' by the efficacy of his own obiter dicta! Other judges were more cautious, though.

Lord Denning's explanation of the development of this doctrine is quoted by Russell LJ in *Williams* v *Roffey* [1990] 2 WLR 1153 at p1167F–H (see Appendix A).

6.4 Distinguishing

Judges are generally very reluctant indeed to disregard the decisions of other judges even when they are not binding on them, either because the judge in the new case is sitting in a superior court or because the court is not a court of record. Sometimes, however, there is a genuine dilemma in that following the previous decision, while preserving certainty of the law, can lead to an inconvenient or an unjust decision. It may be possible to find differences of fact which allow the judge to decide the new case in a different way so that it is not necessary to follow the inconvenient law. This process maintains the fairness and flexibility of the common law but, if it were used too widely, it would undermine the whole system of precedent. If the law should be changed, it is always open to Parliament to do so by legislation.

When you are given problem questions to answer, they will often contain facts which are materially different to those of decided cases. You must identify the facts which are materially different and decide how these differences will affect the outcome. In effect, you are distinguishing your problem from the previously decided cases.

6.5 Overruling and reversing

A decision is overruled when, in a later case, a higher court reaches a different decision on the same material facts. A decision is reversed if it is overturned by a higher court on appeal in the same case.

Before 1966, the House of Lords had to follow the precedent set in its own previous decisions but in 1966 the Law Lords issued the following *Practice Statement* [1966] 1 WLR 1234:

> 'Their Lordships regard the use of precedent as an indispensable foundation upon which to decide what is the law and its application to individual cases. It provides at least some degree of certainty upon which individuals can rely in the conduct of their affairs, as well as a basis for orderly development of legal rules. Their Lordships nevertheless recognise that too rigid adherence to precedent may lead to injustice in a particular case and also unduly restrict the proper development of the law. They propose, therefore, to modify their present practice and, while treating former decisions of this House as normally binding, to depart from a previous decision when it appears right to do so. In this connection they will bear in mind the danger of disturbing retrospectively the basis on which contracts, settlements of property and fiscal arrangements have been entered into and also the special need for certainty as to the criminal law.
>
> This announcement is not intended to affect the use of precedent elsewhere than in this House.'

Note that it starts with a clear statement of the reasons for the doctrine of precedent and of the reasons for their decisions to depart from it. After 1966, the House of Lords used these new powers sparingly. They were used in the case of *Miliangos* v *George Frank (Textiles) Ltd* [1975] 3 All ER 801, in which the House of Lords overruled its previous decision and allowed the award of damages in a foreign currency where the previous rule had been that damages must be awarded in sterling. It should be noted that, in order to effect this change, the case had to go all the way to the House of Lords. The Court of Appeal itself attempted to overrule the earlier decision but, while agreeing that the change should be made, the House of Lords emphasised that the Court of Appeal had no right to do so – only the House of Lords had the necessary authority to overrule its own previous judgments.

6.6 Decisions given per incuriam

A ruling of the court will be unsound if, in reaching its decision, the Court has failed to consider some point of binding authority or statute. This does not necessarily imply a mistake on the part of the judges or the lawyers. It simply means that, for the future, it would be unsafe to follow that decision because of the failure to consider all the law applicable to the case. It must be shown that, not only is there a failure to consider a relevant point of law but also that this omission would be likely to produce serious inconvenience in the administration of justice or serious injustice to the citizen. In these circumstances, the Court of Appeal and the High Court can decide not to follow the previous case if the judgment is given per incuriam.

6.7 Who may overrule and reverse decisions and who must follow them?

The House of Lords	Judgments bind all other courts.
	May overrule decisions of any court, including its own.
The Court of Appeal	Both decisions of the Court of Appeal are bound by divisions of the House of Lords and by their own previous decisions EXCEPT THAT
The Civil Division	a) Where there are two conflicting decisions of the Court of Appeal, the Court may decide which to follow.
	b) It must disregard a decision of the Court of Appeal which conflicts with a decision of the House of Lords.
	c) It is not bound by a decision of the Court of Appeal reached per incuriam.
	See *Young* v *Bristol Aeroplane Co Ltd* (1944).

The Criminal Division	The same principles apply AND in a case involving the liberty of the subject, if a full court considers that the law has been misapplied or misunderstood, then it must reconsider the earlier decision: *R* v *Taylor* (1950).
The High Court	As a court of first instance it is bound to follow the decisions of all superior courts but is not bound by its own decisions, although in practice the judges usually follow previous High Court decisions.
	The divisional courts are similarly bound and bound by their own decisions, subject to the rule in *Young* v *Bristol Aeroplane Co Ltd*.
	In criminal cases, the rule in *R* v *Taylor* applies.
County courts **Magistrates' courts** **Tribunals**	All inferior courts are bound by the decisions of those above.

Decisions of the Commonwealth, Northern Irish and Scottish Courts and of the Privy Council are persuasive authority only.

Decisions of the European Court of Justice are binding on all courts only as to the interpretation of points of European law requested under art 234 EC Treaty (formerly art 177) by all national courts of Member States.

6.8 Codification

The development of the law through the doctrine of precedent can be hazardous. The system is dependent on the nature of the individual cases which come to court and the willingness of the parties to appeal against unsound decisions.

By contrast, the law in many continental jurisdictions was codified when the countries came to maturity as nation states. French law is contained in the Code Napoleon, a codification of French law which is expressed in language which is readily accessible to French citizens. The Emperor Napoleon himself sat at the conference table as the Code was drafted in order to ensure that the law could be understood by everybody.

English law has also been subject to substantial codification in this century. The four great property statutes of 1925 (Law of Property Act, Trustee Act, Administration of Estates Act, Settled Land Act) set out the law of property in one complete code. In 1948, Company law was similarly codified, although further company statutes have been added to accommodate EC company law. The new statutes comprise a consolidation and modernisation of the law, including enactment of existing case law. The Treasure Act 1996 is in part a codification of existing case law (see Appendix C below). Company law and property law are fields of law where the need for certainty is paramount. It is therefore safer to consolidate the law into one statute. Even where the law is codified, however, the case law still provides interpretations of the statute.

6.9 Reading a case

Working from the case reports rather than from the textbook has many advantages, even when time is pressing. To gain practice in finding your way round a case and extracting its meaning, turn to *Williams* v *Roffey Brothers & Nicholls (Contractors) Ltd* in Appendix A. This is copied in full from the Weekly Law Reports and its citation is [1990] 2 WLR 1153. Read the case report, referring to the notes below for guidance. The only way to learn to read a case is to do it! You will find it easier if you work from a photocopy of the case report.

Points to note

1. Williams, whose name appears first, is the **plaintiff** (in cases since 1999 the **claimant**), claiming payment under a revised contract from Roffey Brothers & Nicholls (Contractors) Ltd – the **defendant**.
2. Immediately above the case name, we are told that the hearing took place in the **Court of Appeal** and immediately below we are told that the case was heard over three days in November 1989. The gap between the first two dates and the last indicates that this was a **reserved judgment** – the judges took 20 days to consider their judgment and delivered it in writing, rather than returning to court immediately in order to give an oral judgment. This is also indicated formally by the abbreviation *cur. ad. vult.* at the bottom of p1155 (Latin: *curia advisari vult* – the court wished to consider the matter).
3. The judges are named. The more cases you read for yourself, the more you will learn about the judiciary and you will be able to assess the quality of the judgment and the style of the judge. In this book we shall be considering 'Denning' judgments and 'Diplock' judgments and 'Scarman' judgments. You will add other names to this list: the great chancery judges whose expertise lies in property matters; which judges are known for their pragmatic approach and their common sense; which judges value certainty of the law above social issues, and so on.
4. The paragraph in italics gives a summary of the main areas covered by the case. This is also printed on the cover of the monthly part of the law reports so that the reader can see at a glance which cases might be of interest to them. This summary and the two paragraphs immediately below it are prepared by the author of the report, whose initials appear on the very last page of the report. These paragraphs are known as the **headnotes**.

5. The first of the two paragraphs is a summary of the facts and the second a summary of the judgment. While this summary is useful, it is not authoritative – it is much better to read the information from the judgments, especially when, as in this case, a very clear account of the facts is given in the judgment (see judgment of Glidewell LJ).

   The second paragraph gives the ruling and says that *Stilk* v *Myrick* (1809) 2 Camp 317 was distinguished and *Hoenig* v *Isaacs* [1952] 2 All ER 176 was applied by the court.

6. The All England Law Reports give Notes in which the reporter refers you to *Halsbury's Laws* for an account of the law relating to consideration, which is the subject matter of this case. **Consideration**, as noted elsewhere, is something which is given by one contracting party in return for something given by the other contracting party. This can be something which is physically handed over, a promise to perform a service or it can be a promise to do something in the future. No contract can be binding unless something is given or promised by each side, or unless it is given by deed, which is a more solemn form of promise. We have already met this concept in the equitable maxim 'equity will not assist a volunteer'.

7. There follows a list at p1154, with citations, of the cases referred to in the judgments, together with those cases cited in argument but not referred to in the judgments. This list is useful if you are looking for related cases for research purposes and in order to form your own opinion on the quality of the judgment.

8. The final paragraph gives details of the appeal. The judge in the county court was a deputy assistant recorder, a junior judge.

9. At the bottom of the page, the **names of counsel** are given. When looking at old cases, some star names can be spotted here – early in his career, Lord Denning appears as counsel in *L'Estrange* v *Graucob* [1934] 2 KB 394. Similarly, judges in the lower courts who first heard the cases, often go on to become distinguished senior judges, so what they have to say at this stage in their careers is often a valuable contribution to the academic argument.

10. The Weekly Law Reports contain a system of lettering in the margins for easy reference to parts of the judgment. This system is used below.

The judgments

How do you read the case itself? 'Very carefully!' came the reply when our students asked this of a visiting barrister.

There are three judgments which must all be read and analysed, the first of which is given by Glidewell LJ:

1. First, Glidewell LJ gives the facts and the history and identifies the issues. The facts are of lesser importance – only those which are material to the ratio decidendi of the case are significant.

2. On appeal, the facts on which the judgment is based are those accepted by the

judge at first instance. From pp1156B to 1157H, Glidewell LJ reviews these facts. The trial judge had accepted the facts as those given by the defendant:

> 'The judge found that the defendants' promise to pay an additional £10,300, at the rate of £575 per completed flat, was part of an oral agreement made between the plaintiff and the defendants on 9th April 1986, by way of variation to the original contract.
>
> The judge also found that before the plaintiff ceased work at the end of May 1986 the carpentry in 17 flats had been substantially (but not totally) completed. This means that between the making of the agreement on 9th April and the date when the plaintiff ceased work, eight further flats were substantially completed.'

3. Glidewell LJ then identifies the two issues to be decided by the Court of Appeal (p1158A and B), namely: was the agreement to pay an extra £10,300 void for want of consideration, ie because nothing new was given in return?; and were the plaintiffs entitled to be paid for work which had been substantially, but not fully, completed?

4. The judge then rehearses the arguments put forward by the plaintiff and the defendant on the **second** issue – substantial completion of the work. He reviews the points of law put forward from the previously decided cases. From p1158E down to p1160E you can see the doctrine of precedent in operation. Glidewell LJ reviews the authorities and reaches his conclusion upholding the judge's decision on this point.

5. From p1160F down to p1166D, he repeats the process in relation to the more important issue of consideration. His starting point is the ratio decidendi of the judge at first instance (p1160H). Glidewell LJ's *ratio decidendi* can be found at p1165D–F.

6. At p1165G, the judge **distinguishes** the key case *Stilk* v *Myrick* which established in 1809 that performance of an existing duty cannot be good consideration. He 'refines and limits' the application of this long-established ruling to cases where a party receives no benefit whatsoever from a re-negotiated agreement.

7. Finally, at p1166B, the learned judge cites *Chitty on Contracts*, to meet Counsel's subsidiary argument that 'consideration must move from the promissee' (ie that one of the parties to the contract must have provided the benefit, and if it is provided by someone who is not a party to the contract, it does not count as consideration).

Russell LJ and Purchas LJ substantially agree with Glidewell LJ's judgment.

Russell LJ has some additional points to make about duress and about promissory estoppel. The judge notes that the absence of consideration was never pleaded in the original statement of claim (the written submission accompanying the writ served on the defendant), although the judge at first instance allowed argument on the point in court. Nor was the estoppel argument fully developed before the court. When a case reaches the Court of Appeal, new argument cannot be heard. These remarks about estoppel are therefore *obiter dicta*.

Purchas LJ assesses the importance of *Stilk* v *Myrick* – a 'case of veneration' (p1169H). He observes that the rule is still approved in *Chitty* and in Cheshire, Fifoot & Furmston's *Law of Contract*, Purchas LJ's ratio decidendi appears at p1172C.

Leave to appeal to the House of Lords was granted but no appeal was made.

Williams v *Roffey* was followed in the later case of *Anangel Atlas Naviera SA* v *Ishikawajima Harrima (No 2)* [1990] 2 Lloyd's Rep 526 where the ratio was defined by Hirst J as follows:

> 'Whoever provided the service, where there is a practical conferment of benefit or a practical avoidance of disbenefit for the promisee, there is good consideration and it is no answer to say that the promissor is already bound; where, on the other hand there is a wholly gratuitous promise, *Stilk*'s case remains good law.'

In reaching their decision, the judges have thoroughly reviewed the application of the doctrine of consideration, with an assessment of the case law. In order to meet the needs of the late twentieth century, they have redefined the doctrine first laid down in a case dealing with the working conditions prevailing at the time of the Napoleonic wars.

6.10 Recording a case: writing a casenote

If you have put a lot of effort into reading and analysing a case, it is important that you can use this material in your private study and in your assessed work. You should take a detailed note of its principal features. As you become more experienced in this, you will probably develop your own method but you may like to start in the following way:

1. Give brief details of the **facts** of the case, including the **parties** and the **history** – where it was tried at first instance and what were the decisions of the lower courts.
2. Give details of the points of **law** and how the law has been applied to the facts of the case in the lower courts. List the points for consideration on appeal, if it is an appeal case.
3. Analyse the **legal argument**. Give details of any **dissenting judgments** (when a judge or judges disagree with the majority decision) as well as the arguments of the majority.
4. Say whether the outcome was a **good decision** or whether you disagree, in either case **giving reasons** for your opinion.
5. Are there **any problems** for future cases if this decision is subsequently followed?
6. Has the decision **clarified** the law – if so, how?

7. Why is it an **important** case?
8. What **changes** does it make to the earlier law?
9. If the case was not reported recently, look for references to **journal articles** on the cases and either note the references so that you can read them later or note the opinions of the writers.
10. You may wish to photocopy key cases and articles and highlight the key points in them, making notes on the text itself.

6.11 *Davis* v *Johnson*: a review of the doctrine of precedent

At p558D–562F of the case report of *Davis* v *Johnson* [1978] 2 WLR 553 (see Appendix B), Lord Diplock gives his opinion on whether the Court of Appeal is bound by its own decisions. Make a note of the main points of his argument. What, in particular, are his objections to the views of Lord Denning?

Lord Dilhorne (p569H *ff*) agrees with Lord Diplock and remarks on the 'unique character of the House of Lords sitting judicially' (p570C).

Lord Salmon at p577B takes a more pragmatic approach:

'This House [ie the House of Lords] decides every case that comes before it according to law. If, as in the instant case, the Court of Appeal decides an appeal contrary to one of its previous decisions, this House, much as it may deprecate the Court of Appeal's departure from the rule, will nevertheless dismiss the appeal if it comes to the conclusion that the decision appealed against was right in law.'

Then he goes on to support Lord Diplock's views of the ability of the Court of Appeal to overrule its own decisions.

Davis v *Johnson* is primarily a family law case. Cases may often have to be viewed in a number of different contexts. When reading a report of a case in a textbook, you must be sure that you have a complete picture of what the case is really about and how the various threads of argument relate to and influence each other. When consulting a casebook, make sure that any extract is relevant to the point of law that you are seeking and that it gives you a complete picture of what the case is about.

Specialist training in mediation is available for organisations such as the Centre for Effective Dispute Resolution (CEDR).

7

Principles of Statutory Interpretation

7.1 Introduction

Most statutes are drafted by trained parliamentary draftsmen who are skilled in avoiding ambiguity and uncertainty in the text of Acts of Parliament and, for the most part, the court simply has to judge how a statutory provision applies to the facts of a particular case.

However, uncertainties can arise in the following ways:

1. Private Members Bills are sometimes drafted without professional assistance;
2. the legislation can later be applied to unforeseen circumstances;
3. a 'hard case' may test the validity of the provision.

It then falls to the judges to interpret the words of the statute. In this way, the court is responsible for giving life the letter of the law. The judges must consider the meaning of the **words** used in the statutory provision, not what Parliament intended to say.

As Lord Wilberforce put it:

'Legislation is passed in England and put in the form of written words. The legislation is given legal effect by virtue of judicial decision, and it is the function of the courts to say what the application of the words used to particular cases or individuals is to be.' (*Black-Clawson International Limited* v *Papierwerke Waldhof Aschaffenburg AG* [1975] 1 All ER 810)

But, said Lord Wilberforce, this is not simply a mechanical analysis. The court should take into account 'intelligibility to the citizen, constitutional propriety, considerations of history, comity of nations, reasonable and non-retroactive effect and, no doubt in some contexts ... social needs'. Often this involves fine judgments of the lights and shades of meaning within a word or phrase.

7.2 Rules of interpretation

The common law has provided its own set of principles which govern the way in which the court will interpret statute law. The availability of such rules provides certainty and consistency in statutory interpretation. There are four main rules:

1. the literal rule;
2. the golden rule;
3. the mischief rule;
4. the purposive rule.

The literal rule

The primary rule of statutory interpretation is the literal rule, which simply states that **statutory provisions must be given their ordinary and literal meaning**. The court must not concern itself with the result of the application of the rule, however inconvenient the result may be. This can lead to a result which was plainly not what Parliament intended and to a result which provides an unjust solution. It is not the function of the court to rewrite statutes which do not produce the result that Parliament intended – this requires amending legislation from Parliament itself. The court cannot add words to the statute in order to enable it to fulfil the purpose which Parliament intended.

This is demonstrated by the case of *Magor & St Mellons Rural District Council* v *Newport Corporation* [1951] 2 All ER 839. Under a local government reorganisation, two Welsh local authorities were amalgamated. The Local Government Act 1933 provided compensation for councils which had their boundaries reduced in the reorganisaton. Because of the amalgamation, the two councils were in effect abolished to form a new authority. Newport Corporation argued that the compensation was only payable to surviving councils and the new authority had no claim. This was the effect of applying the literal rule. Lord Denning in a dissenting judgment in the Court of Appeal called on the court to discover and implement the intention of Parliament. This approach was firmly rejected by Lord Simmonds in the House of Lords: 'It appears to me to be a naked usurpation of the legislative function under the thin disguise of interpretation and it is less justifiable when it is guesswork with what material the legislature would, if it had discovered the gap, have filled it in.'

The application of the literal rule does not guarantee certainty, however, since:

1. Interpretation is dependent on the individual style of the judge – some judges are

more ready than others to declare the meaning 'plain', others more ready to play an interpretative role.
2. Words in their context can have a number of possible applicable dictionary meanings.
3. The possibility of different interpretations by different judges encourages claimants to risk litigation.
4. The application of the literal rule can cause injustice.

The golden rule

When the meaning of the words of the statute is uncertain or ambiguous and its application would lead to a 'manifest absurdity' or inconsistency with another part of the statute, the golden rule allows the court to **modify the words so far as is necessary to avoid the absurdity or inconsistency**. Needless to say, judges are very reluctant to declare that the words of Parliament are absurd so the rule is rarely used.

The mischief rule

Where the words of the statute do not produce a clear meaning, the court can look to the mischief which Parliament intended to correct. The mischief rule comes from *Heydon's Case* (1584) 3 Co Rep 74 which laid down four considerations for the court:

> '[1st] What was the Common Law before the Act?
> [2nd] What was the mischief and defect for which the Common Law did not provide?
> [3rd] What remedy the Parliament hath resolved and appointed to cure the disease of the Commonwealth? [ie What has Parliament done in the new legislation to put right the defect in the previous law?]
> [4th] The true reason of the remedy; and then the office of all the judges is always to make such construction as shall suppress the mischief and advance the remedy.'

The mischief rule allows the court to look at the purpose of the legislation and to construe the words accordingly – but **only** when the meaning of the plain words of the statute is unclear.

In *Davis* v *Johnson* [1978] 2 WLR 553 (reproduced as Appendix B), the House of Lords applied the mischief rule to the construction of s1 of the Domestic Violence and Matrimonial Proceeding Act (DVMPA) 1976 (see p563A–D). The problem arose over the true meaning of s1(2). In order to discover the mischief at which the subsection is aimed, Lord Diplock looks at the *travaux preparatoires* – the proceedings which led to the passing of the legislation: in this case the report to the House of Commons Select Committee on Violence in Marriage (July 1975) (see p563H *ff*). He notes that the question of homelessness of unmarried cohabitees is not dealt with fully in the report. On this issue, Lord Diplock therefore dissents from the majority view of the House of Lords and gives s1 DVMPA 1976 a narrow construction – but concedes that Miss Davis has a remedy in tort.

Lord Dilhorne (pp568C–569D) applies the literal rule:

> 'Here the language of the statute is clear and unambiguous and Parliament's intention apparent. Unmarried persons living together in the same household as husband and wife are for the purposes of s1(1) to be treated as if they were married. An unmarried woman to whom subs(2) applies is to have the same rights as a married woman ...'

He identifies the mischief at which the legislation is aimed at p568C–D.

Lord Kilbrandon also looks to the terms of reference of the House of Commons Select Committee (p571D–E) which he considers wide enough to include families in which the parties are not married. He rejects the appellant's argument that the provisions of the Act are merely matters of procedure:

> 'I must decline to hold that Parliament decreed a trifling and illusory remedy for a known disgraceful mischief, and to hold it in the interest of conceptual purity of the law. Leaving that interest aside, the plain fact is that the 1976 Act has authorised county courts to give the married person an injunction excluding from the matrimonial home the other, saying nothing about the property rights of either, and that that authority applies to a household where the parties are not married to each other "as it applies" to one where they are. That is sufficient for the disposal of this case.' (p573C)

Lord Salmon finds the meaning of s1(2) 'as plain as a pikestaff' (p574G), but he goes on to look at the purpose of the legislation:

> 'The whole purpose of the Act was to afford some protection to "battered wives", married or unmarried. And to the unmarried ones in particular. The married already had the full protection afforded by the 1967 Act. The unmarried did not. The married gained little from the 1976 Act save a quicker and cheaper method of protection.'

He goes on to say that, unless the defendant has been guilty of serious molestation, the court should only impose a temporary exclusion to allow the plaintiff to find somewhere to live (p575A) and at p576H *ff* discusses the doctrine of precedent.

Lord Scarman (p578, last line) observes that 'a layman could be forgiven for thinking that the section was tailor-made to enable a county court judge to make the order that was made in this case.' However at p580F *ff* he looks specifically to the mischief for which Parliament has provided the remedies: 'conduct by a family partner, which puts at risk the security, or sense of security, of the other partner in the home'. Note the way in which Lord Scarman develops this concept (p581 *ff*), concluding: 'For these reasons, my conclusion is that s1 of the 1976 Act is concerned to protect not property but human life and limb.'

For three of the judges, the plain wording of the statute was conclusive but, because the provisions had been interpreted in two previous cases, *B v B* [1978] 2 WLR 160 and *Cantliff v Jenkins* [1978] 2 WLR 177, and the judges were now being asked to overrule these interpretations, they all looked to the mischief at which the legislation was aimed. Over the three cases, 16 judges had been called on to interpret the provision, and they were evenly divided in their construction of the statute (eight:eight). As Viscount Dilhorne remarks: 'Few, if any, sections of a modern Act can have given rise to so much litigation in so short a time and to such a difference of opinion. A few more words in the Act would have avoided all this litigation.'

Lord Kilbrandon concludes: 'It may be, I do not know, that the matters it dealt with were deemed to be of such urgency that the usual researches, necessary to anticipate and deal with all contingencies likely to attend reform of a complicated branch of the law, were omitted or abridged.'

Purposive interpretation

There is an overlap between this approach and the application of the mischief rule. The European Court of Justice takes a purposive approach in which the Court looks first to the purpose of the legislation. This approach has had a significant influence on the English courts. When considering points of European law, it *must* be taken. In the case of *Litster* v *Forth Dry Dock Co Ltd* [1989] 1 All ER 1134, Lord Oliver held that, when legislation is enacted to comply with the United Kingdom's EC Treaty obligations, a purposive construction would be applied even though it may involve a construction which departed from the literal interpretation of the words used by Parliament. This means that on points of Community law the English courts must abandon the literal rule if the resulting interpretation does not comply fully with requirements under Community law. EC legislation contains a preamble, stating the purpose of the legislation which is binding in the same way as any other part of the legislation, even though it is a statement of broad policy rather than a substantive statutory provision. The European Convention on Human Rights also requires purposive interpretation and, under s3 of the Human Rights Act 1998, all United Kingdom domestic legislation must be interpreted to give effect to the Convention: again a purposive approach is required.

7.3 General rules of construction

The statute should be read as a whole

The words must be placed in their true context and not read in isolation.

Ejusdem generis rule

This means that when a sequence of words is given, followed by general words, the general words must be construed to include only items of the same type as the specific words. For example, in *Powell* v *Kempton Park Racecourse Co* [1899] AC 143, general words in the Betting Act 1853 were construed *not* to include 'racecourse' within the definition of 'house, office, room or other place' because house, office and room all indicated places which were indoors and a racecourse is an outdoor place.

7.4 Presumptions made by the court when interpreting statutes

1. Statutes are not intended to alter the common law.
2. Statutes are not intended to have retrospective effect – they are only effective from the date of the Royal Assent, or the commencement date provided in the statute.
3. Criminal offences usually require fault.
4. Criminal statutes are construed strictly in favour of the accused.
5. Parliament is presumed not to intend to promote or to reward serious crime.
6. If there is a conflict between provisions in the same statute, the primary provision must be preferred over a subordinate provision.

7.5 Aids to interpretation

Internal aids to interpretation

The conclusive text of the statute is the Queen's Printer's Copy. You will find the Queen's Printer's Copy of the Treasure Act 1996 reproduced as Appendix C. Find the parts of the statute referred to below in the text of the Act.

The court can look to the following parts of the statute when seeking its true meaning:

1. **The long title** – the full description of the act given at the beginning. In the Treasure Act it is: 'An Act to abolish treasure trove and to make fresh provision in relation to treasure.'
2. **The short title** – the title by which the statute is generally known: the Treasure Act 1996.
3. **The section headings** – the first section in the Treasure Act is headed 'Meaning of "treasure"'.
4. **The definition section of the statute** – the statute may provide its own rules of interpretation: see, for example, s1 Treasure Act 1996 and s205 Law of Property Act 1925 which give definitions of key words in the statute. The definition section in one statute is not conclusive as to the meaning of the same word in another statute. The Interpretation Act 1978 contains a limited number of definitions which are applicable to all statutes.

There are two further internal aids to interpretation which do not appear in the Treasure Act:

5. **The preamble** – in older legislation, an explanatory note was given of the reasons, purpose and scope of the legislation. This is rare in modern legislation but modern charity law is based on the Statute of Charitable Uses 1601 which contains the following preamble:

> 'Whereas lands, tenements, rents, annuities, profits, heriditaments, goods, chattels,

money and stock of money, have been heretofore given, limited, appointed, and assigned as well by the Queen's most excellent majesty, and her most noble progenitors, as by sundry other well disposed persons: some for the relief of aged, impotent, and poor people, some for maintenance of sick and maimed soldiers and mariners, schools of learning, free schools, and scholars in universities; some for repair of bridges, ports, havens, causeways, churches, sea banks and highways; some for education and preferment of orphans; some for or towards the relief, stock or maintenance of houses of correction; some for marriages of poor maids; some for supporting, aid and help of young tradesmen, handicraftsmen, and persons decayed; and others for the relief or redemption of prisoners or captives, and for aid or ease of any poor inhabitants concerning payment of fifteens, setting out of soldiers and other taxes; which lands, tenements, rents, annuities, profits, heriditaments, goods, chattels, money, and stocks of money, nevertheless have not been employed according to the charitable intent of the givers and founders thereof, by reason of frauds, breaches of trust, and negligence in those that should pay, deliver and employ the same.'

This preamble is still used by the court today as an aid to construction when deciding whether the purpose of a gift or a trust is charitable.

6. **Schedules** – These have the same force as any section of an Act.

Marginal notes and punctuation must be **disregarded** when interpreting the words of the statute.

History of the legislation

Where provisions of an old statute have been re-enacted, the scope of the new provision may be called into question. For example s53 Law of Property Act 1925 provides:

'(1) Subject to the provisions hereinafter contained with respect to the creation of interests in land by parol –
(a) No interest in land can be created or disposed of except by writing, signed by the person creating or conveying the same, or by his agent thereunto lawfully authorised in writing or by will, or by operation of law;
(b) A declaration of trust respecting any land or any interest therein must be manifested and proved by some writing signed by some person who is able to declare such trust, or by his will;
(c) A disposition of an equitable interest or trust subsisting at the time of the disposition, signed by the person disposing of the same, or by his agent thereunto lawfully authorised in writing or by will.
(2) This section does not affect the creation or operation of resulting, implied or constructive trusts.'

In a number of stamp duty avoidance cases, the court was called upon to construe the nature of the requirement of writing for the disposition of an equitable interest. In *Grey* v *IRC* [1959] 3 All ER 603, it was held that the word 'disposition' must be given its ordinary, dictionary meaning, but it was argued that s53(1)(c) was a consolidation of three sections of the Statute of Frauds, whose purpose was to ensure that the trustees would know who were the true beneficiaries of a trust and to prevent secret and possibly fraudulent transfers of equitable interests. The judge acknowledged the principle that 'a consolidating Act is not to be read as effecting changes in the existing law unless the words it employs are too clear in their effect to admit of any other construction'. However, the judge concluded that the principle did not apply to s53(1)(c), and applied the literal rule.

External aids to interpretation

These can include the following:

1. The court can refer to the dictionary meaning of the words.
2. Reference to Law Commission and Royal Commission reports is permissible to discover the mischief at which the statute was aimed.
3. The court can now refer to Hansard for the reports on parliamentary debates during the passage of the legislation. Traditionally, this was absolutely prohibited – see Lord Diplock's reasoning in *Davis* v *Johnson* at p563F *ff.* Lord Diplock refers to the position of the European Community with regard to *travaux preparatoires*. However, in recent years, this European influence has been much more significant and in the case of *Pepper (Inspector of Taxes)* v *Hart* [1993] 1 All ER 42, where Hansard revealed a clear statement of Parliament's intention with regard to s63 Finance Act 1976, it was finally conceded by a 6:1 majority of the House of Lords that the absolute prohibition should be modified subject to the following provisos:

   a) the legislation is ambiguous, or obscure, or leads to an absurdity;
   b) the material relied upon consists of one or more statements by a minister or other promoter of the Bill, together if necessary with such other parliamentary material as is necessary to understand such statements and their effect;
   c) the statements relied upon are clear.

Use of Hansard is also subject to a requirement in the 1995 *Practice Note* ([1995] 1 All ER 234) that the relevant extracts should be made available to other parties to the litigation and to the court.

7.6 Reading a statute

To get the most out of this exercise, you must follow the text of the Treasure Act 1996 (in Appendix C) while working through the points below. A summary of the provisions is set out below to make it easier for you to follow the text of the Act. If it is fairly straightforward for you, keep reading from the statute until you come to a provision where the meaning is not clear to you and only then consult the summary.

Summary

- The first page is headed with the Royal Arms and its short title.
- The Act is given a chapter number – Chapter 24. This is given for ease of reference but has no legal effect. It means that this is the twenty-fourth piece of legislation to be passed in 1996.
- Below, under 'Arrangement of Sections' is a contents list.
- On the next page, the heading is repeated, followed by the long title to the Act and the date when the Act was given the Royal Assent – 4 July 1996. This is *not* the commencement date of the Act, for which provision is made in **s15**. In fact, the Act came into force on 24 September 1997.
- Then come the enacting words which have no effect on the meaning of the Act, followed by **s1** which, as we have seen, gives the definitions:

  - **s1(1)** defines 'treasure'.
  - **s1(1)(a)** gives a definition of three types of coin which are treasure.
  - **s1(1)(b), (c)** and **(d)** require a reference to other sections and subsections in the Act in order for items of treasure to be identified.
  - **s1(2)** excludes objects from the definition of treasure.

- **s2** delegates powers to the Secretary of State to designate by statutory instrument further classes of objects as treasure. A statutory instrument is a form of delegated legislation – the Act delegates powers to the Secretary of State to designate objects of treasure which he considers to be of 'outstanding historical, archaeological or cultural importance.' Thus, Parliament has not agreed a comprehensive list of items which are treasure – it has given the Secretary of State powers to add items to the list or (by **s2(2)**) to remove items from the list.

  - These alterations to the list can only be made by an order which has been approved by both Houses of Parliament (**s2(4)**).
  - Note that the marginal note to **s2** has **no** legal effect. The note 'power to alter meaning' could not be used to construe Parliament's meaning.

- **s3** gives definitions which are supplementary to **s1**. How will future courts construe **s3(6)**: 'An object which can reasonably be taken to be at least a particular age is to be presumed to be at least that age, unless shown not to be'?

  - **s3(7)** excludes objects found in and on wrecks – the marginal note gives the reference to the Merchant Shipping Act.

- **s4** vests treasure in the Crown or a franchisee unless prior rights to the property can be established. We must look to **s5** for a definition of franchisee.

  - **s4(2)** defines prior rights.
  - **s4(3)** ensures that the Treasure Act applies to all findings of property which would have been treasure trove before the act comes into force.

- **s4(4)** extends the definition of treasure trove beyond its old common law meaning.
- **s6** provides that all treasure trove shall belong to the Crown and form part of the government's funds in accordance with the Civil List Act 1952. This section gives effective control over the disposal of treasure to the Secretary of State.
- **s7** recognises the jurisdiction of the Coroner over treasure.
- **s8** obliges the finder to notify the Coroner of any found objects which might be treasure and provides sanctions for not doing so.
- **s9** gives the procedure for establishing whether or not the objects are treasure.
- **s10** deals with the payment of rewards.
- **s11** says the Secretary of State must propose and keep under review a code of practice relating to treasure.
- **s12** says that the Secretary of State must make an annual report to Parliament on the operation of the Act.
- **ss13 and 14** say how the Act is to apply in Northern Ireland by making the amendments necessary to other legislation to bring it into line with the new Act.
- **s15** gives the citation of the Act, makes provision for its commencement and provides that it shall not apply in Scotland.

There are points in the drafting of this statute which may well give rise to confusion and to litigation. First, in order to understand the structure of the Act, it is necessary to understand the pre-existing common law. Under common law, treasure trove consisted only of items with a significant gold or silver content which had been concealed by an unknown owner with the intention of retrieving them at a later date. This meant that many important discoveries could not be claimed by the Crown. For example, items from burials could not be claimed because the owner did not intend to come back for them, and jewels such as the Middleham jewel, valued at £250,000 and of considerable historical significance, could not be claimed because they had no substantial gold or silver content. Objects such as pottery, base metal coins and gemstones found with a hoard of treasure had to be separated from the gold and silver items because they belonged either to the landowner or to the finder.

When this background is taken into consideration, it is easier to understand the definitions in ss1 and 3. The Act changed the definition by removing the need to prove that objects were intentionally buried; by making it clear how much gold and silver they must contain in order to be treasure; and by including objects associated with treasure. In addition, the Act gives the Secretary of State powers to extend the definition of treasure to catch new categories of property as appropriate.

The Act also sets out the procedures by which treasure is administered and makes non-declaration an offence, and the previous common law is codified and extended. Problems of interpretation are likely to arise unless the Act is set in the context of the pre-existing case law and this may well be an instance where the mischief rule may be applied to the interpretation of the statute.

The Treasure Bill was initially introduced in the House of Lords as a Private

Members Bill. It was then adopted by the Government and reintroduced in its present form. The *travaux preparatoires* to the earlier bill do not therefore provide aids to interpretation because there is no straight path from the Bill as presented in the House of Lords to the legislation which received the Royal Assent on 4 July 1996. Despite the fact that the original House of Lords debate contained informed contributions from some of our most eminent archaeologists and lawyers, it did **not** reflect the intention of Parliament.

Note the use of delegated legislation to extend the categories of treasure, to set guidelines and to provide a commencement date. Any such powers taken by a minister or a statutory body must have a basis in statute law, as here.

Section III
EU Law and Human Rights Law

8

The Law of the European Union

8.1 Historical background

8.2 British membership of the European Union

8.3 Community legislation

8.4 Direct effect

8.5 The institutions of the European Community

8.6 Websites

8.7 Reading a European case

'For three days in 1946 I attended the trial of the Nazi major war criminals in Nuremberg. For six years Europe had experienced destruction, homelessness, hunger and despair at the hands of these men. Now, at last, we were bringing them to justice. Some looked broken, while others appeared as arrogant as ever.

As I left that court, I pledged that I would do everything within my power to prevent the clouds of war from ever gathering again over our continent.' Sir Edward Heath

8.1 Historical background

The idea for a European Community came from the Resistance movement of World War II. In 1944 there was a meeting of resistance groups in Switzerland. The groups came from all the countries caught up in the war, including Germany. They issued a draft declaration saying that a primary cause of wars in Europe was the existence of 30 separate sovereign states. They saw the solution as a federal union for security, foreign policy and defence. At the end of the war, Europe was in chaos – many people were displaced from their country of origin. The infrastructure was largely destroyed, and governments were bankrupted by the war effort.

On 19 September 1946, Winston Churchill made a speech in Zurich in which he too proposed a United States of Europe based on Franco-German co-operation. Britain would not be part of it because of allegiances to the Commonwealth and a special relationship with the United States. However, a new threat to European stability had emerged from the Soviet Union and the Eastern Bloc. The United States therefore had to maintain its support for the failing European economies. In 1947, the Americans brought in their programme of Marshall Aid to rebuild the

European national economies. This aid was given on condition that there was economic co-operation between the European nations. This co-operation manifested itself in the formation of the Organisation for European Economic Co-operation which scheduled repayments of debts between countries and sought to encourage free trade.

The European States acquired a taste for co-operation as the following sequence of events shows:

1. In 1947, the Benelux countries (Belgium, the Netherlands and Luxembourg) agreed to form a customs union and a single market.
2. In 1949, the Council of Europe was formed. Under its auspices the European Convention on Human Rights, the European Court of Human Rights and the European Commission on Human Rights were founded. These are separate organisations from the European Community (see Chapter 9).
3. In 1949, the North Atlantic Treaty Organisation (NATO) was founded for the common defence of Western Europe, Canada and the United States.

All these initiatives were based on co-operation between nation states rather than integration into any form of union. They were inter-governmental rather than federal, ie the governments were acting independently in agreeing to co-operate: there was no question of a decision being taken by the body which they formed which was binding on all of them without their full consent. However, in practice, the co-operation is very close indeed.

The main problem after the war was what to do about Germany. A repetition of the conditions which prevailed after World War I had to be avoided at all costs since German humiliation at the hands of the Allies had created the climate which brought Hitler to power, and further humiliation might have given the communists too much influence in West German politics. There was therefore no demand that Germany pay reparations for the war damage after World War II. However, while the British and Americans wanted to rebuild a strong Germany, the French were very much opposed to this. They had been invaded by Germany three times within living memory. France wanted to keep the Saar and the Rhineland territories which it occupied and to keep the coal and steel producing Ruhr out of German hands.

The solution was found by Jean Monnet, a French civil servant. He advocated the formation of a supra-national authority with powers to take decisions which would bind all the states who joined, to control coal and steel production in France and Germany and in any other European country which wished to join.

• For France, the idea kept the potentially dangerous industries outside German control and Germany accepted because it was better than having no industry at all.
• The Benelux countries were in favour because they had already had a good experience of integration.
• Italy wanted to join to achieve stability.

- The British, though, did **not** because their coal and steel industries were larger than those of all the other countries put together.

Thus, in 1951, the European Coal and Steel Community (ECSC) was formed. Its decisions were legally binding on the Member States. The High Authority of the ECSC could order re-organisation of the national industry and the state would have to obey. The ECSC was successful because there was an enormous demand for coal and steel to rebuild Europe and for the newly emerging industries providing consumer goods. This treaty expired in 2002.

Jean Monnet later proposed a European Atomic Energy Authority – EURATOM – for co-operation in developing the peaceful uses of atomic energy. Again, the United Kingdom declined to join.

The six partners then proposed a European Economic Community. As was stated in the Preamble to the Treaty of Rome 1957 (referred to in this text as the EC Treaty), its purpose was to bring about 'an ever closer union'. Having sat at the conference table in Messina and negotiated substantial changes to the original proposals for an economic community, Britain again chose not to join.

When, in 1961, Britain finally applied to join the Community, President de Gaulle of France opposed and vetoed Britain's membership. De Gaulle's presidency was a troubled time for the Community. In 1969, after the student riots in Paris, he left office and was succeeded by President Pompidou, who formed a good relationship with the British negotiator, Edward Heath, opening the door to British membership in 1973. Denmark and the Republic of Ireland also joined in that year, followed by Greece in 1981, Spain and Portugal in 1986 and Austria, Finland and Sweden in 1995.

8.2 British membership of the European Union

The Treaty of Rome, as amended by subsequent treaties, is, among other things, the Constitution of the European Communities.

At present the European Convention on the Future of Europe meets regularly under the Presidency of the former French President, Giscard D'Estaing, with a Praesidium composed of members of the European Commission, the national parliaments and the European Parliament, to discuss the proposed draft Treaty on a Constitution for the European Union.

The main purpose of the Treaty would be: to amalgamate all the disparate treaty provisions into a single document; to provide a Bill of Rights for the European Union, and to make its law more accessible to the European citizen; to remove the right of individual Member States to veto legislation from a large number of areas of competence, particularly in social legislation; and to appoint European ministers including a President, a Foreign Minister and a Public Prosecutor. In addition, the initiatives for a common foreign and security policy and a common defence policy would be reinforced.

Each new Member State becomes a signatory to the Treaty of Rome when it joins the European Community and has to comply with its own constitutional requirements in order for the provisions of the Treaty to become national law. In the United Kingdom, it was necessary to pass the European Communities Act 1972. With the passing of this act, the British people, in common with those of other Member States 'have limited their sovereign rights, albeit within limited fields': *Van Gend en Loos* Case 26/62 [1963] ECR 1 at p12. Yet in the Government White Paper of 1971 which introduced the European Communities Bill, it was claimed that there was 'no question of any erosion of essential national sovereignty'. Are these positions compatible?

Section 2(1) European Communities Act 1972 provides:

'All such rights, powers, liberties, obligations and restrictions from time to time created or arising by or under the Treaties, and all such remedies and procedures from time to time provided for by or under the Treaties, as in accordance with the Treaties are without further enactment to be given legal effect or used in the United Kingdom shall be recognised and available in law, and be enforced, allowed and followed accordingly.'

Unless the legislation is in a form which specifically provides for implementing measures on the part of the Member State, s2(1) makes Community law directly applicable in the United Kingdom without the need for United Kingdom legislation.

Section 2(4) provides that all United Kingdom law must be construed so as to comply with Community law. Community law must have supremacy over United Kingdom law. This principle has been reaffirmed by the case law of the European Court of Justice, in particular in *Costa* v *ENEL* Case 6/64 [1964] ECR 585:

'By creating a Community of unlimited duration, having its own institutions, its own personality, its own legal capacity of representation on the international plane and, more particularly, real powers stemming from a limitation of sovereignty or transfer of powers from the States to the Community, the Member States have limited their sovereign rights, albeit within limited fields, and have thus created a body of law which binds both their nationals and themselves.'

In *Amministrazione delle Finanze dello Stato* v *Simmenthal SpA* Case 106/77 [1978] ECR 629 the Court stated:

'... in accordance with the principles of the precedence of Community law, the relationship between provisions of the Treaty and directly applicable measures of the institutions on the one hand and the national law of Member States on the other is such that those provisions and measures, not only by their entry into force render automatically inapplicable any current provision of national law but ... insofar as they are an integral part of and take precedence in the legal order applicable to the territory of each of the Member States, also preclude the valid adoption of new national legislative measures to the extent to which they would be incompatible with Community provisions. ...

A national court which is called upon, within the limits of its jurisdiction, to apply provisions of Community law is under a duty to give full effect to those provisions, if necessary refusing of its own motion to apply any conflicting provision of national legislation, even if adopted subsequently, and it is not necessary for the court to request or await the prior setting aside of such provisions by legislative or other constitutional means.'

This means courts must refuse to apply subsequent provisions of national law which are inconsistent with the Community law, even though the general rule is that the most recent statutory provisions supersede those which have gone before. The Court does not interfere with the new legislation – it simply does not apply it if the national government has not fully implemented, or has misunderstood, the scope of the Community provisions.

Section 2(2) European Communities Act 1972 enables the government to give full effect to its EC Treaty obligations. Section 2(4) provides a rule of *construction* that past, present and future enactments in United Kingdom law are to be construed so that they are compatible with Community law.

By signing the Treaty of Rome, the British Government delegated to the Council of Ministers, and other competent institutions of the Community, powers to make law in areas which are strictly within the fields which have been delegated to the Community under the Treaty of Rome and subsequent legislation. The British Government has a vote at the Council table where all major policy decisions are made.

There is a convention that no Member State will ever be called upon to vote for a matter of community policy which is fundamentally against their national interest. This is known as the Luxembourg Accord. Further, following the Treaty on European Union (the Maastricht Treaty), the principle of subsidiarity has been given greater prominence as art 5 (formerly art 3b) of the EC Treaty:

> 'The Community shall act within the limits of the powers conferred upon it by this Treaty and of the objectives assigned to it therein. In areas which do not fall within its executive competence, the Community shall take action, in accordance with the principle of subsidiarity, only if and in so far as the objectives of the proposed action cannot be sufficiently achieved by the Member States and can therefore by reason of the scale or effects of the proposed action, be better achieved by the Community. Any action by the Community shall not go beyond what is necessary to achieve the objectives of the Treaty.'

There is controversy over the true meaning of subsidiarity, but broadly it restricts the power of the Community so that it can act only where absolutely necessary in order to fulfil Community policy objectives. Any acts which can be carried out by the Member States must be left to them. This principle is not new but the Maastricht Treaty gave it greater prominence and art 5 is a restatement of the rule that there are limits to the powers of the Community which are defined by the treaties.

For so long as the United Kingdom is a member of the European Union, it must adhere to laws made for the whole Community and must take the steps necessary to implement Community law in full. No government has power to bind its successors, however, and a future British Parliament could vote to secede from the Treaty of Rome and withdraw altogether.

8.3 Community legislation

Community legislation consists of treaty-based primary legislation and secondary legislation which is found in regulations, directives, decisions, recommendations and opinions. Most of these are made by the Council of Ministers but the Commission has jurisdiction to legislate in some fields of Community law. The European Parliament has no powers to legislate, although it has an increasingly significant role to play in the legislative process.

The treaties

The Communities were founded with the signing of three treaties: The European Coal and Steel Community Treaty, the EURATOM Treaty and the Treaty of Rome. These contain a preamble – a broad policy statement. Those which will be primary concern to you as a law student are **articles 2 and 3** of the Treaty of Rome. These provisions have been substantially expanded by subsequent treaties. Unlike preambles to United Kingdom statutes, these European policy statements are legally binding on the Member States who, by signing the Treaty, agree to work for the furtherance of these policies.

Articles 2 and 3 EC Treaty (as amended by treaties subsequent to the Treaty of Rome) state:

Article 2:

> 'The Community shall have as its task, by establishing a common market and an economic and monetary union and by implementing common policies or activities referred to in arts 3 and 4 (formerly art 3a), to promote throughout the Community a harmonious, balanced and sustainable development of economic activities, a high level of employment and of social protection, equality between men and women, sustainable and non-inflationary growth, a high degree of competitiveness and convergence of economic performance, a high level of protection and improvement of the quality of the environment, the raising of the standard of living and quality of life, and economic and social cohesion and solidarity among Member States.'

Article 3:

> '1. For the purposes set out in art 2, the activities of the Community shall include, as provided in this Treaty and in accordance with the timetable set out therein:
> (a) the prohibition, as between Member States, of customs duties and quantitative restrictions on the import and export of goods, and of all other measures having equivalent effect;
> (b) a common commercial policy;
> (c) an internal market characterised by the abolition, as between Member States, of obstacles to the free movement of goods, persons, services and capital;
> (d) measures concerning the entry and movement of persons as provided for in Title IV [Title IV deals with visas, asylum, immigration and other policies related to Free Movement of Persons];
> (e) a common policy in the sphere of agriculture and fisheries;
> (f) a common policy in the sphere of transport;

(g) a system ensuring that competition in the internal market is not distorted;
(h) the approximation of the laws of Member States to the extent required for the functioning of the common market;
(i) the promotion of coordination between employment policies of the Member States with a view to enhancing the effectiveness by developing a coordinated strategy for employment;
(j) a policy in the social sphere comprising a European Social Fund;
(k) the strengthening of economic cohesion;
(l) a policy in the sphere of the environment;
(m) the strengthening of competitiveness of Community industry;
(n) the promotion of research and technological development;
(o) encouragement for the establishment and development of trans-European networks;
(p) a contribution to the attainment of a high level of health protection;
(q) a contribution to education and training of quality and to the flowering of the cultures of the Member States;
(r) a policy in the sphere of development co-operation;
(s) the association of the overseas countries and territories in order to increase trade and promote jointly economic and social development;
(t) a contribution to the strengthening of consumer protection;
(u) measures in the spheres of energy, civil protection and tourism.
2. In all the activities referred to in this Article, the Community shall aim to eliminate inequalities, and to promote equality, between men and women.'

Under art 10 (formerly art 5) EC Treaty, Member States are obliged to take all appropriate measures, whether general or particular, to ensure the fulfilment of their obligations arising out of the Treaty. Article 12 (formerly art 6) prohibits all discrimination on grounds of nationality as between Member States and their citizens.

No Community legislation will be valid unless jurisdiction to pass such measures can be traced to the provision in the Treaty. Provision for the setting up and functions of the Community institutions is found in the EC Treaty. Other articles govern specific areas of Community law and are to be construed as statutory provisions: art 141 (formerly art 119) contains the community law relating to Equal Pay; arts 81 and 82 (formerly arts 85 and 86) contain the European Competition policy, for example.

The Single European Act 1986

Any major new policy requires a new treaty. In the 1980s the Member States were concerned that the Community was not sufficiently competitive with the United States and Japan. The trade barriers between the Member States were seen to be an impediment to performance in the world markets. So in 1985 the Commission produced a White Paper entitled *Completing the Internal Market* proposing some 350 measures needed to complete the internal market by 31 December 1992. These were adopted in amending treaty legislation known as the Single European Act, which consisted mainly of amendments to the Treaty of Rome.

The Single European Act gave a new focus to existing policies which had been laid down in the Treaty of Rome. The White Paper had identified three types of barriers which needed to be removed: physical, fiscal and technical. The Single European Act proposed the continuing development of the Community based on four pillars of policy:

1. The **free movement** of goods, persons, services and capital between Member States. This obliged Member States not to discriminate in any way against goods, persons, services and capital coming from other Member States.
2. The **harmonisation** of law in the Member States which directly affects 'the establishment and functioning of the common market'. When drafting new legislation, the Member States must make a concerted effort to bring their law into line with that prevailing in other Member States. There is to be a move away from national standards and specifications towards European standards and specifications.
3. The **competition policy** of the Community – prohibitions on restrictive practices, abuse of dominant trading positions and discriminatory state aids.
4. A **common customs tariff** or common external tariff. All Member States should be surrounded by common trade barriers with the rest of the world so that goods enter the Community under exactly the same conditions whether they come in at Piraeus, Hamburg, Rotterdam or Liverpool or any other port in the Community.

The Treaty on European Union 1992 (the Maastricht Treaty)
The Treaty on European Union (TEU) comprised further amendments to the Treaty of Rome and introduced some new policy pillars:

1. A new concept of **European citizenship**.
2. A **common interior policy on justice and home affairs**, including policies on asylum, immigration, drug-related crime, international fraud, and terrorism, and closer contacts between customs officers and co-operation in criminal matters.
3. A **common foreign and security policy**.
4. **Monetary union**.

The Social Chapter, which recognised employment rights of workers, was to have been another pillar introduced by the TEU. When the United Kingdom could not agree to its inclusion in the Treaty itself, the other Member States entered into a separate Agreement on Social Policy. With the change of government, in 1997 the United Kingdom reopened negotiations to ratify the Social Chapter and United Kingdom ratification was incorporated into the Treaty of Amsterdam.

The Treaty of Amsterdam
The European Council met in Amsterdam in June 1997 and agreed the text of the Treaty of Amsterdam whereby:

1. The text of the treaties was to be **simplified** – obsolete provisions were to be deleted and the articles renumbered. Only arts 1, 2, 3 and 105 of the EC Treaty remained unchanged.

2. The **institutions** were to be reformed with a view to the enlargement of the EU. It was agreed that voting in the Council and Parliament would have to be reweighted and that there should only be one Commissioner per Member State but the detail of these changes would be postponed until one year before enlargement. Legislative procedures were simplified, in particular the co-decision procedure.

3. Measures were introduced to give **greater transparency** to the decision-making processes. Citizens would have a right of access to the European Parliament, Council and Commission documents, except where it was in the public or private interest to deny such access.

4. There was to be **greater flexibility** in the future development of the EU. Measures would be introduced to permit closer integration of the 'vanguard group' of Member States seeking closer union so that there could be closer co-operation between smaller groups of Member States.

5. The pillar of justice and home affairs was renamed '**freedom, security and justice**' and under this head measures on asylum, immigration and rights of residence for Community nationals were put in place, some of which were to be adopted within five years and others were under no time limit. All Member States, except for the United Kingdom and Ireland, entered into arrangements to reduce frontier controls (the Schengen Agreement) and separate arrangements for the UK and Ireland were made by Protocol to the Treaty of Amsterdam).

6. Under the common foreign and security policy it was proposed to introduce a **European humanitarian defence, peacekeeping and rescue force**, subject to recognition that the Member States 'see their common defence realised in NATO'.

7. Police and judicial co-operation in criminal matters was **expanded and revised** to include co-operation in combating racism and xenophobia. There is to be harmonisation of criminal law and laws covering organised crime, drug trafficking and terrorism. The European Court of Justice is to be given a wider jurisdiction on interpretation of these matters under art 234 (formerly art 177).

8. A new art 13 was introduced permitting the Council to act 'to combat discrimination based on sex, racial or ethnic origin, religion or belief, disability or sexual orientation'.

9. A new art 6a was introduced giving a commitment to respect for fundamental rights.

10. Provisions were made for an integration of environmental policies and greater protection of the environment.

11. There was clarification of the principle of subsidiarity

12. The UK ratified the Social Agreement.

The Nice Summit

The Nice Summit in December 2000 met to decide the fine detail of the restructuring of the Community institutions in preparation of the enlargement of the Union to include Poland, Romania, the Czech Republic, Hungary, Bulgaria, Slovakia, Lithuania, Latvia, Slovenia, Estonia, Cyprus, Malta – and eventually Turkey. The enlargement will bring the total of Member States to twenty-seven.

1. Under the enlargement protocol, **the votes in the Council and the Parliament were reweighted** according to size of population of the Member States. This was the subject of negotiation at Nice so that Germany, although larger, has parity of voting power with France and the United Kingdom.
2. **The Commission was reduced** to one member per state and a rotation system will be introduced to bring the number of members of the Commission to below 27.
3. Attempts to bring in further qualified majority voting were resisted by the Member States.
4. There was to be a common accord to permit differentiated integration – **closer co-operation**. It was recognised that this would require changes to the institutional structure of the EU.
5. The Court of First Instance is to have **chambers to hear cases in specific fields of EC law**, with an appeal system to hear appeals from these new chambers.
6. **The Charter of Fundamental Rights of the European Union** was approved. This would bring together the fundamental rights from international and European Conventions recognised by the Member States and would be considered further in 2004.
7. German proposals for a **Constitutional Conference in 2004** were approved at Nice. At this summit the Draft Constitution currently in preparation will be considered.

The Treaty of Accession 2003

On 16 April 2003 in Athens, ten of the applicant states signed the Treaty of Accession. The ten new Member States will join the EU on 10 May 2004, leaving only Romania, Bulgaria and eventually Turkey to complete the current round of applications.

Secondary legislation

Secondary Community legislation has its basis in art 249 (formerly art 189) EC Treaty which provides for four types of measure:

1. **Regulations** are binding on the Member States exactly as they are drafted and in their entirety. These are directly applicable in national law. The passing of a regulation requires a high degree of consensus between the Member States.

2. **Directives** are binding on Member States as to the result to be achieved. The Member States must implement the policy fully but they may choose the method of implementation. Normally, the Directive includes a time limit by which the policy must be implemented by national legislation.
3. **Decisions** are binding in their entirety upon those to whom they are addressed. Decisions are usually given by the Commission in response to individual requests for confirmation that a course of action complies with Community law. A dispensation from compliance with Community law may be given by Decision. This may contain conditions which will also be binding on those to whom the decision is addressed.
4. **Recommendations** and **opinions** have no binding force, but carry considerable political and moral weight.

8.4 Direct effect

We have seen that Treaty provisions and regulations, being binding in their entirety, are directly applicable in the jurisdictions of the Member States – as soon as they are passed, they become part of national law. If the provision is **unconditional, clear and precise and intended to confer rights on the individual** it will also have direct effect and can be pleaded in litigation against another individual and is said to have **horizontal direct effect**. This was established in *Van Gend en Loos* Case 26/62 [1963] ECR 1. The Dutch government imposed a customs duty which was contrary to art 12 (now art 25) EC Treaty and the case of *Van Gend en Loos* concerned a court action to recover the sum paid, seeking to rely on art 12. The European Court of Justice upheld the right to do so: 'Article 12 must be interpreted as producing direct effects and creating individual rights which national courts must protect.'

In *Van Duyn* v *Home Office* Case 41/74 [1974] ECR 1337, the European Court of Justice gave criteria on which direct effect could be established:

'These provisions impose on Member States a *precise obligation which does not require the adoption of any further measure* on the part either of the Community institutions or of the Member States and which leaves them, in relation to its implementation, no discretionary power.'

The direct effect of directives

Because they require something to be done on the part of the Member States in order to implement them, directives are not directly applicable. They do not pass automatically into the national law. However, it was established in *Ratti* Case 148/78 [1979] ECR 1629 that they were binding on Member States, who must take steps to implement them within the period set by the directive itself. Directives can have **vertical direct effect**:

'A Member State which has not adopted the implementing measures required by the directive in the prescribed periods may not rely, as against individuals, on its own failure to perform the obligations which the directive entails.'

Thus, if the date by which the directive must be implemented in national law has come and gone, an individual can plead the rights given in the directive in an action against a Member State, provided the directive is intended to confer rights on the individual and the wording of the directive is unconditional, clear and precise.

The difference between horizontal and vertical direct effect are discussed in *Marshall* v *Southampton and South West Hampshire Area Health Authority* Case 152/84 [1986] ECR 723 which we shall study at the end of the chapter. The case is set out in Appendix D.

Note that the State is still liable when sued not in its capacity as the government who should implement the legislation but as employer. The European Court of Justice has given a wide interpretation of 'State' in this context to enable a remedy to be more readily available to individuals.

Indirect effect

Failure of the Member State to implement a Directive on time is a breach of its obligations under art 10 (formerly art 5) EC Treaty:

'Member States shall take all appropriate measures, whether general or particular, to ensure fulfilment of the obligations arising out of this Treaty or resulting from action taken by the institutions of the Community. They shall facilitate the achievement of the Community's tasks.'

In *Francovich and Others* v *Italian State* Joined Cases C–6/90 and C–9/90 [1990] IRLR 84, the individuals were allowed to recover compensation for loss suffered as a result of a breach of Italy's obligation under art 10 EC Treaty. So, although they had no cause of action against their employer – another individual for this purpose – they **could** recover damages against the State whose responsibility it was to implement the directive.

8.5 The institutions of the European Community

The powers which have been transferred by the Member States to the Community are conferred by the Treaty of Rome on the Institutions of the Community. The original Treaty of Rome stated that the tasks entrusted to the Community will be carried out by four institutions: an Assembly (now the European Parliament); a Council (of Ministers of the Member States); a Commission; and a Court of Justice.

The European Parliament

The Parliament sits in the Palais de Justice in Strasbourg. Originally, the Members of the European Parliament (MEPs) were people nominated by their governments but in 1979 direct elections were introduced with elections for the European Parliament in each Member State. MEPs are elected for a term of five years. They have three main functions:

1. to advise the Council about the Commission's proposals for Community legislation;
2. to consider the Community budget; and
3. to exert a measure of control over the Council and the Commission.

Community legislation

Under the Treaty of Rome, Parliament had to be **consulted** about EC legislation. The Council of Ministers must seek and take into consideration the opinion of Parliament but the Council is **not** obliged to follow it. Failure to comply with this consultation procedure can lead to the annulment of the legislation.

The Single European Act introduced provisions so that more measures can be passed by qualified majority voting rather than by unanimous vote. This increased the power of the Council to pass legislation because it was easier to find a majority of Member States to decide to act than to persuade all the Member States to do so. As a check on these increased powers, a **conciliation procedure**, which is found in art 251 (formerly art 189b) EC Treaty gave Parliament greater powers whereby, among other measures, if the Council adopts a common position (agrees to legislate) on the proposal by qualified majority voting, the proposal must go back to Parliament for a second reading before it can become law. If the proposal is then rejected by Parliament, it can only be adopted by the Council by unanimity.

Parliament's powers were further increased in the Maastricht Treaty with the introduction of the **co-decision procedure** found in art 252 (formerly art 189c) under which the Parliament has the power to veto legislation in some circumstances. However, in practice, there is close consultation between the Council, Parliament and Commission on matters concerning legislation.

The budget

Originally the Community was financed by contributions from the budgets of the individual Member States, but since 1970 the Community has been financed from its own resources. At this time Parliament was given supervisory powers over the Budget which were increased in 1977. The European Parliament now has the final say on all non-compulsory expenditure such as administrative and operational expenditure – about 30 per cent of the Community budget – with most of the rest of the expenditure comprising the Common Agricultural Policy budget which is subject to its own rules. Parliament can also propose modifications to the rest of the budget, which the Council can reject by qualified majority vote. Under art 272(8) (formerly art 203(8)), by a majority of the Members or two-thirds of the votes cast, Parliament can reject the Budget in its entirety and require a new draft budget to be submitted. They have only used this power once, in 1979. In order to do so, they must act strictly within the budgeting procedure: *Council* v *Parliament* Case 34/86 [1986] 3 CMLR 94.

The supervisory function of the Parliament

Article 31 (formerly art 37) EC Treaty provides that the Parliament shall exercise **advisory and supervisory powers**. By art 201 (formerly art 144), the Parliament is given power by a two-thirds majority, which must be an actual majority of all MEPs, to compel the entire Commission to resign. This censure motion is subject to a cooling-off period of three days.

The result of a successful censure motion would be to bring the work of the Community to a complete halt. The Commissioners are appointed by their respective national governments, who would then appoint a new Commission of the same persuasion as the old one. In any case, it would be very difficult to achieve the necessary consensus of all political parties for a two-thirds majority. Nevertheless, because of the availability of the censure motion, the Commission is seen to be accountable to the Parliament and this is reinforced by two additional powers:

1. **Annual general report** – the Commission must submit an annual general report on the activities of the Community which must be discussed by Parliament in open session. The President of the Commission also presents a report of the activities proposed for the coming year so that the Parliament is able to monitor the framing of Community policy and, if necessary, can challenge proposals at an early stage.
2. **Questions** – MEPs can raise Parliamentary questions about the work of the Commission. The Commission must reply within a given time. The answers are published in the Official Journal of the Community. MEPs can also ask questions of the Council.

Committees

Much of the work of the Parliament is carried out by its committees. These perform some of the functions of the ministries in a national government. There are **standing committees** which are set up permanently to consider such matters as political affairs, legal affairs, budgets, the environment, women and institutional reform. In addition, Parliament can set up committees on a temporary basis to deal with matters which fall outside the remit of the standing committees. Each committee has a rapporteur who will prepare a report of the Committee's findings and will lead the debate when the report is presented to the Parliament. The reports of the committees serve as a basis for the majority of debates in the Parliament.

The Ombudsman

The office of Ombudsman was set up by the TEU. The function of the Ombudsman is to investigate claims of maladministration on the part of the European institutions other than the European Court of Justice and the Court of First Instance. The appointment is for the term of the current parliament and the Ombudsman has no power to award compensation or any other remedy. When a complaint is made, the Ombudsman forwards the complaint to the institution concerned which then has three months in which to respond. The Ombudsman then makes a report to Parliament, to the individual and to the institution concerned.

The Council

The members of the Council change according to the matter to be considered. The Council is made up of the Ministers responsible in their respective governments for the matter to be debated in the Council meeting. The function of the Council is set out in art 202 (formerly art 145) EC Treaty:

> 'to ensure co-ordination of the general economic policies of the Member States and have power to take decisions.'

The Council's main function is to take the decisions that become Community law. The Council is, in effect, the Community's legislature. The Council enacts regulations and directives. The Commission drafts proposals for legislation and is influential as to the form and content of the proposals but at the end of the day it is the Council that adopts the vast majority of the legislation.

The composition of the Council is a demonstration that the Community is not an autonomous institution which enacts legislation beyond the influence of the Member States. The Member States themselves, through their representatives on the Council pass Community law. The problem is that individual Member States can now be outvoted on more issues with the wider use of qualified majority voting.

The Council must act within the procedural requirements laid down by the EC Treaty. Otherwise the Council will be acting ultra vires (outside the scope of its powers) and the measures may be challenged in the European Court. Article 308 (formerly art 235) gives the Council wide powers to take measures to fulfil the objectives of the Treaty where the Treaty itself does not provide the necessary powers. This must be done in consultation with the Parliament. The Council uses its art 308 powers very sparingly.

The Council is assisted in its functions by the Council of Permanent Representatives (COREPER). This is a committee consisting of the ambassadors from the Member States to the Community. This committee reviews the measures to be considered by the Council and produces an agenda for the meetings of the Council.

The Presidency of the Council is held by a Member State, not by an individual. The Minister from the Member State which holds the Presidency presides over the

Council. Each Member State in turn holds the Presidency for a period of six months. With the enlargement of the membership of the EU to 25 states, one constitutional change under consideration is the appointment of an elected permanent President who would be an individual rather than a state.

Article 205(1) (formerly art 148(1)) provides: 'save as otherwise provided by this Treaty the Council shall act by a majority of its members'. In practice, the Council very rarely acts by a simple majority. Initially most measures required a unanimous vote but this made any progress on the development of the Community very slow. In recent years, the Council has been more ready to act by a qualified majority as defined in art 205(2). The votes are weighted between the individual States so that the larger States cannot automatically outvote or coerce the smaller ones. Unanimity is still required on matters of greater significance, such as the admission of a new Member State or concluding a Treaty with a non-EC State.

No provision was made in the Treaty for summit meetings of the heads of government. A few such meetings took place in the 1960s and 1970s and it was decided in 1974 that such meetings should be given a formal status as the **European Council**, a body which was finally given a Treaty basis in the Maastricht Treaty.

The Commission

The Commission consists of 20 members, two from the United Kingdom, France, Germany, Italy and Spain and one from each of the other Member States. These numbers will change in order to accommodate representatives of the new Member States. Each member is appointed by agreement between the governments of the Member States. They are appointed for five years and this period can be renewed. The Commissioners can only be dismissed or retired for misconduct. They can be removed en masse by a vote of the Parliament. The Commissioners must be completely independent of the Member States and at all times must act in the best interests of the Community; they must neither seek nor take instructions from any government or other body. Each Member State undertakes to respect this principle. The Commissioners' obligation of fidelity to the Community extend beyond their tour of duty and they must continue to act with integrity and discretion, particularly with regard to future employment.

The governments of the Member States, in consultation with the Parliament, nominate the President of the Commission, usually after heated and often lengthy negotiation. Either one or two Vice Presidents are appointed from among their number by the Commissioners themselves.

The Commission has a staff of approximately 16,000 – comparable of that of a city council before privatisation. About 20 per cent of these work in the translation service.

The functions of the Commission are laid down in art 211 (formerly art 155) EC Treaty:

'In order to ensure the proper function and development of the common market, the Commission shall:
- ensure that the provisions of this Treaty and the measures taken by the institutions pursuant thereto are applied;
- formulate recommendations or deliver opinions on matters dealt with in this Treaty, if it expressly so provides or if the Commission considers it necessary;
- have its own power of decision and participate in the shaping of measures taken by the Council and by the European Parliament in the manner provided for in this Treaty;
- exercise the powers conferred on it by the Council for the implementation of the rules laid down by the latter.'

So the function of the Commission is to make sure that the rules of the Community are applied correctly. If a Member State or an individual cannot comply with their obligations under the Treaty, the Commission will decide whether it is appropriate to allow them a derogation (exemption) from the obligation.

The Commission is often called the 'watchdog of the treaties'. In this role the Commission has wide powers of investigation. Article 284 (formerly art 213) empowers the Commission to gather information and carry out checks which are necessary for the performance of its tasks. The Commission receives complaints of non-performance of Treaty obligations from Member States, from Parliament, from the Council or from individuals and pressure groups. If, after investigation by the Commission, a breach of Community law is established, the Commission can impose fines on individuals and organisations. If they disagree with the Commission's findings, they can appeal to the European Court of Justice.

Article 226 (formerly art 169) gives the Commission powers to ensure that Member states comply with their Treaty obligations. The procedure has three stages:

1. An informal stage when the Commission asks the Member State for comments on the complaint.
2. The reasoned opinion stage when the Commission delivers its opinion, giving reasons for that opinion and giving the Member State a time limit within which to remedy the breach. There may be a negotiated settlement at this stage.
3. If the State fails to remedy the breach, the Commission may take proceedings against the Member State in the European Court of Justice. If successful, the Commission suggests a suitable fine to the European Court of Justice and the Court orders the breach to be remedied and the fine to be paid.

Where the Council acts as the legislature of the Community, all proposals for legislation are drafted by the Commission, either on its own initiative, or on the recommendation of Parliament or on matters put forward by the Council of Ministers or European Council.

The Commission itself may issue regulations and directives, take decisions, make recommendations and deliver opinions. This function is limited to matters which are delegated to the Commission, either in the Treaty or by powers delegated by the Council of Ministers.

The Commission negotiates on behalf of the Community on all international matters – on agreements and treaties, such as the GATT agreement on world trade and on applications from other States to join the Community.

The European Council

The European Council is the regular summit meeting comprising Heads of State and their Foreign Ministers. Under the Single European Act, it is required to meet at least twice a year.

The European Court of Justice

Lord Slynn, in his Hamlyn Lecture *Introducing a New Legal Order*, described the European Court of Justice as follows:

> 'The courtroom at Luxembourg is in some ways a microcosm of what is happening outside. The lawyers who come to argue the cases wear their national robes – the English, the Scottish and Irish in their wigs, the Italians with their gold and silver tassels, the Germans with their elegant silk facings and white ties, the Dutch with their long many-buttoned black gowns, the French with the ermine band to the "epinonge" they wear over their shoulder. They address the Court according to their national customs. So the English begin "My Lords", some of the others "Monsieur le President, Messieurs les Juges, Monsieur l'Avocat General" or "Herr Praesident, meine Herren Richter, mein Herr Generalanwalt". They reveal their national characteristics in the manner of their address. In answer to a question from the Court, the staccato Scottish "certainly" is very different from the rolling Italian "assolutamente", pregnant with emphasis and followed by an exuberant explanation. Even to compare the hands of the interpreters in the Dutch and the Danish booths with those in the Italian and French booths – as many visiting students do to their apparent interest – is significant.
>
>   The legal systems and experiences which the lawyers draw on are patently so different, both in the substance of their submissions and in their techniques. A stranger would quickly realise which lawyers come from a country where oral advocacy and debate between the judge and the lawyer is the norm. Even, dare I say it, when one of the 13 judges and the six advocates general speak from the bench, whether in their own language or in French, a lot of national history and tradition and personality is evident which is not hidden behind the identical red gowns which they wear.'

Article 220 (formerly art 164) provides: 'The Court of Justice shall ensure that in the interpretation and application of this Treaty the law is observed.'

Composition and organisation of the Court

Since the enlargement of the Community in 1995, after Lord Slynn had delivered his Hamlyn Lecture, the Court consists of 15 judges and eight advocates-general. Again, these numbers will change as the acceding states join the EU. The judges are appointed by common accord of the governments of the Member States. In practice, each judge has been a national of a different Member State. When the Court sits in plenary session (when there is a full court), either nine or all 15 judges sit depending on the difficulty or importance of the case.

The judges do not deliver separate judgments – one single decision is given following secret deliberations. This may mean that it is a majority decision but this is never recorded. However, sometimes it is possible to detect some dissent from the way in which the judgment is framed.

The Maastricht Treaty amended art 165 (now art 221) so that the Court is also divided into Chambers, or divisions of three judges. This was necessary to cope with the increasing workload of the Court. However, the Court must sit as a full court if a Member State or a Community institution which is party to an action so requests. The Court has adopted French as its working language.

In accordance with art 223 (formerly art 167), the judges and advocates-general are chosen 'from persons whose independence is beyond doubt and who possess the qualifications for appointment to the highest judicial office in their respective countries or who are juris consults of recognised competence; they shall be appointed, by common accord of the Governments of the Member States for a term of six years.' Article 223 goes on to provide that every three years there shall be a partial replacement of the judges. The advocates-general are also partially replaced after three years, but retiring judges and advocates-general are eligible for reappointment. The judges elect a President of the Court of Justice from among themselves for a period of three years. He/she can be re-elected.

The judges come from a number of backgrounds, including membership of their national judiciary, legal practice, political or administrative office, law faculties or with experience of more than one of these fields.

Advocates-general

The role of the advocate-general is to deliver an opinion on the outcome of the case, taking an objective view on behalf of the Community as a whole. Article 222 (formerly art 166) states:

> 'It shall be the duty of the advocate-general, acting with complete impartiality and independence, to make, in open court, reasoned submissions on cases brought before the Court of Justice, in order to assist the Court in the performance of the task assigned to it by Article 164 [now art 220]'

The advocate-general acts as an independent adviser but takes no part in the judges' deliberations. The prime function of the advocate-general is to deliver an impartial and reasoned **opinion**. This opinion is given at the conclusion of the argument and before the Court retires to consider its decision. The judges are **not** obliged to follow his opinion. The Court has complete freedom to decide whether or not to do so. However, the opinion forms an extremely valuable basis on which the Court can arrive at its judgment. As you will see in Appendix D, the opinion is published in the case report alongside the judgment, and in later cases the opinion may be more influential than the decision itself.

The Court is also assisted by a juge-rapporteur who makes a preliminary study of the case and prepares a report for the Court on the facts and the evidence available. This information is used to prepare the case for the court and to decide whether it should be tried by a full court or a chamber. When the advocate-general's opinion has been delivered, the juge-rapporteur prepares a first draft of the Court's judgment which can then be amended or completely rewritten according to the final views of the judges.

The jurisdiction of the Court

1. To establish whether or not a Member State has failed to fulfil an obligation under the Treaty. Actions for this purpose can be brought by the Commission under new art 226 EC or by a Member State under under art 227 EC.
2. To exercise unlimited jurisdiction with regard to penalties in actions brought by the Commission under new arts 228(1) and 229 EC.
3. To review the legality of an act, or of a failure to act, of, inter alia, the Council, the Commission or the Parliament, at the request of the Member States, the Council or the Commission and in limited circumstances from the Parliament and the European Central Bank.
4. To give preliminary rulings under new art 234 (formerly art 177) EC at the request of a national court or tribunal.
5. To grant compensation for damage caused by the institutions in actions brought by Member States, and natural and legal persons under new arts 235 and 388 EC.
6. To act as a Court of Appeal from the Court of First Instance under new art 225(1) EC.

Procedure

The procedure of the Court is laid down in art 245 (formerly art 188) of the Court's Rules of Procedure.

> 'A lawyer from the English Court is likely to find the procedure very strange. The oral and adversarial character of English civil procedure (and its Scottish and Irish counterparts) is in marked contrast with the written and inquisitional features of the Luxembourg procedure.' (Brown and Jacobs: *The Court of Justice of the European Communities*)

The procedure consists of:

1. written proceedings;
2. possibly a preliminary enquiry to establish issues of fact which need further proof and what evidence will be necessary;
3. oral proceedings;
4. judgment.

The written proceedings have much greater significance in a case before a European court than in a case before an English court. Much more of the case is dealt with by written submissions which are submitted to the Registrar of the Court, to the parties and to the institutions whose measures are in dispute. These are the applications, defences, statements of case and all the related papers. Much more of the case is dealt with by documentation than in an English case. The defendant has a month within which to lodge a defence, and if they fail to do so, the Court may give judgment to the other party by default.

The written procedure ends with the juge-rapporteur's preliminary report as to whether a preliminary enquiry is necessary in order to obtain further background information. The Court itself may undertake the enquiry or it may be assigned to a chamber. If no preliminary enquiry is necessary, the Court will fix the date of the oral hearing.

The oral proceedings are very much shorter than in an English trial because so much of the evidence is given in writing, but, as can be seen with the Woolf reforms, the procedure of the English court is changing with incentives to the parties to shorten the submissions made by counsel on their behalf in order to save court time. The oral proceedings before the European Court of Justice consist the reading of the juge-rapporteur's report in open court, followed by submisions from lawyers and advisers to the parties, and from the witnesses and experts. These submissions will be much shorter than those before an English court. Long speeches are discouraged. The oral proceedings end with the report of the advocate-general.

The Court then decides the case. The deliberations are secret and the opinion of the majority of the judges decides the matter. No dissenting judgments are given as in an English case, but where the judgment lacks clarity some dissention may be detected. There may have been a compromise over the final draft. The judgment consists of:

1. a summary of the facts and the arguments presented by the parties;
2. the grounds for the decision – usually very brief by comparison with those given in an English case;
3. the decision; and
4. an order for costs.

Any Member State can be represented in the case, as can the Commission so that national and Community view can be taken into account. Where appropriate, the Court can make interim orders to preserve the status quo or to ensure the production of necessary documents.

The Court of First Instance

A second tier was introduced into the European Court system in 1989 as a measure to deal with the overload of cases waiting to be heard by the European Court of Justice which was causing increasingly long delays. The judges of the ECJ therefore requested the setting up of a second court to take over some of its work.

The Court of First Instance hears cases brought by employees of the Institutions regarding their employment. It also hears competition cases when companies and undertakings challenge the rulings on competition policy made by the Commission.

The TEU introduced a further category of case: claims brought by citizens and companies for judicial review under new arts 230 and 232 EC which are made against organisations other than the Member States and the EU.

There is a right of appeal from the decisions on these cases to the European Court of Justice.

There are no advocates-general, although the Court can choose a judge from among its number to fulfil this function.

Sources of Community law

The European treaties do not identify the sources of Community law. The only direction given to the Court is a requirement that in the interpretation and application of the treaties 'the law' is observed. This means more that observing the primary and secondary legislation in the treaties, regulations and directives which, in any case, are often cryptic.

Lord Slynn, in his Hamlyn Lecture, described the European Court as 'the crucible in which legal principles and developments are to be fused'. He says that the Community has achieved supremacy of its law over national law for decisions of the Court by the consistent application of principles which are fundamental to all legal systems, a practice which has won the respect of the national courts. These principles are:

1. **Uniformity** – the requirement that Community law must be interpreted and applied in exactly the same way throughout the national courts of all the Member States. Interpretation by the European Court of the meaning of words such as 'worker', 'public policy', etc, must take precedence over the interpretations given in national law. There is the additional problem in Community law of translating the law consistently into all the languages of the Member States. This problem is partially overcome by a rule that Community texts should be interpreted in the light of their versions in the official language of the Community. If there is a difference between various translations, an attempt must be made to derive **a meaning which is common to all them all from the scheme, object and purpose of the provision**. In the absence of such a meaning the interpretation which is least onerous to Community citizens must be chosen.
2. **Effectiveness** – where there are alternative possible meanings, preference must be given to the interpretation that tends to promote the effectiveness or validity of fundamental Community principles.
3. **Protection of individual rights** – where a provision is silent or obscure, it must be given a meaning that affords individuals the widest freedom of action that is compatible with Community interests. Provisions of the treaties giving individuals a right of action to enforce their Community rights should be given a wide interpretation in favour of the individual.
4. **Proportionality** – the means used to achieve a given end should be no more than is appropriate and necessary to achieve that end.

5. **Natural justice** – principles such as the right to a hearing when a case is brought against you – the concept of natural justice is derived from English law.
6. **Non-discrimination** – everyone is equal before the law.
7. **Adherence to legality** – the Court will not countenance an interpretation which favours illegality.
8. **Adherence to procedural rights**.
9. **Respect for fundamental human rights**.

The case law of the European Court of Justice

Case law does not have the same prominence in continental legal systems as it does in the jurisdictions of the United Kingdom. The European Court of Justice is **not** obliged to follow its own decisions. The primary duty of the Court is to ensure that Community law is interpreted and applied correctly. Because the Community is relatively new, much of Community law is incomplete and undeveloped. In addition, the law-making process requires considerable compromise in order to achieve any agreed text so that Community statutes contain little detail. Often, the Court has to go beyond a literal interpretation of the words of the legislation. It has to fill gaps in the law in order to clarify it. Nevertheless , in the interests of uniformity, the Court tends to follow its earlier decisions and caselaw is heavily relied upon in argument before the European Court.

National laws of the Member States

The Court will look to the national laws for guidance on the meaning of Community law in the following circumstances:

1. when Community law refers to the laws of the Member States;
2. where Community law has developed in the legal systems of the Member States;
3. it may look to national law to construe the meaning of the words of the Treaty.

Note: the Community is fast developing an international personality of its own similar to those of the Member States and is therefore subject to international law in the same way.

8.6 Websites

For further information on the institutions of the European Union, you can consult their websites:

European Court of Justice: http://www.curia.eu.int/en/index.htm
Commission: http://europa.eu.int/comm/index.en.htm
Council: http://www.ue.eu.int/en.htm
Parliament: http://www.europarl.eu.int/sg/tree/en/default.htm

8.7 Reading a European case

Look now at *Marshall* v *Southampton and South West Hampshire Area Health Authority (Teaching)* Case 152/84 [1986] ECR 723 reproduced as Appendix D. From this you will see how a judgment of the European Court of Justice is set out in the European Court Reports, the official court reports of the European Court. As for *Williams* v *Roffey* in Chapter 6, you should read through the case, noting its structure and the arguments regarding direct effect of directives. This will give you an introduction to reading European cases. The points below are intended to guide you through the case when reading it for yourself.

Points to note

1. Each case is given a number which appears at the top of the first page and is part of the citation of the case – here Case 152/84. 1984 is the year when proceedings were initiated and this is the 152nd case of that year. The case reference is [1986] ECR 723. The European Court Reports are the official record of the proceedings of the ECJ. There is an alternative set of reports of European cases – the Common Market Law Reports, which are commercially produced and appear more quickly than the European Court Reports. The judgment of the Court and the opinion of the advocate-general are also released as A4 typed sheets and can be found in libraries which contain a European Documentation Centre. Brief reports of important cases appear in the Times Law Reports shortly after judgment is given.
2. The case name appears just as in an English case – and indeed this **is** an English case in which proceedings before the English court have been delayed while a reference is made to the European Court of Justice under new art 234 EC Treaty. This case was referred from the Court of Appeal.
3. The case is then given a subject heading: Equality of treatment for men and women – Conditions governing dismissal.
4. The main points of the case are summarised in italics.
5. Then come the headnotes.

The advocate-general's opinion

1. Advocate-general Slynn's opinion is set out before we get to the judgment of the Court. Note that the opinion is given on 18th September 1985, five months before judgment is given. Sometimes the press reports the opinion as if it is the conclusive judgment in the case. Remember that the opinion is merely persuasive – the Court is not obliged to accept it.
2. First the advocate-general gives a summary of the facts.
3. Then in the second column of p726, he sets out the points specifically referred

by the Court of Appeal for interpretation. There are two specific questions which the Court must answer.

4. From p727, the advocate-general summarises the representations which have been made to the Court by Miss Marshall and by the Area Health Authority. Note also that the United Kingdom government intervenes in the proceedings and its representations are considered both by the advocate-general and by the Court. Any Member State may intervene on an art 234 (formerly art 177) reference, not just the Member State in which the case originates. The Commission also intervenes in the case.

5. The advocate-general responds to the **first question** on p728: whether a woman's dismissal because she has passed the normal retirement age applicable to women is an act of discrimination prohibited by Directive 76/207. He sets out the relevant provisions of Directive 76/207 (note that when a directive is cited, the year appears before the number). He draws a distinction between the time when employees retire and their entitlement to a pension and treats these as two separate issues, the first being one of dismissal, the second relating to access to social security entitlement (last paragraph of p729). This argument is developed on p730.

6. The advocate-general then refers to the earlier case of *Burton v British Railways Board* [1982] ECR 555. See how he distinguishes this case (top of p731). Note that, in any event, the Court is **not** bound by its previous decisions, although it usually follows them in the interests of certainty.

7. At the bottom of the first column of p731, the advocate-general gives his answer to the first question – such a practice is discriminatory and thus contrary to art 5(1) of Directive 76/207.

8. The **second question**: Does art 5(1) of Directive 76/270 have direct effect even though it is inconsistent with s6(4) of the Sex Discrimination Act 1975? The advocate-general notes that the two provisions do not have the same effect.

9. Note what he says in the second paragraph on p732 about the construction of UK statutes which implement European directives.

10. At the top of p733 he states the rule. He goes on to conclude that the words of art 5(1) are 'unconditional and sufficiently precise' so that 'they may not be without effects even if in the absence of implementing measures within the prescribed period.'

11. He concludes that, in accordance with the existing case law, the Member State may not escape liability because of its failure to implement Community legislation fully but that the Directive is **only** effective against the Member State. He refuses to give horizontal direct effect to directives (middle, second column, p734).

12. However, on p735, the Advocate-General considers whether the Area Health Authority can be construed as the State and, preferring a broad interpretation, concludes that it can.

13. Furthermore, the State can be sued in the role of employer because 'a State can legislate, a private employer cannot' (top of p735, second column).
14. He construes the Health Authority as an agent for the Minister of Health and concludes that Miss Marshall is an employee of the State who can assert her rights according to Directive 76/207.
15. He ends by giving his answers to the two questions raised by the Court of Appeal and finally makes a recommendation as to costs.

The Judgment

1. The first page (p737), repeats the details given at the beginning of the advocate-general's report but in more detail. The reference is given for Directive 76/707 – OJ 1976 L39, p40. The Official Journal (OJ) publishes all the official documents of the Community including proposals for and final texts of Directives. If your library contains a European Documentation Centre, look this up.
2. The seven judges who form the Court are named. Lord Mackenzie Stuart, the United Kingdom judge, is named as the President.
3. The advocate-general and the Registrar are named.
4. Also given are the names of counsel, both for the written proceedings and for the oral proceedings, including counsel for the United Kingdom and for the Commission.
5. The Court gives its decision at p738. The paragraphs are numbered for ease of reference. The Court of seven judges delivers one unanimous decision.
6. Paragraphs 1–11 summarise the facts and history of the case. Paragraph 12 again sets out the two questions referred to the Court from the Court of Appeal.
7. Paragraphs 13–20 state the law.
8. Paragraphs 21–38 deal with the **first question**. First, the Court summarises Miss Marshall's arguments. Look at paragraph 23. Miss Marshall relies on one of the broad objectives of the Treaty to 'provide for the constant improving of the living and working conditions of the peoples'. This can be found at art 117 (now art 136) EC Treaty.
9. Paragraphs 26 and 27 set out the Commission's views.
10. The respondent's arguments appear in paragraphs 28 and 29 – a claim that the matter is outside the scope of Directive 76/207 and is governed by Directive 79/7 which permits a differential in retirement ages.
11. Then come the United Kingdom's arguments – paragraphs 30 and 31.
12. The decision of the Court on the first question is then delivered in eight short paragraphs. First, the Court notes that this case is not concerned with access to a pension scheme but with termination of employment, which is governed by Directive 76/207 which provides, at art 5(1), for equal treatment in working conditions.
13. Next, the Court deals with the ruling in the *Burton* case and the wide construction of 'dismissal' (paragraph 34).

14. At paragraph 35, it considers the exemption given in Directive 79/7 concerning equal treatment in retirement ages. This is a provision which is contrary to the fundamental right to equal treatment recognised by the Commission in paragraph 27. It must therefore be construed restrictively – given as narrow an application as possible, hence the Court's ruling in paragraph 36, leading on to the answer to the first question in paragraph 38.

15. The Court goes through the same process with the **second question**, considering the doctrine of direct effect in detail. The issue is whether Miss Marshall as an employee of a State authority can rely on the Directive as if it had been fully implemented by the United Kingdom government. If the Area Health Authority is held to be a private employer, she will not be able to plead the Directive against them.

16. The Court's ruling begins at paragraph 46 with a review of the doctrine of direct effect.

17. On the question of whether the State can escape responsibility for its failure to implement the Directive correctly, the Court agrees with the advocate-general (at paragraph 49) that this cannot be permitted, regardless of in what capacity the State is being sued.

18. Note that it was the Court of Appeal which decided that the Health Authority was a public authority (paragraph 50). The European Court of Justice cannot interfere with this finding which is within the jurisdiction of the national court, subject to the guidelines supplied by the European Court in its ruling on the art 177 reference.

19. The Court finds art 5(1) Directive 76/207 to be unconditional and sufficiently precise, despite the limitation of its application in art 1(2) – while the scope of the application of the Directive is limited to exclude equal treatment in social security matters, and the exceptions in art 2 of the Directive are not applicable to this case. Therefore, the requirement that the Directive must be unconditional is met.

20. The Court concludes with the answer to the second question at paragraph 56.

21. Finally, the Court deals with costs. The United Kingdom and the Commission must pay their own costs and, because this is a reference from the national court, the costs of the parties to the action will be dealt with in the context of the national case.

The Court gave its final ruling some two years after the case was referred to them.

To what extent do the answers given by the Advocate-General correspond with those given by the Court? In some cases, there is no relation at all.

9

The Human Rights Act 1998

9.1 Historical background

9.2 The European Convention on Human Rights and the scope of its articles

9.3 The Human Rights Act 1998

9.4 Future applications to the European Court of Human Rights

The Human Rights Act 1998 came into force on 2 October 2000. This legislation implements the European Convention on Human Rights in UK domestic law so that breaches of the provisions of the Convention can be pleaded in English courts.

As one of the founder members of the Council of Europe, the United Kingdom ratified the European Convention on Human Rights in 1951 but, at this stage, did not incorporate the Convention into domestic law in the belief that the English common law provided sufficient protection of the fundamental rights and freedoms guaranteed by the Convention. Thus, UK citizens had to take human rights cases to the European Court of Human Rights in Strasbourg. The new legislation means that these issues may be resolved in the domestic courts.

9.1 Historical background

In 1948 the Congress of Europe met in the Hague and resolved that the Council of Europe should be formed. Membership of the Council of Europe would be open to all European nations which were democratically governed and which undertook to respect a Charter of Human Rights. It was further resolved that a Commission should be set up to draft the Charter and to set standards to which a democratic state should conform.

The Council of Europe was set up in May 1949 and its founding statute contained the following provision:

> 'Every Member of the Council of Europe must accept the principles of the rule of law and of the enjoyment by all persons within its jurisdiction of human rights and fundamental freedoms.'

The first priority of the new body was to draft Charter of Human Rights and, on 3 September 1953, the Convention for the Protection of Human Rights and Fundamental Freedoms came into force.

Implementation of the Convention was originally monitored by three bodies:

1. The European Commission of Human Rights.
2. The European Court of Human Rights.
3. The Committee of Ministers.

States can bring cases against each other and, where states give their citizens the right of 'individual petition', individuals can bring cases to enforce the Convention rights against those states. The United Kingdom granted its citizens the right of individual petition in 1966 with the result that, although individuals could not bring cases in the domestic courts prior to October 2000, they could take their case to the European Court of Human Rights in Strasbourg. This resulted in negative publicity for successive UK governments because of the disproportionate number of cases which went to Strasbourg from the UK when similar cases could be brought in the domestic courts of states which had received the Convention into their national law. Subsequent protocols to the Convention have added further rights to the list of those guaranteed.

9.2 The European Convention on Human Rights and the scope of its articles

Preamble

The Convention begins with a preamble which sets out the principles upon which the Convention is founded:

> 'The governments signatory hereto, being members of the Council of Europe,
> Considering the Universal Declaration of Human Rights proclaimed at the Assembly of the United Nations on 10 December 1948;
> Considering that this Declaration aims at securing the universal and effective recognition and observance of the Rights therein declared;
> Considering that the aim of the Council of Europe is the achievement of greater unity between its members and that one of the methods by which that aim is to be pursued is the maintenance and further realisation of human rights and fundamental freedoms;
> Reaffirming their profound belief in those fundamental freedoms which are the foundation of justice and peace in the world and are best maintained on the one hand by an effective political democracy and on the other by a common understanding and observance of the human rights upon which they depend;
> Being resolved, as the governments of European countries which are likeminded and have a common heritage of political traditions, ideals, freedom and the rule of law, to take the first steps for the collective enforcement of certain of the rights stated in the Universal Declaration,
>
> Have agreed as follows ...'

Key Convention articles

Article 1
Obligation to respect human rights

'The High Contracting Parties shall secure to everyone within their jurisdiction the rights and freedoms defined in Section I of this Convention.'

Article 1 places on the High Contracting Parties (the states who have ratified the Convention) the duty to secure for everyone the rights which are guaranteed by the Convention. It should be noted that this is not a universal guarantee of the rights of the individual – the Convention protects only those rights specifically covered it its provisions. Ratifying states are also under a duty to ensure that the national law is compatible with the Convention.

Article 2
The right to life

'1. Everyone's right to life shall be protected by law. No one shall be deprived of his life intentionally save in the execution of a sentence of a court following his conviction of a crime for which this penalty is provided by law.
2. Deprivation of life shall not be regarded as inflicted in contravention of this article when it results from the use of force which is no more than absolutely necessary:
(a) in defence of an person from unlawful violence;
(b) in order to effect a lawful arrest or to prevent the escape of a person lawfully detained;
(c) in action lawfully taken for the purpose of quelling a riot or insurrection.'

This is the most significant provision of the Convention. Protection of life by the state imposes an obligation to make unlawful killing a criminal offence, but art 2 also places the state under a duty to safeguard life as well as to refrain from taking life intentionally. However, in *Osman* v *United Kingdom* (2000) 29 EHRR 245 the European Court of Human Rights (ECHR) set the limits on the state's duty in this regard:

'Not every claimed risk can entail for the authorities a Convention requirement to take operational measures to prevent that risk from materialising. Another relevant consideration is the need to ensure that the police exercise their powers to control and prevent crime in a manner which fully respects the due process and other guarantees which legitimately place restraints on the scope of their action to investigate crime and bring offenders to justice, including the guarantees contained in arts 5 and 8 of the Convention.'

In that case, the police had been notified of a number of incidents leading up to the death of Ahmed Osman but had taken no action. None of the incidents were life-threatening and the ECHR held that this did not amount to a breach of art 2. However, art 2 places the police under a duty to make proper investigation in cases of suspicious death.

The second paragraph of art 2 provides exception to the state's duty to protect human life. The ECHR defined force which 'absolutely necessary' in *McCann* v

United Kingdom (1995) 21 EHRR 97. This was the case concerning the three IRA members who were killed in Gibraltar in 1988 by the Special Air Service. The court said that all the surrounding circumstances of the action must be taken into consideration, including the planning and control of the action. This placed a duty on the state to ensure that its agents received proper training, briefing and instructions when lethal force was contemplated. In such circumstances, the state must exercise 'strict control' over the operation. In this case, it was held by a very narrow majority that the UK government had failed to keep sufficient control and was thus in breach of art 2.

There have been attempts to bring cases concerning abortion under art 2, but the ECHR has held that art 2 only relates to post-natal human life and the life of the foetus cannot be regarded in isolation from the life of the pregnant woman.

Now that the Human Rights Act is in force, it is envisaged that art 2 may be relied on in cases relating to adequate provision of medical treatment in state-run hospitals.

The provisions of art 2 are supplemented by Protocol 6 to the Convention which provides:

> '1. The death penalty shall be abolished. No one shall be condemned to such penalty or executed.
> 2. A State may make provision in its law for the death penalty in respect of acts committed in time of war or of imminent threat of war; such penalty shall be applied only in the instances laid down in the law and in accordance with its provisions. The State shall communicate to the Secretary General of the Council of Europe the relevant provisions of that law.
> 3. No derogation from the provisions of this Protocol shall be made under art 15 of the Convention.
> 4. No reservation may be made under art 64 in respect of the provisions of this Protocol.'

Article 3
Torture and degrading treatment

'No-one shall be subjected to torture or to inhuman or degrading treatment or punishment'

In *Ireland* v *United Kingdom* (1978) 2 EHRR 25 the ECHR defined the terms of art 3 as follows:

1. Torture: deliberate inhuman treatment causing very serious and cruel suffering.
2. Inhuman treatment or punishment: the infliction of intense physical and mental suffering.
3. Degrading treatment: ill-treatment designed to arouse in victims feelings of fear, anguish and inferiority capable of humiliating and debasing them and possibly breaking their physical and moral resistance.

Not only does this article prohibit absolutely the inflicting of such treatment by the state, the state is also under a positive duty to prevent individuals within its borders from doing so. Deportation of someone who will be subject to such treatment in the receiving country is also in breach of art 3.

The Turkish state was held liable under art 3 for rapes committed by its soldiers and cases have been brought in relation to treatment of prisoners, those in police custody and those in mental institutions and in relation to corporal punishment inflicted by parents on children.

Article 4
Prohibition of slavery and forced labour

'1. No one shall be held in slavery or servitude.

2. No one shall be required to perform forced or compulsory labour.

3. For the purpose of this article the term "forced or compulsory labour" shall not include:

(a) any work required to be done in the ordinary course of detention imposed according to the provisions of art 5 of this Convention or during conditional release from such detention;

(b) any service of military character or, in case of conscientious objectors in countries where they are recognised, service exacted instead of compulsory military service.

(c) any service exacted in case of an emergency or calamity threatening the life or well-being of the community.

(d) Any work or service which forms part of normal civic obligations.'

Slavery implies ownership of the person and servitude implies that the person lives on the property of the master and that it is impossible to change his/her condition. There can be no derogation from this article and its interpretation derives from the Convention of the International Labour Organisation. Few cases have been brought to the ECHR and few of those which have been brought have been successful. Unsuccessful attempts to rely on art 4 have been made: in relation to duties imposed by professional bodies; in relation to prisoners' work programmes; and by boy entrants to the Royal Navy who were refused the right to an early discharge from a nine-year period of service.

Article 5
The right to liberty and security of the person

'1. Everyone has the right to liberty and security of person. No one shall be deprived of his liberty save in the following cases and in accordance with a procedure prescribed by law:

(a) the lawful detention of a person after conviction by a competent court;

(b) the lawful arrest or detention of a person for non-compliance with the lawful order of a court or in order to secure the fulfilment of any obligation prescribed by law;

(c) the lawful arrest or detention of a person effected for the purpose of bringing him before the competent legal authority on reasonable suspicion of having committed an offence or when it is reasonably considered necessary to prevent his committing an offence or fleeing after having done so;

(d) the detention of a minor by lawful order for the purpose of educational supervision or his lawful detention for the purpose of bringing him before the competent legal authority;

(e) the lawful detention of persons for the prevention of the spreading of infectious diseases, of persons of unsound mind, alcoholics or drug addicts or vagrants;

(f) the lawful arrest or detention of a person to prevent his effecting an unauthorised entry into the country or of a person against whom action is being taken with a view to deportation or extradition.

2. Everyone who is arrested shall be informed promptly, in a language which he understands, of the reasons for his arrest and of any charge against him.

3. Everyone arrested or detained in accordance with the provisions of paragraph 1.c of this article shall be brought promptly before a judge or other officer authorised by law to exercise judicial power and shall be entitled to trial within a reasonable time or to release pending trial. Release may be conditioned by guarantees to appear for trial.

4. Everyone who is deprived of his liberty by arrest or detention shall be entitled to take proceedings by which the lawfulness of his detention shall be decided speedily by a court and his release ordered if the detention is not lawful.

5. Everyone who has been the victim of arrest or detention in contravention of this article shall have an enforceable right to compensation.'

Article 5 is supplemented by art 1 of Protocol 4:

'No one shall be deprived of his liberty merely on the ground of inability to fulfil a contractual obligation.'

Article 5 is intended to protect the individual from arbitrary arrest and detention but not against less serious restrictions on liberty. The list of exceptions to the right to liberty and security in paras (a)–(c) is a finite list and the state cannot provide for further exceptions.

Article 6
The right to a fair trial

'1. In the determination of his civil rights and obligations or of any criminal charge against him, everyone is entitled to a fair and public hearing within a reasonable time by an independent and impartial tribunal established by law. Judgment shall be pronounced publicly but the press and public may be excluded from all or part of the trial in the interests of morals, public order or national security in a democratic society, where the interests of juveniles or the protection of the private life of the parties so require, or to the extent strictly necessary in the opinion of the court in special circumstances where publicity would prejudice the interests of justice.

2. Everyone charged with a criminal offence shall be presumed innocent until proved guilty according to law.

3. Everyone charged with a criminal offence has the following minimum rights:

(a) to be informed promptly, in a language which he understands and in detail of the nature and cause of the accusation against him;

(b) to have adequate time and facilities for the preparation of his defence;

(c) to defend himself in person or through legal assistance of his own choosing or, if he has not sufficient means to pay for legal assistance, to be given it free when the interests of justice so require;

(d) to examine or have examined witnesses against him and to obtain the attendance and examination of witnesses on his behalf under the same conditions as witnesses against him;

(e) to have the free assistance of an interpreter if he cannot understand or speak the language used in court.'

Article 6 applies to both civil and criminal proceedings. Its provisions are supplemented by arts 2–4 of Protocol 7 and by art 13 of the Convention itself.

Articles 2–4 of Protocal 7 provide:

'*Article 2*

1. Everyone convicted of a criminal offence by a tribunal shall have the right to have his conviction or sentence reviewed by a higher tribunal. The exercise of this right, including the grounds on which it may be exercised, shall be governed by law.

2. This right may be subject to exceptions in regard to offences of a minor character, as prescribed by law, or in cases in which the person concerned was tried in the first instance by the highest tribunal or was convicted following an appeal against acquittal.

Article 3

When a person has by a final decision been convicted of a criminal offence and when subsequently his conviction has been reversed, or he has been pardoned, on the ground that a new or newly discovered fact shows conclusively that there has been a miscarriage of justice, the person who has suffered punishment as a result of such conviction shall be compensated according to the law or the practice of the State concerned, unless it is proved that the non-disclosure of the unknown fact in time is wholly or partly attributable to him.

Article 4

1. No one shall be liable to be tried or punished again in criminal proceedings under the jurisdiction of the same State for an offence for which he has already been finally acquitted or convicted in accordance with the law and penal procedure of that State.

2. The provisions of the preceding paragraph shall not prevent the reopening of the case in accordance with the law and penal procedure of the State concerned., if there has been a fundamental defect in the discovered facts, or if there has been a fundamental defect in the previous proceedings, which could affect the outcome of the case.

3. No derogation from this Article shall be made under art 15 of the Convention.'

In *Delcourt* v *Belgium* (1970) 1 EHRR 355 the ECHR declared:

'In a democratic society within the meaning of the Convention, the right to a fair administration of justice holds such a prominent place that a restrictive interpretation of art 6.1 would not correspond to the purpose of that provision.'

Under art 6, each party must have an equal opportunity to present their case. Access to justice may include a right to legal aid (*Airey v Ireland* (1979) 2 EHRR 305). The article also gives the right to parties to object on questions of impartiality, for example when the case is heard by the party's employer.

In another case, a new trial was ordered in the Scottish Court of Appeal because one member of the bench was Lord McCluskey, who had written an article in which he had said that the Canadian equivalent of the Convention was providing 'a field day for crackpots, a pain in the neck for judges and legislators and a gold mine for lawyers' (*Hockstra and Others* v *HM Advocate* (2000) The Times 14 April).

On the question of presumption of innocence (art 6.2), the ECHR declared in *Barbera, Messegue and Jabardo* v *Spain* (1988) 11 ECRR 360:

'When carrying out their duties, the members of a court should not start with the preconceived idea that the accused has committed the offence charged; the burden of proof is on the prosecution, and any doubt should benefit the accused. It also follows that it is for the prosecution to inform the accused of the case that will be made against him, so that he may prepare and present his defence accordingly and to adduce evidence sufficient to convict him.'

Article 7
Freedom from the effects of retrospective criminal legislation

'1. No one shall be held guilty of any criminal offence on account of any act or omission which did not constitute a criminal offence under national or international law at the time when it was committed. Nor shall a heavier penalty be imposed than the one that was applicable at the time when the criminal offence was committed.
2. This article shall not prejudice the trial and punishment of an person for any act or omission which, at the time when it was committed, was criminal according to the general principles of law recognised by civilised nations.'

In addition to protection from the application of new heads of criminal liability to acts which predate the legislation, art 7 protects parties from changes in the criminal law which adversely affect their position. For example, the defendant may only receive a sentence which was in force at the time the offence was committed, regardless of any later change in the law.

It should also be noted that art 7.2 allows the prosecution of 'any act or omission which, at the time when it was committed, was criminal according to general principles of law recognised by civilised nations', so that offences such as war crimes will be prosecuted even if no formal provision has been made for them within international law or the law of the member state.

Article 8
The right to a private and family life

'1. Everyone has the right to respect for his private and family life, his home and his correspondence.
2. There shall be no interference by a public authority with the exercise of this right except such as is in accordance with the law and is necessary in a democratic society in the interests of national security, public safety or the economic well-being of the country, for the prevention of disorder or crime, for the protection of health or morals, or for the protection of the rights and freedoms of others.'

In *Van Oosterijk* v *Belgium* (1979), the European Commission on Human Rights defined the right to a private life as follows:

' "The right to respect for a private life" is the right to privacy, the right to live as one wishes, protected from publicity ... It comprises also, to a certain degree, the right to establish and develop relationships with other human beings especially in the emotional field, for the development and fulfilment of one's own personality.'

Cases have been brought under art 8 to establish the rights of illegitimate children, homosexual couples, transsexuals and the rights of grandparents, the rights of children of one family separated into different foster homes to maintain links with one another and the right of foster children to maintain links with their birth parents.

Article 8 has also established the rights of individuals who are under surveillance by the state. In *Malone* v *United Kingdom* (1984) 7 EHRR 14 the United Kingdom was held to be in breach of art 8 for telephone tapping which at the time was not only a breach of the right to privacy but also an interference with Mr Malone's correspondence. Correspondence in this context includes all forms of communication. Privacy is guaranteed not only in the home but also in the workplace and elsewhere. In *Halford* v *United Kingdom* (1997) 24 EHRR 523 Ms Halford's office telephone was tapped and this was held to be a breach of her privacy.

Most recently, Michael Douglas and Catherine Zeta Jones sought an injunction against *Hello!* magazine to try to prevent unauthorised publication of their wedding photographs (*Michael Douglas and Catherine Zeta Jones, Northern and Shell plc* v *Hello! Ltd* (2001) The Times 16 January (CA)). The happy couple had entered into an exclusive contract with *OK* magazine for the publication of the photographs, and *Hello!* were aware of this. The terms of the contract granted the couple some control over which pictures would be published and in return they had agreed to do their best to ensure that no unauthorised photographs were taken. The effect of the injunction, if it continued in force, would have been to prevent publication of the entire issue of *Hello!* While the court recognised that the couple had a right to privacy under the Human Rights Act 1998, and that such a right could be enforced through the courts under s6 Human Rights Act 1998, they also recognised that Michael Douglas and Catherine Zeta Jones had already sold their privacy elsewhere and refused the injunction.

Article 9
Freedom of thought, conscience and religion

'1. Everyone has the right to freedom of thought, conscience and religion; this right includes freedom to change his religion or belief and freedom, either alone or in community with others and in public or private, to manifest his religion or belief, in worship, teaching, practice and observance.
2. Freedom to manifest one's religion or beliefs shall be subject only to such limitations as are prescribed by law and are necessary in a democratic society in the interests of public safety, for the protection of public order, health or morals, or for the protection of the rights and freedoms of others.'

Article 9.1 protects the freedom to practise a religion and to promote religious belief (*Kotinakis* v *Greece* (1993) 17 EHRR 397). However, in employment cases, the requirements of employers are also recognised under art 9.2 so that the requirement for a Muslim to attend the mosque on Friday or for a Christian to go to church on Sundays have not precluded their employers from stipulating that they work on those days.

Pacificists and conscientious objectors are granted the right to freedom of thought and conscience but any state action to limit their activities in promoting their beliefs will be viewed in the light of art 9.2.

Article 10
Freedom of expression

'1. Everyone has the right to freedom of expression. This right shall include freedom to hold opinions and to receive and impart information and ideas without interference by public authority and regardless of frontiers. This article shall not prevent States from requiring the licensing of broadcasting, television or cinema enterprises.
2. The exercise of these freedoms, since it carries with it duties and responsibilities, may be subject to such formalities, conditions, restrictions or penalties as are prescribed by law and are necessary in a democratic society, in the interests of national security, territorial integrity or public safety, for the prevention of disorder or crime, for the protection of health or morals, for the protection of the reputation or rights of others, for preventing the disclosure of information received in confidence, or for maintaining the authority and impartiality of the judiciary.'

In *Handyside* v *United Kingdom* (1976) 1 EHRR 737, a case concerning a handbook of sex advice for children, the ECHR held that freedom of expression constitutes one of the essential foundations of a democratic society:

'... one of the basic conditions for its progress and for the development of every man. It is applicable not only to "information" or "ideas" that are favourably received as inoffensive, or as a matter of indifference, but also to those that offend, shock or disturb the state or any sector of the population. Such are the demands of that pluralism, tolerance and broadmindedness without which there is no "democratic society".'

Article 10 provides for some state control over broadcasting and the press. It also recognises in art 10.2 that, where freedom of expression is exercised, it carries duties and responsibilities. In Appeals Nos 11553/85 and 11658/85 the European Commission on Human Rights defined freedom of expression as follows:

'Freedom of expression constitutes one of the essential foundations of a democratic society and one of the basic conditions for its progress and for each individual's self-fulfilment. Of particular importance, in this context, is the freedom of the press to impart information and ideas and the right of the public to receive them.'

The exercise of this freedom may be in conflict with the right of another to a fair trial or to respect for their family life, as well as with the rights specifically mentioned in art 10.2 which recognise the duty of the state to intervene to protect these conflicting interests. However, such intervention must be proportionate.

The Commission has recognised the right of the state to place limits on its employees' freedom of expression, including the rights of the armed forces:

'The proper functioning of an army is hardly imaginable without legal rules designed to prevent servicemen from undermining military discipline, for example by writings ...

The Court must not disregard either the particular characteristics of military life ... the specific "duties" and "responsibilities" incumbent on members of the armed forces, or the margin of appreciation that art 10.2 leaves to the Contracting States' (*Engel v Netherlands* (1976) 1 EHRR 647).

Perhaps the most significant cases concern freedom of the press. The court will take into consideration whether the interference with freedom of expression can be justified as necessary in a democratic society. In the 1970s the *Sunday Times* published an article on the effects of the drug thalidomide. The article gave details of the research and testing methods used by the pharmaceutical company who, at the time, were negotiating an out-of-court settlement with families who were affected by the tragic side-effects of the drug. In the English court, the company was granted an injunction against publication on the grounds that publication would be in contempt of court. The ECHR held that the grant of the injunction was an interference with the newspaper's right to freedom of expression. Although the availability of an injunction was 'prescribed by law', the UK government had failed to show that the enforcement of the injunction fulfilled a 'pressing social need' or that its imposition was 'proportionate to the legitimate aim pursued'. The Court continued:

> 'Whilst the mass media must not overstep the bounds imposed in the interests of the proper administration of justice, it is incumbent on them to impart information and ideas concerning matters that come before the courts just as in other areas of public interest. Not only do the media have the task of imparting such information and ideas, the public also has a right to receive them': *Sunday Times* v *United Kingdom* (1979) 2 EHRR 245.

The Court further pointed out that, in this case, the families had a right to the information revealed by the newspaper's investigative journalism.

Article 11
Freedom of association

> '1. Everyone has the right to freedom of peaceful assembly and to freedom of association with others, including the right to form and to join trade unions for the protection of his interests.
> 2. No restriction shall be placed on the exercise of these rights other than such as are prescribed by law and are necessary in a democratic society in the interests of national security or public safety, for the prevention of disorder or crime, for the protection of health or morals or for the protection of the rights and freedoms of others. This article shall not prevent the imposition of lawful restrictions on the exercise of these rights by members of the armed forces, of the police or of the administration of the state.'

Article 11 puts the state under a duty to both permit and make possible trade union activity and other rights of assembly. The article also covers political parties. Rights *not* to join a trade union are also protected under this head so that 'closed shops' imposed by the unions are in breach of art 11. The trade union's right to strike is also protected. However, as was demonstrated by the GCHQ case (*Council of Civil Service Unions* v *United Kingdom* (1987) 50 DR 228), trade union members who are part of the state's administration can be forbidden by the state to join a trade union in the interests of national security (art 11.2).

Article 12
The right to marry

'Men and women of marriageable age have the right to marry and to found a family, according to the national laws governing the exercise of this right.'

The right to marry under art 12 is strictly subject to national laws and protects male/female relationships only. Caroline Cossey, a transsexual seeking to marry her male partner, was unsuccessful when she sought to assert this right under art 12 (*Cossey v United Kingdom* (1990) 12 EHRR 632), and in *Rees v United Kingdom* (1986) 9 EHRR 56 the ECHR said that:

'Article 12 was mainly concerned to protect marriage as a basis of the family.'

Other articles and protocols

Articles 13 (right to an effective remedy) and 15 (derogation in time of emergency) are not incorporated into UK law by the Human Rights Act 1998, Parliament having taken the view that they are sufficiently covered by domestic law.

Article 14 (prohibition of discrimination), art 16 (restrictions on political activity of aliens), art 17 (prohibition on abuse of rights) and art 18 (limitation on use of restrictions on rights) are provisions which apply to the concrete Convention rights, so that freedom from discrimination, for example, is only protected in relation to the other freedoms specified in the Convention and in the protocols.

The protocols guarantee further rights, of which the following are now enforceable in the UK courts. Protocols 4 and 7 are set out above. Protocol 1 states:

'*Article 1: Protection of property*
Every natural or legal person is entitled to the peaceful enjoyment of his possessions. No one shall be deprived of his possessions except in the public interest and subject to the conditions provided for by law and by the general principles of international law.
The preceding provision shall not, however, in any way impair the right of a State to enforce such laws as it deems necessary to control the use of property in accordance with the general interest or to secure the payment of taxes or other contributions or penalties.
Article 2: Right to education
No person shall be denied the right to education. In the exercise of any function which it assumes in relation to education and to teaching, the State shall respect the right of parents to ensure such education and teaching in conformity with their own religious and philosophical convictions.
Article 3: Right to free elections
The High Contracting Parties undertake to hold free elections at reasonable intervals by secret ballot, under conditions which will ensure the free expression of the opinion of the people in the choice of the legislature.'

The margin of appreciation

This is a doctrine which has similarities to subsidiarity in EC law. It recognises that states have a closer knowledge than the Strasbourg court of the cultural and moral values of its citizens and allows a limited discretion to the state to limit the application of the Convention rights. This doctrine does not apply in the state's own courts but only when a case is taken to Strasbourg.

Derogations and reservations

Article 15 of the Convention permits states to apply for derogations:

> 'In time of war or other public emergency threatening the life of the nation the High Contracting Party may take measures derogating from its obligations under this Convention to the extent strictly required by the exigencies of the situation.'

At present, the United Kingdom has only one derogation in force – rights of detention under the Prevention of Terrorism (Temporary Provisions) Act 1989. Section 1(2) of the Human Rights Act 1998 exempts the government from incorporation of the Convention in accordance with any derogation for a period of up to five years (s16). Section 15 of the Human Rights Act 1998 permits 'designated reservations' of matters which the UK government declined to ratify with the rest of the Convention. The only current designated reservation relates to Protocol 1, art 2:

> 'At the time of signing of the present (First) Protocol, I declare that, in view of certain provisions of the Education Acts in the United Kingdom, the principle affirmed in the second sentence of art 2 is accepted by the United Kingdom only so far as it is compatible with the provision of efficient instruction and training, and the avoidance of unreasonably public expenditure.'

9.3 The Human Rights Act 1998

The Human Rights Act (HRA) 1998 directs the courts to interpret domestic legislation so that it is compatible with the rights guaranteed by the European Convention on Human Rights. The Convention rights do not pass directly into UK law. They appear in the HRA 1998 as a schedule and the sections of the Act provide the machinery for their application, so that the procedural articles of the Convention are not received into domestic law.

Section 3(1) of the HRA 1998 provides that:

> 'So far as it is possible to do so, primary legislation and subordinate legislation must be read and given effect in a way which is compatible with Convention rights.'

If the UK court finds that the provision is not compatible with the Convention, under s4, they may issue a certificate of incompatibility but this does not affect the validity, continuing operation or enforcement of the provision. When a court is considering the issue of a declaration of incompatibility the Crown has a right to intervene in the proceedings (and can appear before the court to argue a case even though it is not a party to the proceedings). Once any possible appeal against the declaration has been dealt with, s10 and Schedule 2 provide for 'fast track' remedial action to make amendments to the legislation without delay. Schedule 2 provides the machinery for making a 'remedial order' without going through all the usual stages for the passing of legislation. However, the certificate of incompatibility speaks to the future and does not assist the claimant bringing the case in which it is granted.

As regards future legislation, s19 provides that there is a presumption that all future domestic legislation will be Convention compatible. A Joint Committee has been set up to scrutinise all primary and subordinate legislation passing through the House of Commons and the House of Lords to ensure compatibility with the Convention and to issue a certificate to that effect in respect of each piece of legislation.

Section 6 makes it unlawful for a public authority to act in a way which is incompatible with the Convention. 'Public authority' in this context includes the courts and this enables the claimant to invoke the Convention indirectly against individuals, giving the Convention horizontal effect, as well as directly against state institutions under s7. However, the act of a public authority will not be unlawful if the public authority is acting on legislation which is incompatible, which is why the claimant will have no claim in that particular case. As with EC law, 'public authority' is given a wide meaning.

When interpreting domestic legislation, the court must consider the Strasbourg case law of the European Court of Human Rights and must give an interpretation which is compatible with the Convention rights. In this way, the Convention will permeate UK domestic law through interpretation by the court. This arrangement raises questions of the separation of powers. Will the judiciary, in effect, become part of the legislature? Convention rights must be given a purposive interpretation. Section 2 of the HRA 1998 provides that the Strasbourg case law must be taken into account by the UK court. However, the Strasbourg jurisprudence is not binding on the UK court.

Under s7(1) only a victim of the unlawful act complained of may bring proceedings against a public authority. According to Strasbourg case law, a victim is someone who is actually and directly affected by the act or omission complained of. However, it was held in *Klass v Germany* (1978) 2 EHRR 214 that this would include anyone who was under a real risk of being directly affected. However, the European Court of Human Rights does not recognise the standing of members of the public who are not victims to bring cases, and this includes public interest groups unless they are truly representative of victims. These groups have been permitted to intervene in UK domestic cases in recent years (the most notable example being the intervention of Amnesty International in *R v Bow Street Metropolitan Stipendiary Magistrate, ex parte Pinochet Ugarte* [1998] 4 All ER 897.

Section 8 of the HRA 1998 gives the courts powers to award compensation for the unlawful act of the public authority. Such an award must be made in accordance with the principles laid down by the European Court of Human Rights and must take into consideration any other relief or remedy granted and the consequences of any decision in respect of the act complained of. 'Relief' would include the granting of an injunction, or any of the orders following from judicial review.

There are two governing concepts of the Strasbourg court which will now be received into our domestic law: the concepts of legitimate aim and proportionality. These are the mechanisms by which the necessity that the state must at times interfere with the freedom of the individual is accommodated.

Legitimate aim

We have already seen that the Convention articles provide exceptions to the guarantees of fundamental rights and freedoms (the qualified rights granted in arts 4.2, 4.3, 5, 6, 7, 12 and 14) and also provide in some cases that the state cannot impose exceptions (as in the case of art 3, the absolute prohibition of torture). Where exceptions are permitted, the interference with human rights must be prescribed by law. Articles 8–11 specify legitimate aims which can be pleaded by states wishing to defend actions for breach of the Convention. These are similar to those which can be claimed under art 30 (formerly art 36) of the EC Treaty – issues of public health, safety and morality and issues of national security. The state can also rely on a legitimate aim which leads to the protection of the rights of others and on economic grounds.

Proportionality

The interference in the qualified human rights must be 'necessary in a democratic society'. The state will be justified in interfering with human rights only to the extent which is absolutely necessary to serve its legitimate aim – there must be a 'pressing social need' for such action by the state.

9.4 Future applications to the European Court of Human Rights

A claimant may still apply to the Strasbourg court if it can be established that all domestic procedures have been exhausted without a remedy. This might arise if the government declined to legislate or to amend existing legislation or if the domestic courts had failed to uphold the claimant's human rights. It is possible that when seeking a remedy for incompatible legislation, the claimant may first have to obtain a certificate of incompatibility.

Section IV
Academic Study Skills

10

Research and Preparation Skills

10.1 Preparation

The essence of any good legal work is good preparation. A thorough knowledge of your subject will give you confidence, will enable you to cope with unexpected points which may arise, and, most importantly, will enable you to develop your arguments in depth.

Good preparation entails an effective interaction with the materials which keeps your mind alert to the possibilities of the subject.

10.2 Understanding

First, you must be sure that you know what is expected of you. You must be sure you understand the task set and all its implications. Second, you must be familiar with the criteria by which your work will be assessed. The formal criteria by which all university departments are judged are the Benchmarks for Law.

Benchmarks for Law

The Quality Assurance Agency for Higher Education has set benchmarks as the minimum level of performance required to pass an honours degree in law. Any student graduating in law must show achievement in all of the following areas of performance:

Subject specific abilities

1. Knowledge: A student should demonstrate a basic knowledge and understanding of the principal features of the legal system(s) studied, ie she/he should be able:

   • to demonstrate knowledge of a substantial range of major concepts, values, principles and rules of that system;
   • to explain the main legal institutions and procedures of that system;
   • to demonstrate the main legal institutions and procedures of that system.

2. Application and problem-solving: A student should demonstrate a basic ability to apply his or her knowledge to a situation of limited complexity in order to provide arguable conclusions for concrete problems (actual or hypothetical).

3. Sources and research: A student should demonstrate a basic ability:

   • to identify accurately the issue(s) which require researching;
   • to identify and retrieve up-to-date legal information, using paper and electronic sources;
   • to use primary and secondary legal sources relevant to the topic under study.

General transferable intellectual skills

4. Analysis, synthesis, critical judgement and evaluation: A student should demonstrate a basic ability:

   • to recognise and rank items and issues in terms of relevance and importance;
   • to bring together information and materials from a variety of different relations to a topic;
   • to produce a synthesis of relevant doctrinal and policy issues in relation to a topic;
   • to make a critical judgement of merits of particular arguments;
   • to present and make a reasoned choice between alternative solutions.

5. Autonomy and ability to learn: A student should demonstrate a basic ability, with limited guidance:

   • to act independently in planning and undertaking tasks in areas of law which she or he has already studied;
   • to be able to undertake independent research in areas of law which he or she has not previously studied starting from standard legal information sources;
   • to reflect on his or her own learning and to seek and make use of feedback.

Key skills

6. Communication and Literacy: Both orally and in wiriting, a student should demonstrate a basic ability:

   - to understand and use the English language (or, where appropriate the Welsh language) proficiently in relation to legal matters;
   - to present knowledge or an argument in a way which is comprehensible to others and which is directed at their concerns
   - to read and discuss legal materials which are written in technical and complex language.

7. Numeracy, information technology and teamwork: A student should demonstrate a basic ability:

   - where relevant and as the basis for an argument, to use, present and evaluate information provided in numerical or statistical form;
   - to produce a word-processed essay or other text and to present such work in an appropriate form;
   - to use the world-wide web and e-mail;
   - to use some form of electronic retrieval system;
   - to work in groups as a participant who contributes effectively to the group's task.

Note that these are the *minimum* standards for an honours degree: It has been suggested that this translates into the following degree classifications:

First class: excellent work
The student has attained, in all areas of performance tested by assessment, a standard that cannot be improved upon within the practical constraints of the assessment process.

Upper Second class: meritorious work
Superior understanding of the principal features of the subject in its factual, doctrinal and policy aspects. High level of ability to evaluate and analyse material, to solve problems and to identify and assess, and use appropriately, primary and secondary sources. Very good communication skills and skills in reflective learning. High level of performance in other relevant key skills (IT, group work, presentation skills).

Lower Second class: good work
Good knowledge of the principal features of the subject in its factual, doctrinal and policy aspects, including relevant doctrinal and policy issues, and ability to evaluate issues and to make reasoned choices between alternative solutions. Good communication skills. Good IT and other key skills.

Third Class: benchmark pass
Basic knowledge of the principal features of the subject, including doctrinal and policy issues, ability to evaluate issues in terms of importance and to make reasoned choices between alternative solutions. Some ability to work independently, undertake personal research, use primary and secondary sources and reflect on own performance. Minimum acceptable standard of communication skills (including use of English language and presentational skills). Basic competence in IT skills.

Levels of performance on essay questions

Look at the example in *Figure 7* and the way the question is interpreted to represent different levels of approach. These are often described as a 'deep' and a 'surface' approach to learning. (The example is non-legal, to make it more accessible to all readers new to the study of law.)

First Class Answer

Original Question:

'*Compare and contrast the effects of blindness and deafness on language development.*'

First class answer:

'*Identify the consequences of blindness and deafness for language development. Compare and contrast these consequences, drawing conclusions about the nature of language development and commenting on the adequacy of theories of language development.*'

Upper second class answer:

'*Identify the consequences of blindness and deafness for language development. Compare and contrast these consequences.*'

Lower second class answer:

'*List some of the features of blindness and deafness. List some consequences for language development.*'

Third class answer:

'*Write down anything you can think of about blindness, deafness, child development and language development in the order in which you think of things. Draw no justified conclusions.*'

Figure 7

A deep approach to learning generates a deep response to the material you are given to study during the course. The first class answer shows much more than a knowledge of the basic subject material. The more facets you can see to the question, the deeper your approach – so long as they are relevant.

By contrast, a surface approach to the material simply gives back to the lecturer what they have given you in the first place with little interaction or critical comment on your part – you show that you can get by in the subject but with little interest or enthusiasm.

Part of your preparation must be to reflect on the question from the moment that it is issued to you – to discover potential conflicts and to assemble data to enable you to respond to it in depth.

The assessment criteria

Many law departments will issue assessment criteria to their students in a course handbook or with the assessment itself. Sometimes criteria are given in lectures or tutorials and not written down. Generally, lecturers and examiners expect to receive answers which:

1. Identify the legal issues or the issues which are most relevant to resolving the problem *or* in an essay question the elements of the question which require a response.
2. Accurately state the law in enough detail about the constituent elements of the rules so the rules can be effectively used to analyse a problem or to assess the hypothesis in the essay title.
3. Analyse the problem or the hypothesis in the light of the rules, including clear statements of how the factual issues correspond to the elements of the legal rules.
4. See where the elements of the rules might be used to different effect and to support different results, depending on which facts, how many facts and which rules are used; explaining in clear language the best result in the light of the available facts and rules.
5. Identify issues of policy in the rules, such as the policies that the rules are supposed to support, and identifying the consequences of the rules, whether intended or not, that may be criticised on policy grounds.
6. State a conclusion as to the best result in a problem or as to the strengths/weaknesses of the hypothesis.

Marks will also be given for:

1. good structure;
2. accuracy in answering the question exactly as set; and
3. evidence that you have given an appropriate response to the question, including, most importantly, your own critical analysis and conclusion.

Evidence of good research and familiarity with the source materials will also gain marks. If you select the relevant issues and law, the lecturer can safely assume that you understand the subject as a whole. If you write everything down, this shows little understanding.

10.3 Researching your subject

If your lecturer has supplied a reading list, this should be your starting point. Make sure you assemble your materials early – there will be pressure on the available resources if the same essay has been set for the whole year group. If the volumes you require are missing from the library shelves for a long period, you should tell your lecturer and ask for other arrangements to be made to supply the materials to students. Remember that cases and statutes appear in more than one set of volumes and on databases.

If no reading list is given, work from your lecture handouts and textbooks. Useful source materials are often quoted in textbooks and their references given in footnotes. Some textbooks give bibliographies and recommended further reading.

You may need to consult the Index of Legal Periodicals for a list of relevant articles. This is an American index but contains listings of British publications. *Halsbury's Laws of England* also contains details of recently published articles – these can be found in the Noter Up and Annual Abridgement under subject headings. The current monthly parts should also be consulted. Current Law also gives details of new publications. At the very least, you should look through the recent volumes of the relevant periodicals on the library shelves. Note too the references of articles which will be of use on other assignments. These voyages of discovery can be very satisfying in themselves if you allow yourself plenty of time. Your ability to use the law library will be improved with each assignment. If the facilities are available to you, carry out a search of the Internet and the law databases.

When you find an article on a related topic, skim-read it to make sure that it is relevant – some parts may be more relevant than others. Do not waste time on material that is not strictly relevant other than for your own interest. If you find a seminal article (one of fundamental importance to your research), you may wish to make your own photocopy or to photocopy the most relevant pages. Once you have assessed its value to your work, then read it more carefully and take notes and quotations.

One danger is that you spend so much time on this preliminary research that you don't leave enough time to write the essay. Set yourself a deadline by which you will start to prepare your essay even if you feel your research is incomplete. Learn to manage your research time efficiently.

10.4 Constructing your answer

Read through all your assembled material and sort out what is relevant. Read generally in the initial stages, but if you discover key points which you wish to use in your answer, note these, together with an accurate reference to the source of the material which should then be put in a footnote so that the source is correctly attributed.

Subdivide the essay topic into a number of subject areas and note your material under the appropriate heading. As you read, note your own reaction to the subject matter. Record these thoughts separately from your noting of the source material – put them in brackets, in a different coloured ink, or with your initials and a colon.

10.5 Reflection

No matter how good your time management, inevitably there will be times when you will find it difficult to make any real progress on your assignment – just at the time when you had planned to get it done. This is **normal** but it requires some discipline and some strategy to keep your programme on course.

If this happens to you, you must **pause for reflection**. Instead of studying the subject intensely, let your mind go free. It is often a good idea to have more than one project in hand at any one time. Indeed, it can be difficult to avoid this on a law degree! Staring at the page or at the blank paper will achieve nothing. Make a start on something else – or take a complete break from all your work and come back to the task in hand later. Your mind will continue subconsciously to work on the problem area.

It may be difficult to find a suitable beginning to your essay or to put the issues into an appropriate order – or you may be unable to see the answer to one part of the question or to express your own opinions lucidly. You will find these problems easier to resolve after a break. With experience, you can allow for these breaks in your timetable.

When you have taken a break, come back and try to define the problem you have been experiencing. In your mind (or in reality), try to explain the subject matter as simply as possible to a person who has little or no knowledge of the subject. Try a little lateral thinking to find an alternative approach. Whatever you try, you will have distanced yourself from the immediate problem and may now be able to see the wood for the trees.

10.6 Reasoning

When I left the firm at the end of my articles, I was presented with a crystal paperweight. My principal said that this was the end to all my troubles in practice –

when a client asked what their chances were, all I had to do was to look into my new crystal ball!

If you develop good critical reasoning skills, you will have no need of a crystal ball – you will be able to give a reasoned assessment of the strengths and weaknesses of the client's case or the judge's likely opinion. This is what you are asked to do in your assessments. The symbol of justice as a set of scales is a pertinent one – all the arguments must be carefully weighed and a balance struck.

In the academic debate, dissenting opinions and judgments in the lower courts must be examined, as must the reports of the Law Commission – even if the recommendations never pass into legislation. You must also have a good working knowledge of the principles of statutory interpretation and the doctrine of precedent so that you can assess the significance of a judgment.

You will begin to recognise the style of the judges as individuals – you will soon learn to recognise a Denning judgment or a Diplock judgment and to know when the decision rests in 'a safe pair of hands' – ie which judges can be relied upon to bring a measure of common sense into the equation.

It is important that you check that the law in your textbooks is up to date – either by consulting *Halsbury's Laws* or *Current Law* or by making a LEXIS search if this is available to you. Attention to detail is an important element of good preparation.

With a problem question, the scenario will closely resemble the facts of cases you have studied on the course but there will be subtle differences in some of the facts given. A close analysis of the facts is very important to the accuracy of your answer. Where you observe discrepancies between the facts given and those of the cases, you must note them and draw a conclusion as to their significance. Some significant facts will be omitted deliberately from the problem. For example, in land law, you may not be told whether or not a couple who occupy property are married, so on no account make an assumption. Answer in the alternative, discussing rules which apply if they are married and the alternative outcome if they are not married.

Avoid sweeping statements. **Don't** say in your introductory paragraph that you strongly agree or disagree with the statement given in your essay title. Your argument must be **balanced**. Your essay should test your own opinions and those of the writers in the subject area and draw a reasoned conclusion based on a thorough examination of the subject and founded on established legal rules. All students should be passionate in their beliefs but a law essay is not the place to show that passion.

Note down the connections you make or the inconsistencies in arguments. Read critically and reflectively. Follow the academic debate and identify your own view on the subject matter. Record this carefully: your relevant observations which can be backed by legal authority are key evidence of the depth of your approach. Dare to be critical of the key players in the academic debate. **Don't** read their work as gospel truth. Dare to be critical of the approach of the judges too. But make sure that your views are impartial and logical.

10.7 Structure

List the key issues in a logical structure. Make sure every one of them is relevant to the required answer. Use the structure indicated in the list of assessment criteria, above – this is a development of the ISAC structure discussed in Chapter 2.

You may prefer to use a structure suggested by the essay question and to apply the criteria to each element of the answer in turn. What you must **not** do is give a catalogue of the law as delivered to you in lectures or in your textbook. Marks are allocated for the way in which you select your material and for your informed response to the question set.

As you prepare your work, make sure you follow **all** the instructions given for your assignment.

10.8 The need to write

It is vital that you recognise the point at which you are ready to start writing your answer. If paragraphs or sentences begin to form in your mind which are your direct response to the question, write them down immediately. Try to avoid the habit of having to read everything before you start to write. This is self-indulgent and counter-productive.

The insights which come to you during your preliminary study are valuable and, even if you eventually decide not to include them in the finished work, they may stimulate other thoughts. It is better to record those you decide not to use than to lose those which you need.

Keep a note of any useful quotations and of key words which show you have a knowledge of the language of the subject. Try to avoid the use of Latin phrases unless they are technical terms. The examiner needs to know that you understand the principle – not that you can copy Latin out of your textbook.

10.9 Reviewing your structure

As you begin to write your assignment, you will be given fresh insights into the issues – new arguments and connections will become clear to you. These are very important and should be incorporated into your answer. This means that your essay plan will have to be revised and restructured so that the new ideas appear to their best advantage in the appropriate place.

10.10 Evaluation

When you are happy with your structure and your essay plan, evaluate the results and continue this process until the essay is finally written. Read and re-read your text, test your theories and alter your phrasing as necessary.

Allow yourself twice the time you think the assignment will take. Dr Dale Griffin of the University of Sussex spent five years researching into 'Task Completion Wishful Thinking Syndrome' (reported in *The Times*, 29 February 1996). He discovered that students often grossly underestimated the time they needed in which to finish important tasks and failed to learn from their experience. When asked to estimate how long a colleague would take to complete the task, they were able to assess this accurately. If it is difficult to be realistic, it is best to err on the side of caution.

10.11 Plagiarism

Universities have very strict rules about plagiarism. It is forbidden to copy the work of others without attributing it. It is vital that you adapt source materials at least by paraphrasing them – and even then you must attribute the source of your material in a footnote. If you quote directly from the material you **must** put the quotation in quotation marks or in a different typeface and attribute the source in a footnote, giving the name of the author, the work and the page reference. You should also include a bibliography of all works you have consulted, giving enough details for the reader to check your sources if necessary. Claiming someone else's work as your own is **cheating** – it is theft of ideas of another.

Similarly, although group work generally is to be encouraged, there comes a point when you must work independently on any assessed work. The line is drawn at different points in different institutions but generally, while as a group you may wish to share source materials – articles you have found or a different textbook – what you make of this material must be your own work.

If your work is too similar to that of another student, you may have to take part in a viva (oral examination) or to rewrite the essay or be disqualified. Beware!

All university departments have access to software which makes it very easy to check the authorship of passages from student essays, so never be tempted to use work which is not your own, even if you think there is no better way of expressing the concepts.

This is especially important for law students because the law department is under a duty to disclose such incidents to the Law Society and the Bar Council and this may prevent the person concerned from entering professional practice.

SO REMEMBER: PLAGIARISM WILL SERIOUSLY DAMAGE YOUR CAREER PROSPECTS!

11

Legal Writing Skills

Good preparation is the key to good writing – it will give your work a sound structure. You will be able to present your ideas in a logical order which will be easy for the reader to follow. This book is primarily concerned with the writing and presentation of student essays and projects in an academic environment. The skills acquired in the academic stage of your education and training should be the foundation for the specialist writing skills required for professional life.

The very fact that you have been accepted on to a law course is evidence that you have an aptitude for good communication, but many students believe that something more is expected of them. Lawyers are notorious for communicating with clients and with each other in ways which preserve a mystique and enable them to claim possession of the expert knowledge. Fortunately, with the wider dissemination of legal information through radio, television and newspapers and on management courses, lawyers have had to abandon the barricades of obscure language and must now communicate like the rest of the human race. In law schools today, the emphasis is on clarity of expression and accessibility of language.

You must find a writing style in which you can express yourself clearly and appropriately so that your reader is engaged in the material which you wish to communicate. Most of us are taught to choose our language carefully from an early age. When you embark on your first steps in legal writing you must choose again. You must take control of the language you use and develop your own style. This style will evolve as your grasp of legal concepts becomes more complex. How do you choose a style? When you decide what you like and dislike in the writing of others you are making that choice.

Look at the judgments of Lord Diplock and Lord Scarman in *Davis v Johnson* (Appendix B). Lord Diplock applies the law to the facts of the case at pp562G–565B. He refers to Miss Davis as 'his mistress' and to Mr Johnson as 'her paramour'. He disapproves of the modern term 'cohabitees'. Look in particular at the complicated structure of Lord Diplock's sentences.

By contrast, Lord Scarman at p579E *ff* describes Miss Davis's plight in a more straightforward way. He uses simple language and short sentences. He does not use pejorative terms like 'paramour' and 'mistress'. He describes Miss Davis's plight in detail. Her desperate situation is not masked by obsolete, archaic language. Lord Scarman shows he is familiar with the plight of women like Jennifer Davis. So ask yourself these questions:

1. Whose language is more effective? Why?
2. What did Lord Diplock and Lord Scarman intend to achieve in their choice of language?
3. How would you present the facts of the case?
4. How could you best identify the issues in the case by your choice of language?

Then, ask yourself these questions about your *own* writing.

Here is an extract from Lord Denning's judgment in *Burgess v Rawnsley* [1975] Ch 429:

> 'In 1966 there was a scripture rally in Trafalgar Square. A widower, Mr Honick, went to it. A widow, Mrs Rawnsley, the defendant, also went. She was about 60. He went up to her and introduced himself. He was not much to look at. "He looked like a tramp" she said. "He had been picking up fag ends." They got on well enough, however, to exchange addresses ... Next day he went to her house with a gift for her. It was a rose wrapped in a newspaper. Afterwards, their friendship grew apace. She was sorry for him, she said. She smartened him up with better clothes. She had him to meals. She went to his house: he went to hers. They wrote to each other in terms of endearment. We were not shown the letters, but counsel described them as love letters.'

Why is this clear? There are several reasons:

1. The immediacy of the language makes it accessible. This is common law for the common people at its best.
2. The sentence structure is simple and logical. Count the number of words of more than two syllables. Sentences which are too long can detract from clarity. Here the story unfolds in short sentences.
3. This passage comes from a case concerning the severance of a joint tenancy of land, a complex area of law which you will meet in your land law course. This

account of the facts of the case, which goes on to describe how Mr Honick and Mrs Rawnsley bought a house together, sets the law in an understandable human context.

Here is another example from Megarry J, one of our greatest Chancery judges:

'Errol Flynn was a film actor whose performance gave pleasure to many millions. On 20 June 1909 he was born in Hobart, Tasmania; and on 14 October 1959 he died in Vancouver, British Columbia. When he was 17 he was expelled from school in Sydney; and in the next thirty-three years he lived a life which was full, lusty, restless and colourful. In his career, in his three marriages, in his friendships, in his quarrels, and in bed with the many women he took there, he lived with zest and irregularity. The lives of film stars are not cast in the ordinary mould and in some respects Errol Flynn was more stellar than most. When he died he posed the only question that I have to decide: Where was he domiciled at the date of his death?' (Megarry J: *Re Flynn* [1968] 1 All ER 49 at p50)

11.1 Developing your own style

The best way of developing your own writing style is to be aware of styles adopted by others. If you can analyse the differences in form and language between a Scarman judgment and a Diplock judgment, you can adopt and adapt the techniques which please you for your own writing. However this does *not* mean slavishly following someone else's writing style.

Before you start to write, be clear in your mind about what you want to say. Get your thoughts in order and write them down in simple language. Many students think they must use obscure legal terms in order to impress. This is not so. If you understand the rules of spelling, grammar and syntax and know how to construct sentences and paragraphs, you will write more clearly than if you ignore these fundamental rules, which no doubt have dogged you through primary and secondary education. In tertiary education, they are of paramount importance, especially for law students. Effective presentation of argument is fundamental to successful practice of law. Arguments will not be presented effectively if the audience, whether judge, lecturer or ordinary mortal is distracted by poor spelling, poor grammar or by irritating habits of expression. The effort required to learn the rules will be more than repaid.

1. Essays and problem answers should be written in the third person. Even if you are asked to 'Advise Fred', **don't** start 'Well Fred, you have a good case ...'. This is over-familiar. Write as if you were explaining Fred's case to a colleague.
2. Avoid the use of the first person – 'I think that'. Some tutors dismiss the use of the phrase 'It is submitted that ...' as a preface to the student's own opinion, but others encourage it because it lends objectivity to the views expressed. It is also a signal to the reader that this is your own opinion. Which style do your lecturers prefer?

3. The purpose of a law essay is analysis rather than description. When discussing cases, do not give too many facts. Concentrate on the issues and only give facts when they are essential to the understanding of the issues.
4. In formal legal writing, do not use abbreviations – 'it is', not 'it's'; 'do not, will not' not 'don't, won't'.
5. The introduction to your essay should set the context and summarise the main points of your argument. If the essay title includes a quotation, the introduction could set the quotation in context and analyse its meaning in order to introduce the topics to be covered later in the essay.
6. An introduction along the following lines should be **avoided at all costs**: 'This essay is about the investment powers and duties of trustees. It will be necessary to discuss the Trustee Investment Act 1961. Then I will discuss the cases…'.
7. **Your introduction must engage the attention of the reader and encourage them to read on.**
8. Your essay must have a conclusion which summarises **your** arguments and **your** assessment of the issues. Don't introduce new arguments in your conclusion. When answering a problem question, say what the outcome of the case is likely to be – don't sit on the fence.
9. **In both written and oral presentation, the rules are**:

  – say what you are going to say – the introduction;
  – say it – body of the essay/presentation;
  – say what you have said – conclusion.

10. Use the active voice: 'Mary invested her inheritance in BT shares' not 'The inheritance was invested by Mary in BT shares.'
11. Use the positive rather than the negative: 'The postman usually calls at 9am' not 'It was not unusual for the postman to call at 9am.'
12. Watch the word order of your sentences: 'The boy's red jumper' not 'The red boy's jumper.'

11.2 Gender-free language

Wherever possible, use gender-free language. Watch out for and note ways of doing this. Richard Nobles wrote his book *Pensions, Employment and the Law* (Clarendon Press, Oxford 1993) entirely in the third person feminine. Is this gender-free? It certainly challenges the reader's assumptions. Some authors write alternate chapters using masculine and feminine pronouns.

'One' may sound pompous. 'He or she' is inelegant. But it may be preferable to use 'he or she' rather than offend the reader – even then readers might prefer 'She or he'.

Also, use 'staffing', not 'manning'; 'police officer', not 'policeman'; plural 'they', not singular 'he, she'.

When in doubt, bend the rules – risk using 'they' with a singular verb, rather than repeating 'he or she' a number of times. It is important to be aware of the problem and use your judgment – it's your essay!

Legal writing must be objective – the expression of religious views, however sincerely held, is not appropriate.

11.3 Structure

The order in which ideas are presented is crucial to the reader's understanding. The necessity of spending a considerable time in planning and preparation has already been emphasised, as has the need to revise the plan throughout the writing and editing process. You must start with a logical order for your ideas. It is often helpful if your writing is divided by sub-headings.

Each **paragraph** should contain a sentence which states its theme or point. This should come first unless there is a sentence which links this paragraph with the preceding one. The other sentences in the paragraph should support and develop the theme with facts, examples, citations, analogies, contrasts, limitations, practical consequences and so on. If all these were included in one paragraph, the paragraph would be far too long. They are suggestions of ways in which to develop a theme from your theme sentence.

Some judgment has to be made as to the length of a paragraph. If paragraphs are too short, they will interrupt the flow of your argument. If they are too long, your ideas may be lost. This is a matter for your judgment. If you tend to write short paragraphs, experiment with joining them up. If your paragraphs cover most of a page, try dividing them up.

Sentence construction is also important. We have already examined the effects of using long or short sentences. Sentences are structured by the use of good grammar, the appropriate use of punctuation and the correct word order. Sentences should not normally be of more than 20 words. If you express more than one idea, and the two parts of the sentence are joined with a conjunction (and, but, if, etc), consider breaking the sentence at the point of the conjunction.

Each sentence must have a subject and a verb. The noun and the verb must agree – a singular noun requires the singular form of the verb. For example:

- 'Of the students waiting to see Professor Jones at 11am, none *was* there at 11.30.'
- 'Of the students waiting to see Professor Jones at 11am, all *were* gone by 11.30.'

It is dangerous to **split infinitives**. While you may defend to the death the right of the *Star Trek* adventurers 'to boldly go' to the ends of the universe, academics and judges do not approve of split infinitives. Keep the parts of the verb in the correct sequence and the reader will pay attention to the point of law you are making rather than to your breach of a rule of syntax now considered by many to be outdated.

Correct word order keeps your language simple. For example, drafting a notice or a byelaw which has consequences for the public is an exact science. Look at the way in which the meaning can be altered as the order of the words in a sentence is changed or the use of words varied slightly. It is important that you check your own writing to see how the structure can be improved by rearranging paragraphs, sentences and words.

Sentences can be clarified by the use of **punctuation**:

- Every sentence should end with a **full stop**.
- **Commas** should be used to separate items in a list or phrases which make up a sentence.
- **Colons** mark the beginning of a new idea or of someone else's idea. They can be also be used as an abbreviation for 'which is' or 'there are'. They widen the scope of the theme which you are discussing.

  - "As Catherine McKinnon observes: 'No man is ever in the same position as a woman is, because he is not in it as a woman.'"
  - "There are four varieties of rose in my garden: Paul Scarlett, Frensham, Peace and Zepherine Drouain."
  - "She studied the view: a new world opened before her of farms and fields, hamlets and villages."

- A **semicolon** allows you to add another linked idea or an emphasis to a closed sentence: "She asked him to bring her a glass of wine; he went immediately."
- **Apostrophes** are used either to indicate the possessive or to abbreviate words:

  - "Mary's house is the one next to the Post Office."
  - "We're going to the theatre tonight."
  - "It's raining" but "The dog is playing with *its* bone." There is no apostrophe to indicate the possessive here.

- **Inverted commas** indicate speech or quotations. They are also used to indicate unusual usage. The are **not** used to indicate a technical term or a proper noun (name):

  - The policeman said in evidence "I was proceeding along the highway in an orderly fashion."
  - As Margaret Thatcher said: "There is no such thing as society."
  - This "hotchpotch" as she called it ...

But not

  - "Lord Denning" developed "the doctrine of promissory estoppel".

Sometimes it is necessary to use another set of inverted commas within the quotation. Single quotation marks are then used: "When I saw John, he said 'I am going to London on Wednesday.'" This is a convention which is observed less often nowadays.

- When using quotations, it may not be necessary to use the whole text – you may wish to abbreviate it. Where you omit a passage from the quotation, insert **three full stops**. When you omit the final part of the quotation or where the quotation forms the end of your sentence, insert four to indicate a full stop:

  '... citizens of advanced industrial democracies ... have difficulty in forging a personal and social identity.'

- Subsidiary ideas can be put in **parentheses** (brackets): "The footpath (part of the Icknield Way) crossed the main road at the entrance to the village."
- If you wish to expand a theme, you may use dashes in a similar way: "Quality of working conditions for all – rather than equality of the sexes – is the European Commission's new objective."

Punctuation will give space to your ideas so that they are less likely to be overlooked by the reader.

11.4 Presentation

Examiners will claim that students do not lose marks for poor presentation but this is a dangerous assertion. If work is presented with care, it is pleasing to the eye, easy to read, key points are apparent without close scrutiny and it shows that the writer has taken some trouble. Anything you do to make the marker's life easier is likely to count in your favour. Moreover, standards of spelling and grammar are still perceived as an indication of educational ability.

Here are some do's and don'ts:

Do

- Make sure your handwriting is easy to read – it is less important that it is tidy than that it is legible. Neat handwriting can be the most illegible. Make sure that your letters and words are adequately spaced and that your writing is neither too large nor too small. If possible, invest in a fountain pen and use black ink. Alternatively, use a black roller ball pen. Avoid using a blue ball point pen – especially in examinations when you have to write at speed. Work should *never* be submitted in pencil unless this is a specific instruction, as may be the case on a multiple choice paper. Use a pen with a wide barrel if your writing is otherwise too small. Experiment with different pens before making a final selection.
- Invest in a word processor or make sure that you can use the university's computer facilities for students. All universities nowadays run training courses. Make sure you know how long you must allow for work to be processed by computer services in order to meet essay deadlines.

- Use plenty of paper – use wide margins, double spacing and leave an extra line between each paragraph. It is particularly helpful if you separate your paragraphs on your examination script.
- Use bullet points to highlight your key points.
- Underline and embolden case names.
- Put quotations in different type, in bold or in indented paragraphs.
- Use a dictionary and a thesaurus to help you to use words appropriately and to give you a choice of words. If you have difficulty with grammar and spelling, invest in a grammar book and a spelling dictionary and **learn** from your mistakes.

Don't

- Leave everything to the last minute so that you have no time to check spelling or prepare a clean copy.
- Prepare a clean copy in the examination – crossings-out are permissible as long as your script is legible.
- Mis-spell rec*ei*ved, sep*a*rate, there/their/they're, principle/principal, ie *do* learn the rules of spelling.
- Rely on your spell check – it will let words through which are typographical errors and wrong in this context. If your spelling is too far off the mark, it may select an entirely different word.
- Adopt an over-familiar or an over-formal style.

11.5 Footnotes and bibliography

Each idea or quotation which comes from someone else's work must be attributable in the text itself. There are alternative ways of doing this:

- 'Research by Smith (1994) demonstrates that …' (accompanied by a reference to the written paper in the bibliography).
- 'The rule was confirmed by the court in *Barber* v *Guardian Royal Exchange* Case C–262/88 [1990] IRLR 240, para 44', ie full case reference in text itself.
- 'Gray observes (at p292)' – again with a reference to the full work in the bibliography.
- 'Christine Littleton observes[21]' – with a footnote or endnote giving the reference to her article.

If your essay is handwritten, or if your word processor has the facility to do so, full references should be inserted as footnotes on the page where the reference appears. If your word processor cannot do this easily, a list of endnotes at the end of the essay is acceptable.

Even if you make extensive use of footnotes, you should include a bibliography for any assessed essay. List all the books and articles you have consulted during the preparation of your essay, not just the ones from which you have quoted. Books, articles and reports should be cited separately and each category listed in alphabetical order according to the author's name. There is no need to include your lecture notes in the bibliography. Whether or not you include Nutshells and other superficial textbooks is a matter for your conscience, but in any case these are not suitable sources for material for assessed work.

11.6 Citing academic sources

In a footnote, the surname of the author appears first, followed by initials or first name, then the title of the chapter or article, next the publication (usually underlined or in italics), the publisher and the year of publication:

Book:	Bercusson, Brian, Equality and (Re)Conciliation of Working and Family Life, *European Labour Law*, Butterworths, 1996
Article:	Fitzpatrick, B, Equality in Occupational Pensions: The New Frontier after *Barber,* 54 MLR 271
Case:	You may wish to refer to a case by an abbreviation – *High Trees*. This should be accompanied by the full case name and reference in a footnote the first time you use the abbreviation.
If you have already quoted from the same source:	Fitzpatrick, B, op cit, at p272.
If your next quotation is from the same source:	ibid, p273 – ibid means from the same source.

11.7 Editing

As each draft comes off your word processor, read it through carefully. Make sure that you have answered the question, that all your points are relevant and that your work makes sense. Is your essay repetitive? Is it accurate?

Paragraphs:

• Are your paragraphs too short/too long?
• Could you improve the text by rearranging the paragraph breaks?
• Identify the key sentence in each paragraph.
• Have you supported your hypothesis with rules of law?
• Are there ambiguities/inconsistencies?
• Does each paragraph lead naturally into the next or do you need to make further connections?

Sentences:

- Could you break your sentences into shorter ones?
- Is your style too staccato – do you use too many very short sentences or paragraphs?
- Are there any words which can be cut out?
- Does each sentence have a subject and a verb?
- Could the structure of your sentence be improved by altering the word order?
- Have you used foreign phrases or jargon where plain English would make the meaning clearer?
- Could you improve the flow of the text by simplifying the sentence structure – active rather than passive, positive rather than negative, nouns rather than noun phrases, etc. for example, 'writing' rather than 'the writing game'.
- Is your writing gender-free?

Read the text through separately, line by line, to check for spelling mistakes and typographical errors. Finally, check that the numbering of your footnotes is correct and that all sources have been attributed.

11.8 Thinking like a lawyer

Throughout your time as a law student, you will be exhorted to 'think like a lawyer'. It is unlikely that anyone in your law department will come up with a clear explanation of what this means. See *Figure 8* (opposite) for some suggestions.

I am thinking like a lawyer when I

- Use my analytical skills to discover all the legal issues which arise on the information given
- Make sure that my knowledge of the substantive law is fully up to date
- Apply the law in the context of the principles of statutory interpretation and the doctrine of precedent
- Consider the political issues and other issues of policy behind the black letter law
- Consider the ethical issues and the issues of human rights in the matters I am asked to consider
- Consider the historical context which has dictated the state of the current law
- Understand the court system and parliamentary system through which changes in the law are brought about and the approaches of individual judges and parliamentarians to the laws under consideration
- Follow the academic debate on the state of the law and am prepared with well considered views of my own on whether the law needs to be changed
- Am aware of my own prejudices and am able to put these to one side in order to take an objective approach
- Grasp the fact that law in its application is never certain and that legal problems may have more than one solution and am willing to address the uncertainties
- Adopt the vocabulary of law
- Take all these aspects of law into consideration, make a considered and balanced judgment on the state of the existing law, apply the existing law to the problem or issue under consideration and present my conclusions after engaging in a logical, well structured argument
- Never lose sight of the human context to which the law applies.

This means that when I practise as a lawyer I will

- Take responsibility for the advice I give
- Give the client an accurate, objective account of their legal rights and responsibilities
- Use my enhanced powers of communication to present a case effectively
- Consider the issues of policy behind the black letter law and, where necessary, work for change
- Observe at all times the codes of professional conduct to which the legal professions subscribe
- Be clear about my own ethical standards and work within them

Figure 8

11.9 Writing skills self-assessment exercise

When your marked assessments are returned to you, the marker will make comments on the way in which you present your written work. Before you start work on your next round of assessment, you should take a long, hard look at these comments to make sure you don't make the same mistakes again. Use (or adapt) the chart in *Figure 9* (opposite) to bring together all the comments which have been made about your work (including the positive comments showing where you have done well). Then you can get a clearer picture of the changes you should make and the ideas which your lecturers have given you to help you to improve your work for the future. If you do not understand the comments made on your work, you should *always* make an appointment with the marker in order to be given a full explanation. This is especially important where you fail the assessment. Where more than one marker makes the same comments you should pay particular attention to what has been said. Most unfortunately, the feedback you receive can seem very negative – a catalogue of things you have failed to do. It is important to remember that the marker is on your side! The points are made in order to enable you to get the best possible class of degree at the end of your course. Reviewing your work in this way will make you a truly reflective learner.

Writing Skill	Subject 1		Subject 2		Subject 3		Subject 4	
	Tutor's Comments	Own Comments	Tutor's Comments	Own Comments	Tutor's Comments	Own Comments	Tutor's Comments	Own Comments
Presentation								
Legibility								
Spelling								
Punctuation								
Grammar								
Style								
Structure								
Research								
Bibliography								

Figure 9

11.10 Self-assessment checklist

Each time you write an essay, give a presentation or sit an examination, that in itself is a learning process. Although post mortems are not generally a good idea, especially in the middle of a number of assessments, some reflection on your performance will help you to do better next time round.

You should be given some feedback if you make a presentation in class or if you hand in an essay, but feedback after examinations is less common. However, experience in secondary education has shown that students are surprisingly accurate in assessing their own performance. If, when you receive your mark for the assessment, you feel you deserve better, talk to the person who marked your work. Often it is possible for someone else to mark it. If you do this, you must be able to justify your opinion of your performance.

If you record your experiences of performing set tasks which will have to be repeated in the future, you can benefit by the lessons learned in the process. We all gain insights into what we could do better next time, but if these are not recorded, more often than not they are lost. For each of your subjects and for each type of assessment, you could use the checklist in *Figure 10* (opposite) to record ways in which you can benefit from your experience.

Self-assessment checklist

SUBJECT

PREPARATION

- What did I do well?

- What can I do better/differently next time?

WRITTEN WORK

- What did I do well?

- What can I do better/differently next time?

REVISION

- What did I do well?

- What could I do better/differently next time?

THE EXAM

- What did I do well?

- What could I do better/differently next time?

MY TARGETS FOR NEXT TERM/NEXT YEAR:

WHAT SKILLS DID I USE IN THIS TERM'S/YEAR'S WORK?

Figure 10

11.11 Postscript

Having given you all the rules for good academic writing, I am conscious that I have broken most of them in this text! Why? The purpose of this book is to give you information in a non-legal way. There are many, truly excellent, academic texts on the theory and practice of good legal skills. I hope you will read them. However, they are sometimes aimed over the heads of those taking their first steps in law. I hope a less formal style will encourage you to read and act on the information in this book.

'A word is not a crystal, transparent and unchanged; it is the skin of a living thought and may vary greatly in color and context according to the circumstances at the time in which it is used.'

(Holmes J in *Towne* v *Eisner* 245 US 418, 425 (1910))

A House

'References in this Part of this Act to a house do not apply to a house which is not structurally detached and of which a material part lies above or below a part of the structure not comprised in this house.'

(Leasehold Reform Act 1967)

Plain Wayne, Gift of an Orange

'When an ordinary man wants to give an orange to another, he would merely say "I give you this orange". But when a lawyer does it, he says it this way: "Know all men by these presents that I hereby give, grant, bargain, sell, release, convey, transfer, and quitclaim all my right, title, interest, benefit, and use whatever in, of, and concerning this chattel, otherwise known as an orange, or citrus orantium, together with all the appurtanances thereto of skin, pulp, pip, rind, seeds, and juice, to have and to hold the said orange together with its skin, pulp, pip, rind, seeds, and juice for his own use and behalf, to himself and his heirs in fee simple forever, free from all liens, encumbrances, easements, limitations, restraints, or conditions whatsoever, now or anywhere made to the contrary notwithstanding, with full power to bite, cut, suck, or otherwise eat the said orange or to give away the same with or without its skin, pulp, pip, rind, seeds, or juice." '

(From *Wisconsin Bar Bulletin*, February 1975, p61)

12

Presentation Skills

The successful study and practice of law is heavily dependent on the development of good presentation skills. The skills which you acquire on the law degree should be transferable not only into legal practice but into any future career and into your personal life. There are three areas where presentation skills are of paramount importance:

1. Whenever you have to give any kind of formal presentation: as part of an assessment, in student debate, or when giving a talk on behalf of a student society or on one of your particular interests.
2. In tutorial work on your law course, when good communication skills can enhance the experience for everyone and ensure that you really learn something in the limited time available.
3. At interview.

12.1 Presentation skills generally

Many of us have an inherent fear of speaking in public but good public speakers are made, not born and these fears can be overcome. Indeed, a good performance requires some stage nerves – the adrenaline lifts your performance provided that you learn to keep your nerves under control.

In fact, the aim is not so much to give a performance as to share information – you must want to give your audience the benefit of your knowledge. Most audiences come to share that knowledge, not to criticise your appearance or your delivery. If you are overcome by nerves, analyse **exactly** what it is you are afraid of. Some of these fears are entirely rational and can be overcome – fear that the overhead projector or Powerpoint won't work, fear that you will forget what you have to say. Such calamities can be avoided by good preparation. Familiarise yourself with all your equipment and prepare good, legible notes and you will cope effectively with such eventualities which happen every now and then to even the most experienced speakers.

Most of us have a fear of negative criticism, a fear of failure; that what we say will not match the listener's expectations. Or is the fear that the presentation won't match our own expectations which are far too high? Don't waste time agonising about the outcome of your presentation – spend the time in good, thorough preparation instead.

Whatever your objective, write it down in **one sentence**. The sentence should describe an objective that is clear, precise and attainable – what it is that you wish your audience to think, say or do.

Choose the **three to five most important issues** from your subject matter. Choose those which support your thesis most strongly. The issues should be of equal importance. If some are weaker than others, expand the weaker ones to incorporate other material so that all points are equally balanced.

Start by writing your conclusion. This should be the information and ideas of which you wish to convince your audience – a summary of your main thesis. Next, draw **up to five themes** out of this and order them in a **logical sequence**. Write a **complete sentence** to describe each theme. Then expand on the theme with support for your thesis.

When selecting your themes, think about **which themes can best be put across to an audience**. Which will make your presentation most effective? It is often difficult to articulate technical points of law but quite easy to speak on background materials from the Law Commission reports, for example. Consider putting the difficult material into a handout.

Communication of ideas to an audience is a **two-way process**. With practice, you should be able to vary your script in response to the reaction of your audience. If they appear to be confused by what you are saying, you must be able to clarify your material. Again, this is much easier if you are fully familiar with your subject matter. You must be able to think on your feet.

12.2 Choosing your language

Your language must be clear. It must not get in the way of the message you are trying to convey. Use a thesaurus to find the words which convey your meaning most accurately but **keep your language as simple as possible**.

Don't mix your metaphors. Order your thoughts and images into a logical sequence. Your arguments will be more convincing is you use concrete examples rather than abstract images. And avoid cliches. Use fresh, stimulating language and avoid words and phrases like 'ball park', 'bottom line' and 'prioritise'.

Listen to the rhythm of your sentences. You will get lost in sentences that are too long. Just as in written work, too many short sentences strung together will give a staccato effect. Vary the rhythm and use it to emphasise your key points.

Be aware of the sound of your language.

12.3 Know your audience

There are a number of steps you can take in order to prepare to meet your audience. You can ask the person who has asked you to speak what is required of you – the level of knowledge of the subject which the audience has, likely numbers, whether there are experts (or novices) so that you can pitch the level of your talk to meet their needs. If you are speaking to a group of which you are a member, you will already have much of the required information.

Think specifically who will be in the audience – will they expect a formal or a relaxed approach? What will best suit your subject matter? When selecting your material, think of what your audience needs to know. How will they absorb this new information? Can you give them visual aids or anecdotes which will help them to grasp the points you are making? If you are giving the same presentation to different audiences, it is essential that you make changes to your material.

In order to communicate with the audience, you must engage with them. Although you are doing the talking, you must evoke a response in them:

- Use pauses so that they can absorb the new ideas.
- If appropriate, engage them in discussion.
- Simplify your style – do not let technical terms or jargon get in the way.
- Speak slowly to enable the listener to absorb your new ideas.
- Set up your presentation – and close it – with a strong introduction and conclusion.
- Treat your audience with respect – be sensitive to their age, gender and ethnic background.

12.4 Personal delivery skills

Know yourself

Do you help the audience to receive what you are trying to communicate? If your eyes are glued to your written script or you are searching frantically for the next point, you will not show sufficient concern for them to enable you to communicate properly. You can help them to receive your communication by:

- Wanting them to understand what you say.
- Speaking clearly and slowly.
- Maintaining eye contact.
- Controlling your body language – for example, arms folded indicates both aggression and defensiveness.
- Controlling your personal habits. On no account: jingle change in your pocket; play with your hair; make distracting movements – moving papers, shifting weight from one foot to the other, rocking on your heels; or scratch anything!

Develop good personal delivery skills

- Stand up and stand still – or sit up and sit still.
- Take a firm stance – balance your weight evenly on both feet.
- Wait for others to stop talking.
- Take a breath – pause.
- Establish eye contact with the audience – if there is a member of the audience who is the 'top person', start by making eye contact with them.
- Welcome the audience.
- Keep your voice strong and maintain your energy level – this is critical to gain and hold the interest of the audience.

In response to a first-year questionnaire, students said they wanted lecturers to:

- speak more slowly;
- use simpler language;
- emphasise key ideas;
- allow time for effective and accurate note-taking; and
- give detailed handouts which helped the student follow the lecture.

Bear these points in mind when you are making your presentation.

Establishing and maintaining eye contact

Keep up eye contact with the audience at all times. This means you must have short, legible notes which are easy to follow at a glance and you must know them well. And look at each member of the audience in turn when speaking, especially in a small group.

Don't overdo it – don't fix one poor soul with your gaze so that they feel you are accusing them of not paying attention – the purpose of eye contact is to make the audience feel included in the exercise.

Maintaining eye contact will make you more interesting and more credible. Eye contact enables you to gauge your audience's understanding of and response to what you are saying.

Using your voice

- The right volume will sound a bit loud to you.
- Don't rush – this is new information.
- Your voice is the key instrument – use pitch and tone for emphasis and to sustain interest, but don't overdo it!
- Use pauses to allow the audience to react to what you say.
- Do *not* lower your voice at the end of the sentence – often your key point comes at the end.
- Keep your voice strong – it builds and reinforces your advocacy.
- Use your hands to emphasise key points.

Using visual aids

You can enhance your powers of communication dramatically by using overhead transparencies and/or a handout. If you can use Powerpoint and it is available, this gives a professional edge to your presentation BUT only if you are fully competent and confident with the technology and you are sure that this will be available to you.

12.5 Rehearse and refine

Preparation of material and good delivery are important, but so, too, is presentation. The following pointers will be helpful:

- If possible, familiarise yourself with the room where you will be speaking.
- Learn how to work the visual aids and equipment if you intend to use them.
- Make brief notes of key points on index cards.
- Rehearse out loud from the notes on the cards so that you are accustomed to using the notes while still maintaining eye contact. If you cannot practice with a friend, look at yourself in the mirror.
- On no account use a full written script.
- Precis your key objectives in your mind – keep them simple.
- When rehearsing, review, edit, simplify and shorten wherever possible.
- As you practice, visualise giving the speech.
- Then rehearse again!

Remember to watch your time! Often, you will be given an allotted time and it is important that you keep to this, especially if your presentation is assessed. In any case, if you keep the audience too long, they will not pay attention to the closing passages of your talk.

When preparing, you should allow approximately **one minute for every normal-sized paragraph**.

12.6 Presentation skills in tutorials and seminars

Every week during your course, you must come prepared to contribute to the discussion in tutorials and seminars. The success of small group learning and teaching is heavily dependent on the presentation skills of the participants. Tutorials are not a competition – they are a meeting of minds to share ideas.

According to our student survey, the vast majority of students resent their colleagues who tend to dominate tutorial groups – the ones who jump in first to answer every question and then won't let other members of the group get a word in edgeways. Our survey also showed that the students who were perceived as dominating the group resented the others for not being prepared to contribute!

A tutorial is, in effect, a group presentation of any work set and a general discussion of the topic. If each participant came properly prepared, was aware of other members of the group and paid attention to the way in which they presented their own views to the group, tutorials might be a more rewarding experience for everyone.

When you volunteer to answer (or are invited to do so), **present your ideas to the whole group and make eye contact with them in turn**. This means that the room must be arranged in a way which makes this possible. Ideas should be presented to the group as a whole, **with pauses to invite contributions from other students**. This avoids the problem of the tutorial which degenerates into a dialogue between the dominant student (who naturally sits as close as possible to the tutor) and the tutor.

When it is your turn to speak, try not to bury your head in your notes: look up, speak slowly and clearly, keeping your voice strong, and make **one key point** before inviting another student to take over.

Tutorials are not like classes at school – this is the students' time to review their recent work. It is an exercise in working with a group as much as a test of your knowledge and the skills developed in tutorials will be invaluable for later life when you have to participate in business meetings.

If the group is able to work together to share the information, the tutor will not have to revert to the schoolroom method of asking each individual in turn to answer part of the set work, something which can be tedious and can inhibit any deep discussion of the issues.

12.7 Presentation skills for interview

Law students need work experience. This means that they must develop interview skills at a much earlier stage than other students. Many firms use work experience as part of their graduate entry selection process which starts in earnest in the second year of the LLB course. In the first year, students who are serious about a career in law seek some preliminary work experience. In order to be successful, you must perform well at interview – another situation when good presentation skills are essential.

The interview is your chance to convince the interviewer that you would fit in well to their organisation and that they could trust you with their clients. Those firms which use work experience as a selection process will test this very thoroughly, not only in a formal interview, but when you are shown round, at any seemingly informal meetings and over lunch.

In the selection process for traineeships and pupillage, you may be asked to take isometric or numeracy tests or to give a presentation. For example, one firm recently asked candidates to put forward plans for staging the next Olympic Games. You also may be asked to take part in a group exercise, when your ability to relate well to a group of people will be assessed, and indeed your interaction with members of staff and with your fellow candidates will be under scrutiny at all times.

This means that, in order to be successful at a time when there is stiff competition for every work experience opportunity, training contract and pupillage and on the job market generally, you must pay close attention to the way in which you conduct yourself at interview.

Your appearance is very important. To do well, you must obey the dress code – that means in most cases, a sober suit and a light coloured shirt for either sex. Take trouble with your appearance – make sure your hair is neat and your shoes are polished, that your clothes are ironed. Take any papers with you in a briefcase or a good bag and make sure you can find them easily. Take a calculator, a pen, a pencil and a notepad.

When you arrive, relax and smile, however nervous you may be feeling. But don't walk around all day with an inane grin! Remember that the receptionist may be asked for input on your performance. When you are called for interview, greet the panel of interviewers when you enter the room and wait to be asked before you sit down. Sit up straight in your chair with feet planted on the ground. **Don't** sit as if you are strapped into the electric chair! Make a conscious effort to relax. Watch your body language.

An interview is as much about listening as it is about speaking. Listen carefully to the questions asked of you. Take your time to answer and ask for further clarification if necessary. Don't rush in with an answer. Think ahead to identify questions which you might be asked. There will inevitably be questions for which you are not prepared. Take your time and give the best answer you can. Be prepared to admit that you don't know, but only after you have considered the possible answers.

Dealing with questions

Treat all questions as sincere – even if you suspect that the questioner is trying to catch you out. Be seen to join forces with the questioner. Focus on the **issues** raised by the question. Treat your questioner with courtesy and include all the interviewers when you answer. If you haven't a clue what the answer is, own up!

Be prepared to ask questions of your own about the firm or chambers – remember that interviewing is a two-way process and that **you** are free to decide that this is not the place for you. Finally, remember to thank the interviewers for giving you their time.

13

Preparing for Examinations

13.1 Preparation

13.2 What do you need to know?

13.3 The examination

13.4 Exam stress

A sensible approach to the examinations can improve your marks significantly. Nobody likes to place their work under scrutiny, but techniques can be learnt to enable you to produce your best work. When you think of examinations, what do you see? Do you see an opportunity to show how hard you have worked over the past year, a chance to engage with the examiner on some interesting aspects of the course you have undertaken and to use the knowledge and skills you have acquired over the year? Or do you see the whole examination process as a threat, with examiners poised to catch you out as final disclosure of the fact that you are not fit to be on the course? Or something in between?

Do you plan revision schedules which are unrealistic about the amount of work that you can do in a day, that leave no time for recreation? Or, worse still, do you fail to make any plan at all?

The more carefully you plan your revision time, the more control you will take over your exam performance.

13.1 Preparation

From the very beginning of the course, you should be aware of the way in which it will be assessed. Remember that the majority of the material which you study will be included in the examination unless you are specifically told otherwise. You can therefore begin to judge which subject areas will give you the best chance of success – which interest you and seem logical and straightforward.

The run-up to the examinations falls into two parts. In the first part, you are aware of the impending exams but they will not be near enough for you to treat them as a matter of urgency. In any case, on modular and semesterised degree courses, you may have little time between the last lectures and the first examinations. In the early stages of revision, you should put your work in order in preparation for revision. Assemble all the notes, textbooks, articles and source materials for each course and put them in subject order. Select the materials which are most suitable for revision. If you were told to read the full text of a case or article, make sure that you have done so.

Once all your materials are in order, plan a revision timetable, setting aside blocks of time for each of your subjects, allocating the same amount of time to each subject. At this stage, you should read to refresh your memory, to gain a complete picture of the subject and to start to identify which topics you will choose to revise. You should also fill in any gaps in your reading which are worrying you.

Nearer the date of the examination, you will be ready for the final stages of revision. Plan another timetable, taking into account the fact that the original timetable has probably slipped a bit by now and you will have a more realistic idea of how long it takes to revise each subject area. How this timetable is made up is entirely up to you – choose blocks of time which will enable you to study effectively – one hour, two hours, half a day or a day at a time. This is a matter of personal preference.

Study each subject in turn. Otherwise, by the time of the examination you may have forgotten the first subject and left insufficient time for the last. It is rarely possible to stick to the revision timetable – review your progress and divide up the remaining time between the subjects at regular intervals. Try to be realistic about how long the work takes. If you allow time in your timetable for relaxation and for unexpected calls on your time, it will be easier to keep your morale high and your revision on course.

13.2 What do you need to know?

You should study enough topics in each subject to give yourself a real choice of questions. Generally speaking, you should study two or three more than the number of questions you have to answer. This depends on the nature of the paper. Look at past examination papers to help you to decide how many topics you should cover. Check with your lecturer or tutor that the format of this year's paper will be the same.

- If you attend lectures and tutorials regularly throughout the year, you will already have gathered quite a lot of information about what is expected of you in the examination as most lecturers give indications of the required standard and the possible content of the paper. If your tutors or lecturers give revision classes, you should go to these. Usually the class looks at old examination papers and guidance is given on how to answer them. If you have any doubts about what is expected of you, **ask!**
- You **don't** need to know every case on the handout.
- You **do** need to be able to explain and illustrate the key concepts in each subject area by reference to decided cases.

- You must show that you can *use* the material you have covered in the course.
- You must show that you have worked on the subject for yourself – to do well, it is not enough simply to give back on the examination paper what the lecturer gave you in the first place.
- This *doesn't* mean that you must invent argument or develop original theories – simply that you must show a sufficient understanding of the subject to enable you to respond appropriately to the question actually set and, in doing so, to apply the law and to draw your own conclusion on the subject.
- When your are asked to 'discuss' or to 'examine critically' or to 'evaluate', you must do just that – a description of the law is not enough.
- If, during the course, you have been given copies of any materials – cases, articles from journals – it will be assumed that you have read them.

13.3 The examination

Remember to find out well beforehand where your examinations are to be held and how long it takes you to get there. Make sure you have all your materials ready – pens, pencils to write rough notes. Make sure your pen makes your handwriting legible – avoid blue ball point pens, and, if possible, avoid ball point pens altogether. And make sure you have the correct documentation with you. Usually you are allocated a particular seat, according to your registration and examination number.

If you are permitted to take a statute book into the examination room, ensure that you have complied with the regulations with regard to marking it up. Usually, written notes in the statute book are not permitted, although underlining and highlighting of key passages usually are. Overseas students are often permitted to take dictionaries into the examination. If you choose an electronic dictionary, make sure it is one approved by the university – dictionaries with programmable memories are not usually permitted for obvious reasons.

Any books which can be taken into the examination room will be checked by the invigilator before the examination begins.

Be punctual or, better still, be a little early. If you are too early, the waiting may cause you to panic. Make sure you are physically comfortable – layers of clothing are best. In May and June, when examinations normally take place, the weather can be changeable. Tie your hair back if this tends to be a distraction. Once inside the examination room, leave your bag away from your desk. Make sure you have all you need. Make sure, too, that your desk and chair don't wobble. If they do, ask to change.

Listen carefully to the announcements at the beginning of the examination. Don't turn over the exam paper until you are told to do so. When you do turn it over, read the rubric (the instructions) carefully – note how many questions you have to answer and the extent of the choice. Look to see if there are any compulsory

questions and whether you are obliged to choose questions from different parts of the paper. If nothing is said to this effect, you have a free choice of questions.

When you look at the questions, **don't panic**. Read the paper right through slowly and carefully and take time to consider which questions will be best for you. Spend up to ten minutes on this.

When you have chosen your questions, divide up the remaining time between them. On your exam paper, note down the time at which you have to begin each new question and **stick to it**. Most of the marks for each question are gained in the first 15 minutes you spend answering it. **You must answer all the questions if you are to do yourself justice** so spending all your time answering three instead of four is totally counter-productive. When you begin an answer, spend the first five or ten minutes planning and structuring your answer. Make sure you have answered all parts of the question in a sensible order. Answer the question specifically set, using key words in the question. Don't be intimidated by students who start to write without planning. If you do spend too much time on a question, divide up the remaining time again between the remaining questions. If your mind goes blank, think of a way of explaining the law to your mum or to a friend – this may be less terrifying than thinking of the examiner and may clear the blockage. If you run out of time, complete the answer in note form.

Remember, though, that the examiner is on your side. Most papers are marked initially by those who have taught the course and they have already invested a great deal of time and effort in helping you to succeed on the course. Examination scripts are then moderated by an external examiner who ensures that standards are maintained.

13.4 Exam stress

Students tend to view the exams as one monolithic whole rather than breaking the experience down into manageable component parts. Some have a phobia about the whole experience, with a belief that exam success is a matter of luck and beyond their reach. The real problem is not the examination itself but the anticipation of the event. Research has shown that the highest anxiety is experienced in the time immediately before the examinations begin and during the first exam. By the time students have taken one or two more, they are more in control and less nervous.

In extreme cases, examination stress can lead to suicide or to thoughts of suicide. Very sadly, it is often the brightest, most conscientious and popular students who take this way out, almost always because they are under some other pressure at the same time – death of a loved one, breakup of a relationship. The examination period is one where everyone should be especially vigilant in watching for the signs of extreme stress; we should never be afraid to offer support or to seek help for others or for ourselves. Universities do not keep records of instances of stress, except to take them into account in the student's favour when grades are finally decided.

Some levels of stress are healthy. University life is intended to stretch students to their full potential and adrenaline is an essential ingredient for peak performance. In any event, a fairly high stress level is a **normal** reaction to assessment. Unhealthy stress lies in setting expectations of performance too high, sometimes a sense of letting everyone down if the expected grades do not materialise. The most intense pressure comes, not from parents or lecturers, but from the student. If you can put aside thoughts of grades and concentrate on the subject, this can relieve some of the pressure, although it can be very hard to do this when jobs depend on a higher class of degree. But you chose to study this subject and, if you have put in the work through the year, you will have enough material with which to answer the exam questions, and your revision should release that acquired knowledge into your short-term memory.

There is also a danger in comparing your progress with that of your peers – there are many successful methods of revision – theirs may be right for them but not for you. If preparation for the examinations can be broken down into a series of achievable tasks, your confidence will increase as each task is successfully completed. This is another use of the revision timetable. Each subject area can be revised and understood and crossed off the list as a job well done. If, after the allotted revision time you still do not understand it, consider abandoning this subject area in the course in favour of something you do understand. If you have difficulty in understanding the course as a whole, seek help from a lecturer or tutor. As each piece of revision is completed successfully, you are free to move on to something new and repeat the process. By the time you have to sit the exams, you should be able to point to a list of things which you *can* do rather than panicking about the ones which you can't.

Exam nerves are a waste of precious energy. They are a sign that you are standing in your own way to success. Think of the worst thing that can possibly happen – that you fail and have to take the exam again. In this unlikely event, your tutors would help you to overcome your difficulties and prepare you to take the exam again.

Taking exams is like any other test of ability – **you need to go into training to do well**. This means increasing your skill and knowledge, being properly prepared for all eventualities and keeping fit and healthy. **A tired mind will impede your performance**. Get to bed early, eat regularly, take fresh air and exercise and build into your revision programme time for sport, relaxation and trips to the pub. If you still feel overwhelmed by the whole process, seek help.

Section V
The Legal Professions

14

Legal Professionals

14.1 Solicitors

14.2 Barristers

14.3 The judiciary

14.1 Solicitors

Solicitors deal with the general public. They are the first port of call for anyone needing professional legal advice. They deal with contentious matters – criminal and matrimonial cases, negligence, breach of contract – matters which may end up in court proceedings. They also deal with non-contentious matters – those which are unlikely to end in court proceedings, such as property matters, wills and probate, preparation of contracts, and so on. Much of a solicitor's work is concerned with keeping disputes out of court and with negotiating settlements between the parties. Nearly all litigation (court proceedings) is settled.

There are approximately 66,000 practising solicitors in England and Wales who work in 8,600 firms, in the legal departments of companies, local authorities, government departments and in law centres and Citizens' Advice Bureaux. With the growth of the financial services industries in the 1980s and the 'big bang' in the City of London, divisions between the city firms and high street practices became clear-cut and the different areas of practice were seen to have different training needs. Professional training for solicitors therefore became more specialised.

The profession is now perceived to be divided into a number of distinct categories:

- Top City firms with international connections who specialise in high-calibre corporate work. These firms bring in £500 million in overseas earnings.
- National commercial firms with branches in the major commercial centres in England and Wales.
- Large commercial firms centred in London.
- Niche practices offering a specialism such as intellectual property, entertainment law or professional negligence law.
- High Street practices offering services to small businesses and private clients.

- Sole practitioners – solicitors who practice on their own. They can only do this when they have five years' post-qualification experience.

The nature of solicitors' work has changed in recent years. The Administration of Justice Act 1985 ended the solicitors' monopoly on conveyancing (sale and purchase of property). In return, solicitors with three years' post-qualification experience, at least two of which must be in advocacy, were given more extensive rights of audience in the Crown Court and in all higher courts in civil matters, but not in criminal matters. This work is carried out by solicitor-advocates who have to undergo further training and have to pass an examination in order to qualify.

Solicitors' work has become more specialised, especially in the City practices, so that solicitors may be trained in only a limited number of fields of law, whereas up until the 1980s all solicitors had a common general training in both private client and commercial law.

On completion of their training contract, solicitors start practice as assistants in a firm which is run by partners. After some experience, they hope to be offered a partnership. In order to achieve this, they must have proved their worth to the firm by attracting valuable clients, or because they specialise in a useful area of law. They must be in a position to put in some capital in order to be full equity (profit sharing) partners. Some firms allow partners to be salaried initially in order to ease the financial burden at the outset.

Under the Courts and Legal Services Act 1990 solicitors may now enter into multi-disciplinary partnerships with accountants and/or other professionals, although at present the rules of professional practice still preclude this.

Under the Courts and Legal Services Act 2000 solicitors can enter into conditional fee arrangements – no win, no fee. Under the 2000 Act these are subject to stringent formalities.

Legal Aid work has been completely reorganised. The Community Legal Service has replaced the legal aid scheme and the work is carried out by solicitors under contract. At present, a Salaried Defence Service is being set up on similar lines to the Crown Prosecution Service. It is believed that these changes will mean less work for high street firms and a resulting loss to the public of legal representation in other fields.

New rules have also been brought in to allow the Crown Prosecution Service to conduct prosecutions in court, which will lead to a contraction in barristers' work.

The Woolf reforms have led to a significant reduction in the number of cases which reach a court hearing. This, too, means less work for the legal professions.

14.2 Barristers

There are approximately 8,000 barristers called to the Bar in England and Wales. It is often said that, where the solicitor performs a function similar to that of a general practitioner of medicine, a barrister performs the function of a specialist.

As yet, there is no direct public access to a barrister's services. The client must first consult a solicitor, who in turn instructs counsel (the barrister). Usually, barristers are called in very late in the proceedings – perhaps only a day or two before trial in criminal cases, by which time the solicitor will have dealt with all the procedural matters and prepared the case for trial, interviewing witnesses and taking statements, preparing all the papers for the hearing. The solicitor also briefs counsel, writing an extensive report on the proceedings to date, the evidence available and suggesting possible lines of argument.

Barristers have an automatic right of audience in all courts, but some barristers rarely go to court. They are experts in very specialised fields of law who advise on very complex commercial, property tax or trusts matters. Their advice will be sought at the outset of the matter when a trust or a company is set up, for example. They will then be asked for an opinion on a point of law or to draft the documentation necessary to put into effect the arrangement which has been proposed by the client.

Barristers work very long hours: they are in court all day and they have to familiarise themselves with the case in which they are appearing the following day. In addition, at the end of their day in court, they often have to meet solicitors and their clients for conferences about forthcoming proceedings, so constraints on their time are often pressing and the life can be very stressful.

The barristers' profession has two levels – initially they practise as junior barristers but, when they are established in practice, they can apply to take silk – to practice as Queen's Counsel who wear silk robes. QCs lead the court proceedings and are employed for the high level of their advocacy skills. The appointment is made by the Lord Chancellor's Department, who consult other members of the profession as to the suitability of the candidate. It is a matter of delicate judgment for a barrister to decide what is the appropriate time at which to apply to take silk as the services of a QC are much more expensive than those of a junior and the same financial success in practice is not automatically guaranteed.

The higher rights of advocacy granted to solicitors and the withdrawal of legal aid for personal injury claims have resulted in a reduction in the work available to barristers, making it more difficult for students to find pupillage.

14.3 The judiciary

In some continental jurisdictions, the judiciary forms a third branch of the legal profession which has its own vocational training. Judges hear cases from an early stage in their professional lives without the need for long experience in practice before becoming a judge. In England and Wales, judges are selected by the Lord Chancellor's Department from the ranks of barristers and some senior solicitors. As with Queen's Counsel, the Lord Chancellor's Department consults widely among the candidate's associates in the profession before making an appointment. Often judges sit as assistant recorders or deputy judges as a trial of their suitability to be judges. Once selected, judges receive a special training to equip them for life on the judge's bench, together with in-service training to keep them up to date with the law and procedure.

Barristers who have been called to the bar for at least ten years can be selected to be circuit judges, who sit in the Crown Court and the county court. Barristers of 15 years' standing can be admitted as High Court judges and, from there, may be promoted to sit in the Court of Appeal and eventually to be Law Lords if they have a distinguished career in the Court of Appeal. Senior solicitors can also be appointed to sit as judges. Most district judges in the county court and High Court were solicitors earlier in their careers. The current system of judicial appointment by invitation from the Lord Chancellor's Department is currently under review to ensure more open competition.

In addition to presiding over court hearings, much of a judge's work is carried out in chambers – in a private room where proceedings are less formal. Sometimes this is done for reasons of privacy, for example in family matters. Interlocutory proceedings before the case comes to full trial are heard in chambers. The judge may even consider a matter at home in the case of a very urgent application for an injunction – for example to prevent the removal of a child abroad, out of the jurisdiction of the courts.

The judge must also give prior consideration to the papers relating to a case set down for trial. This takes considerable time and effort outside the times when the court sits.

The Woolf reforms have given the judge's role greater significance in the management of the cases which come to court.

15

The Professional Ethic

Professional values and conduct

'I don't want to be "shown the money". That isn't what I'm about. I just want to be one of those lawyers that actually still care about the word "justice". We all know the ones I mean, the lawyer who likes to have a cleaner pair of hands at the end of the day by knowing that he hasn't sold his soul to the devil. We all appreciate that income is a necessity, but it cannot and must not overlap with justice.' (First year law student, University of Essex, October 2000)

Reading law will give you a complex knowledge base and a range of skills to enable you to apply it. As you study law you will also be aware of a distinct set of values which are shared by its practitioners. These are values which will be expected of you when you enter professional life, either as a solicitor or barrister, or in one of the other professions listed at the end of Chapter 16.

Philip Jones and a team of researchers from Leeds University have identified the qualities which are expected of a graduate in law:

- A broad knowledge and understanding of the subject with an ability to communicate information to others.
- The ability to analyse the subject matter and to apply the knowledge.
- Synthesis – an ability to put different facets of the subject together in coherent ways.
- An ability to weigh up evidence in a professional and fair way and to make critical comments – to exercise professional judgement.
- Creativity.
- Good presentation.
- An ability to operate practically and appropriately as a practitioner of law.
- An ability to work with others.

As a professional, you must be able to take a lead in the workplace. You must be able to take responsibility and perform difficult tasks to a high level. You must be able to think beyond the immediate problem and be able to take responsibility for others.

Professional values generally impose a duty:

- to act impartially and disinterestedly;
- to show a regard for truth;

- to perform services over and above those which you are strictly obliged to perform;
- to act always in the interests of natural justice;
- to give a personal service to a high standard;
- to carry out work promptly and with care and skill;
- not to discriminate on grounds of race, ethnicity or national origin;
- to keep the client properly informed even when it may not be in the professional's own best interests to do so;
- to keep up to date on all matters relating to their professional practice – in the case of a lawyer, this would include keeping up with all the changes in the law.

Legal professional values require more than this, however. These are enshrined in the professional codes of conduct.

In Roman times, lawyers represented their clients for the honour alone – they did not take fees. Even today, barristers' gowns have a small bag sewn into the back of the neck on the outside. In the Middle Ages the convention of voluntary service was still recognised – grateful clients would slip payments into this bag rather than insult the lawyer by offering money for his services. Legal fees today are governed by strict rules of professional practice.

At a time when lawyers are being asked to enter the marketplace and adjust their fees and services accordingly, they are still bound by professional obligations to deliver more than simply what they are paid to do. For example, if a client's interests are in jeopardy, the lawyer must take steps to protect them without considering whether he/she is likely to be paid for the work.

The lawyer must at all times put the client's interest before his/her own. If the lawyer makes a mistake in the client's work, or if he/she discovers information which he/she could withhold from the client in order to serve her own interests, he/she must make full and immediate disclosure of all relevant facts to the client.

If the lawyer earns a commission from another source when placing work on behalf of the client, the commission must be paid to the client. No such obligation is placed on independent financial advisers who can keep the commission on any business they place.

The lawyer owes the client a duty of confidentiality. In some circumstances communications between client and lawyer are privileged: they do not have to be disclosed in evidence before the court. Solicitors must treat the matters as completely confidential. This includes a duty not even to disclose whether or not the solicitor acts for the client. However, confidentiality is guaranteed within the solicitor's firm – the client's concerns can normally be disclosed to personnel with the same firm.

Solicitors are in a fiduciary relationship with their clients. This means that they are in a position of trust which is particularly sensitive because they can exert undue influence by virtue of their expertise and their knowledge of the client's private affairs. If the solicitor abuses this position of trust, he/she must pay over to the client any profit that is made as a result of the breach of fiduciary duty or make good any resulting loss.

Solicitors must never allow themselves to be in a position where there is a conflict of interests over their clients' matters. This may arise if their own personal interests are in conflict with those of their clients or where the interests of two clients are in conflict. The solicitors' professional conduct rules forbid firms to act on two sides of the same matter and most firms have procedures to check that they have never acted for the party on the opposite side to their established client. However, if the matter concerns two existing clients, the firm may, with the consent of the client and where there is only a potential rather than an actual conflict, operate a 'Chinese Walls' procedure. The solicitors in the action operate as if they work for entirely separate firms and are at pains to ensure that the confidentiality of each client is scrupulously maintained. The object of these rules is to ensure that no information which is of value to the other side is disclosed other than with the client's express permission. Confidentiality extends after the client has left the firm or after the client's death. Where an actual conflict of interests arises, the firm is under a duty to send both clients elsewhere for legal advice in case the solicitor can use information on the departing client to the advantage of the one who stays. One application of this rule which has received particular attention from the Law Society is the rule that the solicitor cannot act for both vendor and purchaser on a conveyancing transaction.

Solicitors must keep client's money in an account which is entirely separate from their own money and which must be operated on the same basis as a trust fund.

The duty to the client subsists only so far as it does not conflict with the solicitor's duty to the court and to the legal profession. The full title of a solicitor is 'Solicitor of the Supreme Court'. This means that the solicitor's paramount duty is owed to the court. The solicitor must never knowingly mislead the court and is under a duty not to act for the client if the client has committed perjury. This also means that he/she must refuse to act if he/she knows the client intends to lie to the court.

Barristers must accept instructions on behalf of any client who seeks their professional services. This is known as the 'cab rank principle' – the barrister must act for the first in the queue. The reason for this rule is to ensure that everyone, however heinous their crime, will be represented in court.

Lawyers must act towards other lawyers in good faith and are under a duty not to communicate with the clients of another lawyer who is acting in the same matter. As between solicitor and barrister, the solicitor is under a duty to send full instructions to the barrister and is personally liable for the barrister's fees unless the client is legally aided. The solicitor is the barrister's client.

The sanctions for breach of the professional codes are heavy. If the code is broken, court proceedings in negligence can be brought against the offending practitioner or they may be subject to disciplinary proceedings taken by their professional body.

One criticism of the monitoring of lawyers' professional conduct is that, since it is undertaken by the Law Society and the Bar Council, the process is self-regulatory and not subject to supervision from outside the professions. In 1986, in response to this criticism, the Law Society set up the Solicitors Complaints Bureau which had a limited independence, and in 1996 this was replaced by the Office for the Supervision of Solicitors. Many cases come through this procedure because of neglect on the part of an overworked solicitor. Solicitors are under a duty to treat each client as if they were the only client and to give their work top priority, a real dilemma in a busy office. Complaints are heard by the Solicitors Disciplinary Tribunal with a bench of one lay member and two solicitors who have power to remove the names of offending solicitors from the Roll of solicitors, which bars them from practice. Appeal lies from the Solicitors Disciplinary Tribunal to the Divisional Court of the Queen's Bench Division or to the Master of the Rolls, one of whose functions is to keep the Roll of practising solicitors.

In order to avoid a breach of professional conduct the solicitor can seek the advice of the Law Society's Professional Ethics Division. Lawyers themselves feel a strong sense of shame when they have neglected to protect a client's interests and perhaps this is the strongest sanction of all.

To avoid getting yourself into such a situation, as an intending lawyer, you should be aware of the professional duties, and their full implications, at the earliest possible stage of your legal career so that you will know instinctively when these duties must be observed.

The rules themselves are a minimum requirement containing the lowest common denominator of professional conduct. They tell the professional what they cannot do, rather than laying down a code of positive values by which all lawyers should abide. When doctors are received into their profession, they swear the Hippocratic Oath. After an oath of loyalty to the profession and its members, it continues:

> 'I will follow that system or regimen which, according to my ability and judgement, I consider to be for the benefit of my patients, and abstain from whatever is deleterious and mischievous. I will give no deadly medicine to anyone if asked nor suggest any such counsel, and in like manner I will not give to a woman the means to produce an abortion. Whenever I go into a house, I will go for the benefit of the sick and will abstain from the seduction of females or males, whether freemen or slaves. Whatever, in connection with my professional practice, I see or hear which ought not to be spoken abroad, I will keep secret. So long as I continue to carry out this oath unviolated, may it be granted to me to enjoy life and the practice of the art, respected by all men in all times, but should I violate this oath, may the reverse be my lot.'

A growing number of lawyers would prefer a similar code for their professional bodies, one that tells them what they should do rather than only what is forbidden. What do you consider to be the essentials of a code of professional ethics for lawyers?

The professional codes of practice for lawyers are also in need of reform to take account of the changing moral values of society and the changing methods of practice. The present codes are addressed to individuals, whereas in large modern firms work is undertaken by teams of solicitors assisted by paralegal staff. This means that one individual member of the team rarely sees the work through from start to finish. Further, clients have much more sophisticated legal and commercial backgrounds and may choose the services of one expert to act on both sides of a matter. This would be in breach of the rules of professional conduct.

The professional values of lawyers were summarised in the McCrate Report as follows:

'... the value of providing competent representation – the responsibility to clients; the value of striving to promote fairness and morality – the public responsibility for the legal system; the value of maintaining and striving to improve the legal profession – the responsibility of one's profession; and finally the value of professional self-development – the responsibility to one's self.'

16

Careers in Law

16.1 Qualifying as a solicitor

16.2 Qualifying as a barrister

16.3 Making a successful application

16.4 Alternative careers with law

16.5 Alternative ways to practise law

The legal profession has two main branches – to enter the legal profession you become either a solicitor or a barrister. Judges are selected from either of these professions, but most judges enter the profession as barristers. The professions are supported by paralegal staff, many of whom now have their own professional career structure and public qualifications.

In recent years, there has been a dramatic increase in graduates from law schools. In 1985, 3,236 students sat the Law Society's final professional examination; by 1995, this figure had risen to 6,829. Although by 2000 the figure had fallen again to 6,490, the professions have been unable to absorb this increase, and law graduates have had to seek alternative careers in which a law degree is useful.

16.1 Qualifying as a solicitor

Most law degree programmes qualify the graduate for exemption from the first stage of professional training. If your degree is made up of law and another component, you should ensure that it has been approved by the Law Society for the purposes of this exemption. If your degree is not a qualifying law degree, you must first enrol for the CPE course – the course leading to the Common Professional Examination. This course is offered by approximately 30 institutions, including the six centres of the College of Law. In some institutions the CPE is known as the LLDip (Diploma in Law).

All students must then take the Legal Practice Course (LPC), which is the second stage of training. This course prepares students to take up a training contract and to enter the world of work in the professions, so that they are useful members of the firm as soon as they join it. Tuition on the LPC is given in workshops, with supporting lectures. The students work in groups to reflect the working patterns of practice. The course comprises three compulsory modules – Business Law,

Litigation and Advocacy and Conveyancing – and courses from a choice of electives which vary according to the institution which offers the LPC course.

In addition to these subject modules, the course includes training in Professional Conduct and Client Care, Financial Services, Revenue Law, Accounts, Probate and Administration and Community Law. Training is also given in Legal Writing, Legal Drafting, Practical Legal Research, Advocacy and Interviewing.

The LPC lasts for one year and costs between £5,000 and £8,000, to which living expenses must be added. It is virtually impossible to obtain local authority funding for this course. The larger firms, including some provincial firms, will sponsor their trainees for the LPC. If sponsorship is not available, it is possible to take a career development loan from a bank, but banks may only be prepared to lend to students who have already secured training contracts.

Some institutions offer the LPC course on a part-time or distance-learning basis which enables the student to earn while studying. These courses have additional advantages in that the student is exposed to the training for two years rather than one and has more time to absorb the skills and the knowledge. Annual fees on these courses are usually half the full-time fee. If you can find legal work while studying part-time on the LPC, this work experience can count for up to one year of your training contract.

Applications for the LPC

- Part-time and distance-learning courses – apply direct to the institution.
- Full-time courses – apply to the College of Law for all institutions which provide the course including universities. Applications will then be dealt with through a clearing system. All students must first register as student members of the Law Society who will then issue an application form.

The Common Professional Examination (CPE)

As has been mentioned above, if your law course is not part of a qualifying law degree, you undertake two years of vocational training rather than the one which comprises the LPC. The first stage of vocational training comprises a course teaching the core subjects which are taught on a qualifying law degree: Obligations 1 – Contract, Obligations 2 – Tort, Land Law, Equity and Trusts, Criminal Law, Constitutional and Administrative Law and the Law of the European Union. Some universities offer an alternative course covering the same subjects which leads to a postgraduate Diploma in Law. The fees are at similar levels to those for the LPC.

Professional training

Before being admitted as a fully qualified solicitor, you must complete a two-year training contract after the LPC (unless you can count periods of legal work undertaken before or during the LPC course). Obtaining a training contract is the most difficult part of the qualification process. The boom years of the 1980s, when the profession could not find enough graduates from law schools to fill the available places, were followed by a deep recession in the property market during which, for the first time, the legal profession faced significant numbers of redundancies. At the same time, the LPC became available from institutions other than the Law Society, releasing increased numbers of students seeking training contracts when firms were no longer willing or able to offer them. Subsequently there has been a revival in the property market, but at the time of writing a downturn is expected so the prospects for traineeships are once more uncertain, and at the moment there is still a significant difference between the number of training contracts available and the number of students seeking them. **If you want a training contract, you must be very determined in your efforts to obtain one.** This means making up to 50 applications, each tailored to address the requirements of the individual firm.

Law students begin to apply for training contracts from the spring or summer of their second year. If you are hoping for good examination results, you should make your applications immediately after the summer results are available. If you leave it to the autumn term, you may be too late for some deadlines. If you are taking a four-year degree course, you can wait until the spring or summer of your third year.

The pattern of recruitment has changed however. Firms may not know their requirements three years before the student will start work with them. They are prepared to recruit in the final year and from the LPC Courses. So all is not lost if you are unsuccessful in obtaining a contract as a second year student, although there are considerable advantages in having this settled before your final year of academic study. Many larger firms attract recruits through graduate careers fairs and graduate law fairs, so it is worth attending these in your later years at university and law school. If you have no offer of a contract before you are due to start your LPC, you must consider very carefully whether it is advisable to take on the financial commitment of the course with the possibility of no job at the end of it.

An alternative route to becoming a solicitor

It is possible to qualify as a legal executive and then to become a solicitor after five years' experience. Legal executives have a more limited training which qualifies them to specialise in a limited field of practice. In effect, practice as a legal executive can be as fulfilling as practice as a solicitor. A qualifying law degree approved by the Institute of Legal Executives can exempt you from the substantive law content of the Parts I and II of the ILEX qualifying examinations. Candidates must submit a portfolio to show that they have covered the practice elements of the course. Some universities now offer conversion courses to enable students to become Fellows of the Institute (FILEX). After five years' practice as a legal executive, it is possible to qualify as a solicitor without the need to complete a traineeship. This mode of entry into the profession can provide an alternative which does not involve the heavy expense of the LPC course, or the need to obtain a training contract when these are hard to come by.

16.2 Qualifying as a barrister

Students intending to be barristers undertake the Bar Vocational Course (BVC) after their qualifying law degree. The course is offered at the Inns of Court School of Law, the College of Law and BPP Law School in London, at Nottingham Law School, the University of Northumbria, Manchester Metropolitan University, the University of the West of England and Cardiff University. The BVC course comprises civil procedure, criminal procedure and evidence. Students can choose to specialise in general practice, chancery practice or commercial practice. Sixty per cent of the course is devoted to professional skills.

Students on the BVC must be admitted to membership of one of the Inns of Court. There are advantages in applying for membership while you are still an undergraduate as membership obliges you to dine in the Inn at regular intervals. This enables you to meet members of the profession who may have valuable advice and contacts, and who may offer you work experience.

The course costs between £7,000 and £10,000. There are additional fees for completion of the academic stage of training, membership of the Inn and call to the Bar, as well as the costs of dining. There are some bursaries and interest-free loans which are available for BVC students from the Inns of Court and from the Bar Council. Local authority grants are rarely given, but banks may be prepared to make career development loans.

Applications for the BVC

Applications are processed through a BVC Online (www.bvconline.co.uk). Students apply at the beginning of their final year.

Professional training

Barristers are called to the Bar on successful completion of the BVC. This is when they receive the barrister's qualification. If they wish to practice, however, they must complete a professional stage of training. This comprises two pupillages each lasting six months. Students apply for pupillage in the spring term of the BVC. The Bar Council has introduced an Online Pupillage Application Service (OLPAS). Applicants use the website (www.olpas.co.uk) to apply for pupillage online. In order to be successful, the applicants must have a good academic record and have undertaken mini-pupillages (work experience) while at university.

16.3 Making a successful application

A successful application for a traineeship with solicitors or in chambers requires more than an excellent academic record. If your final mark is likely to be lower than a 2:1, you may have difficulty in securing training, although you will be able to take a place on the LPC or BVC. This is a dangerous trap for the unwary. The larger firms who are registered to offer training contracts receive far too many applications to allow them to consider each in detail. They have systems to screen out the majority on the basis of A level and degree results. This is very unfair, particularly as most partners did not attain the required levels in their own education. This practice may well change, however, if the demand for trainees becomes higher with improvements in the economic situation.

To give yourself the best chance of success, you must build a profile which shows that you would be an asset to the firm because you have a well-rounded personality and will be able to work comfortably and effectively in a business environment. This means that, in addition to your studies, you must take on other responsibilities.

Building your CV

CV stands for curriculum vitae and is an account of your experience to date. You should start by giving personal details – name, address, telephone number, date of birth, nationality, marital status. Then give details of your secondary education and of your university course, giving full details of GCSE and A level subjects and results. As your degree results become available, these should be added. Give the information in chronological order, starting with the most recent. There is no need to give details of primary education. You do not need to write complete sentences – a narrative style can be off-putting. Give brief details and use bullet points for clarity.

List any work experience with the most recent experience first. Separate relevant work experience – for example, list solicitors' work experience and mini-pupillages first. List all positions of responsibility. Remember work in a bank, an insurance company, with an accountant or a stockbroker could all be relevant to legal practice.

List your voluntary activities: fundraising for a charity and office-holding for a student society can demonstrate a business-like approach; sport indicates that you are good at teamwork; voluntary work on a play scheme or community project shows commitment; travel shows independence of mind. Positions of responsibility, such as school prefect or student representative, should also be listed.

Make sure that all your time is accounted for. If you took a year out between school and university, say what you did with it.

When we talk about building a CV, what is really meant is a determination to seek out opportunities like those listed above. You should seek office in the student societies or the clubs you belong to. If you cannot get legal work experience in the vacations, fill your time with activities which show that you would be useful in a legal practice – go on a course to learn a skill or a language. Make sure you are fully computer literate.

If you are a mature student, your work experience may be more impressive than your academic record to date. Emphasise the work experience rather than the academic record by putting this first. If you are a very mature student, summarise parts of your career if they are not relevant – eg 1975–1980: employment in the aircraft industry – rather than listing all the jobs individually.

Have a master copy of your CV on your word processor and update it regularly. Before you send it out, edit it so that if responds to the likely needs of the organisation to which you are applying.

Firms may like you to identify the skills which you learned on the courses and in the activities listed in your CV. For example, working with the elderly would give you valuable skills for dealing with clients in a probate department. Working in a community centre might give you insights which would be valuable in a legal aid practice.

Give the names of two referees, if possible one who knows your academic record and one who can speak to your employment record or is a member of the profession which you wish to join. Two academic references will be acceptable if you don't know anyone who can give you a work-related reference.

If your department runs additional courses in negotiation, client interviewing, advocacy, mediation, for example, attend these and put them on your CV. These are skills which practitioners understand and value. Ask the person who runs the course to issue a certificate to the participants.

Ask a number of people to read the CV before you send it off and to give you constructive feedback. Show it to a careers adviser. And make sure that the grammar, spelling and presentation are immaculate. Use good quality paper and a clear typeface. Look out for the booklets on writing CVs which are available from the university careers service. If the careers advisory service runs workshops on writing CVs, attend these.

Remember that employers often check the details on application forms and CVs – do not lie or exaggerate.

Application forms

Larger firms have printed application forms. If the employer has an application form, this must be used. It cannot be returned with a CV attached and nothing filled in. The form will be specially designed to meet the needs of the employer's selection system. Keep copies of application forms which you fill in – this will help you with future applications, but each application should be tailored to answer the requirements of the organisation.

Read through the application form before you start to complete it. It is best to take a photocopy on which to draft your application. Make sure that you fill the information in the most appropriate place on the form. Read the firm's brochure before applying because this will give you an idea of the qualities they value and the ethos of the firm, to which you can then respond more effectively.

It is important to obey all the instructions on the form and to fill in all the sections. If they are not applicable to your circumstances, put 'N/A'. Remember to be positive about your achievements.

Make sure you keep a photocopy of the form and take this with you to the interview.

The letter of application

Send a covering letter with your application form or CV. Some employers prefer this to be handwritten (although thankfully handwriting analysis as part of the selection process is going out of fashion). If you have unimpressive handwriting, a well-typed letter may improve your chances. If the employer asks specifically for a handwritten letter, the letter **must** be written.

The letter should be no longer than one sheet of A4 paper and should be on good quality paper. It should give the employer a good reason to take your application form off the pile and invite you for interview – list the skills, abilities and experience which will make you attractive to them.

Make references in the letter to show that you know about the firm and that this is not just a mailshot to all firms who might offer a training contract, which in any case is usually a complete waste of time.

The interview

We have already looked at ways of presenting yourself well at interview in Chapter 11. Now we are going to look at the content of the presentation.

*   Make sure that you read a good newspaper and a law journal such as *The Lawyer* so that you are up to date with current affairs and legal news.
*   Read through the employer's literature again – make a note of any pertinent questions you will be able to ask at interview.
*   Read through your CV or application form and make sure that you can substantiate the claims that you make, that you are able to examples of using the skills you claim, for example.
*   Anticipate the questions which you are likely to be asked – the careers service will have lists of these. They may also keep feedback forms which have been completed by students who have been interviewed by the firm in the past.
*   Don't give 'yes' or 'no' answers – answer in detail. Interviewers usually ask open questions in order to evoke a longer response. Don't take this to extremes though.
*   Think about points which you wish to get across. If they do not come up in the

interview, make them when you are asked whether there is anything else you wish to say.

- After the interview, review your performance – note what went well and what could be improved.

16.4 Alternative careers with law

A law degree is an excellent training for many careers. Highly developed skills of critical analysis are invaluable in many fields. Many students take law degrees with no intention of practising. Here are some alternative careers:

- Commercial management
- Accountancy and tax consultancy
- The civil service – eg in the Home Office or Foreign and Commonwealth Office etc
- Local authorities – eg in housing, social services, or administration
- Management consultancy
- Publishing, journalism, librarianship
- Graduate entry to the armed forces
- Work in the Institutions of the European Community
- Politician, parliamentary official
- Insurance, loss adjusters, actuary
- Human resources and personnel
- Journalism

16.5 Alternative ways to practise law

- Justices' clerk
- Local authority lawyer
- Advice worker in legal centre or with the Citizens' Advice Bureau
- Licenced conveyancer
- Legal executive
- Law reporter
- Barristers' clerk
- Police and Crown Prosecution Service
- Government Legal Service
- Company lawyer
- Legal research/teaching
- Appointment in the Lord Chancellor's Department
- Work with a mediation service
- Court officers

- Work in the Institutions of the European Community
- Law Commission researchers
- Law reporting
- Paralegal work (for which CLT now offer a certificate)
- The Probation Service
- Community Welfare Advice Centres

Appendix A
Williams v *Roffey Brothers & Nicholls (Contractors) Ltd* [1990] 2 WLR 1153

The Weekly Law Reports 11 May 1990

1153

2 W.L.R.   Holden & Co. v. C.P.S. (C.A.)

A   agree therefore with the judge that the solicitors were in breach of their
duty to the court.

If the breach is serious, then it is no excuse that it came about
through carelessness or ignorance on the part of the solicitor of what
every competent solicitor should know. But in this case there seems no
doubt that Mr. McClosky acted as he did in the genuine belief that he
was not in breach of his duty to the court, because of what he conceived
B   to be his duty to his client. Moreover he appears to have been supported
in this view by counsel.

In the absence of clear authority we do not think his argument was
so untenable that it could not properly be advanced. Mr. McClosky
made a genuine mistake as to the law. In such a case, in our judgment,
it is not appropriate that what is still in part a penal order should be
C   made. We would allow the appeal.

> *Appeal by Holden & Co. dismissed*
> *with costs.*
> *All other appeals allowed; costs*
> *adjourned generally.*

D   Solicitors: *Holden & Co., Hastings; Steele Ford & Newton, Burnley;*
McGoldrick & Co.; Robin Murray & Co.; Bradburys.

[Reported by JAMES KELLY, ESQ., Barrister-at-Law]

E   ―――――――

[COURT OF APPEAL]

F   WILLIAMS v. ROFFEY BROS. & NICHOLLS (CONTRACTORS)
LTD.

1989   Nov. 2, 3; 23   Purchas, Glidewell and Russell L.JJ.

Contract—Consideration—Performance of existing duty—Subcontract
G   *for carpentry work—Agreed price too low for subcontractor to*
operate satisfactorily and at profit—Oral agreement by main
contractors to pay subcontractor additional sum for performance
of existing contractual obligations on time—Whether agreement
enforceable—Whether sufficient consideration

The plaintiff entered into a subcontract with the defendants,
who held the main building contract, to carry out carpentry
H   work in a block of 27 flats for an agreed price of £20,000. The
plaintiff got into financial difficulty because the agreed price was
too low for him to operate satisfactorily and at a profit. The
main contract contained a time penalty clause and the defendants,
worried lest the plaintiff did not complete the carpentry work
on time, made an oral agreement to pay the plaintiff an
additional sum of £10,300 at the rate of £575 for each flat on
which the carpentry work had been completed. Approximately
seven weeks later, when the plaintiff had substantially completed

The Weekly Law Reports 11 May 1990

1154

Williams v. Roffey Bros. Ltd. (C.A.)   [1990]

eight more flats, the defendants had made only one further   A
payment of £1,500 whereupon the plaintiff ceased work on the
flats. The plaintiff then sued the defendants for the additional
sum promised. The judge held that the agreement for payment
of the additional sum was enforceable and did not fail for lack
of consideration, and gave judgment for the plaintiff.

On appeal by the defendants:—

Held, dismissing the appeal, (1) that where a party to a
contract promised to make an additional payment in return for   B
the other party's promise to perform his existing contractual
obligations and as a result secured a benefit or avoided a
detriment, the advantage secured by the promise to make the
additional payment was capable of constituting consideration
therefor, provided that it was not secured by economic duress
or fraud; that the defendants' promise to pay the plaintiff the
additional sum of £10,300, in return for the plaintiff's promise   C
to perform his existing contractual obligations on time, resulted
in a commercial advantage to the defendants; that the benefit
accruing to the defendants provided sufficient consideration to
support the defendants' promise to pay the additional sum; and
that, accordingly, the agreement for payment of the additional
sum was enforceable (post, pp. 1165c–H, 1166c–D, 1168c–H,
1171H—1172D).

Stilk v. Myrick (1809) 2 Camp. 317 distinguished.   D

(2) That substantial completion on the eight flats entitled the
plaintiff to be paid part of the £10,300 promised; and that, in
the absence of payment, he had properly ceased further work
on the remaining flats (post, pp. 1160D, 1166D–F, 1172D–E).

Hoenig v. Isaacs [1952] 2 All E.R. 176, C.A. applied.

The following cases are referred to in the judgments: E

*Amalgamated Investment & Property Co. Ltd. v. Texas Commerce
International Bank Ltd.* [1982] Q.B. 84; [1981] 2 W.L.R. 554; [1981] 1
All E.R. 923; [1981] 3 W.L.R. 565; [1981] 3 All E.R. 577, Robert Goff
J. and C.A.
De la Bere v. Pearson Ltd. [1908] 1 K.B. 280, C.A.
Harris v. Watson (1791) 5 Peake 102
Hoenig v. Isaacs [1952] 2 All E.R. 176, C.A.
North Ocean Shipping Co. Ltd. v. Hyundai Construction Co. Ltd. [1979]   F
Q.B. 705; [1979] 3 W.L.R. 419; [1978] 3 All E.R. 1170
Pao On v. Lau Yiu Long [1980] A.C. 614; [1979] 3 W.L.R. 435; [1979] 3
All E.R. 65, P.C.
Stilk v. Myrick (1809) 2 Camp. 317
Syros Shipping Co. S.A. v. Elaghill Trading Co. [1980] 2 Lloyd's Rep. 390
Tweddle v. Atkinson (1861) 1 B. & S. 393
Ward v. Byham [1956] 1 W.L.R. 496; [1956] 2 All E.R. 318, C.A.   G
Watkins & Sons Inc. v. Carrig (1941) 21 A. 2d 591
Williams v. Williams [1957] 1 W.L.R. 148; [1957] 1 All E.R. 305, C.A.
*Woodhouse A.C. Israel Cocoa Ltd. S.A. v. Nigerian Produce Marketing Co.
Ltd.* [1972] A.C. 741; [1972] 2 W.L.R. 1090; [1972] 2 All E.R. 271,
H.L.(E.)

The following additional cases were cited in argument: H

Atlas Express Ltd. v. Kafco (Importers and Distributors) Ltd. [1989] 3
W.L.R. 389; [1989] 1 All E.R. 641
Bush v. Whitehaven Port & Town Trustees (1888) 2 Hudson's B.C., 4th ed.
122, C.A.
Davis Contractors Ltd. v. Fareham Urban District Council [1956] A.C. 696;
[1956] 3 W.L.R. 37; [1956] 2 All E.R. 145, H.L.(E.)
Finland Steamship Co. Ltd. v. Felixstowe Dock and Railway Co. [1980] 2
Lloyd's Rep. 287

The Weekly Law Reports 11 May 1990

1155

2 W.L.R.   **Williams v. Roffey Bros. Ltd. (C.A.)**

A   APPEAL from the assistant recorder, Mr. R. Jackson Q.C., sitting at Kingston-upon-Thames County Court.

By specially indorsed writ dated 10 March 1987 the plaintiff, Lester Williams, claimed against the defendants, Roffey Bros. & Nicholls (Contractors) Ltd., the sum of £32,708.70. By re-amended statement of claim dated 3 March 1988 the sum claimed was reduced to £10,847.07. Subsequently, the action was transferred for trial to the county court.

B   The assistant recorder gave judgment for the plaintiff.

By notice of appeal dated 22 February 1989 and amended on 3 November 1989 the defendants appealed on the grounds (1) that the assistant recorder erred in law in holding (i) that an agreement between the parties reached on 9 April 1986 whereby the defendants agreed to pay to the plaintiff a sum of £10,300 over and above the contract price originally agreed of £20,000 was enforceable by the plaintiff and did not

C   fail for lack of consideration; (ii) that the plaintiff's pre-existing contractual obligation to the defendants to carry out works was capable in law of constituting good consideration for an additional sum of £10,300 in respect of identical works; (iii) that notwithstanding the lack of consideration moving from the plaintiff promisee, the benefit to the defendant promisors which might result from payment of an increased

D   contract price was itself capable of constituting good consideration for the increase; and (iv) that a main contractor who agreed too low a price with a subcontractor was acting contrary to his own interests, and that if the parties subsequently agreed that additional moneys should be paid, such agreement was in the interests of both parties and for that reason did not fail for lack of consideration; (2) that, alternatively, in the event

E   that the plaintiff was contractually entitled to the sum of £10,300 the assistant recorder erred in not holding that such entitlement was limited to the sum of £575 per flat as and when the plaintiff's work in each flat had been completed in its entirety, and that since no flats had been so completed no money was owing by the defendants to the plaintiff; and (3) that the assistant recorder was wrong in holding (i) that the defendants repudiated the contract between the parties by their failure

F   to pay the plaintiff interim payments after 17 April 1986; and (ii) that the plaintiff was entitled to leave the site.

By a respondent's notice the plaintiff contended that the judgment of the assistant recorder should be affirmed on the additional grounds that (i) when a new price was agreed between the parties, in the absence of duress and in the case of a commercially reasonable renegotiation, the promise to pay that new price was enforceable and *Stilk v. Myrick*

G   (1809) 2 Camp. 317 did not correctly state the position in English law; (2) on the facts as found, the assistant recorder should have held that there was a termination of the earlier agreement by mutual consent and that the parties entered into a new agreement on 9 April 1986; and (3) alternatively, the assistant recorder should have held that there was an implied term in the first agreement to the effect that in the event of both

H   parties agreeing that the price was too low, a higher price would be agreed and substituted for it.

The facts are stated in the judgment of Glidewell L.J.

Franklin Evans for the defendants.
Christopher Makey for the plaintiff.

Cur. adv. vult.

The Weekly Law Reports 11 May 1990

1156

Williams v. Roffey Bros. Ltd. (C.A.)   [1990]

23 November. The following judgments were handed down.   A

GLIDEWELL L.J. This is an appeal against the decision of Mr.
Rupert Jackson Q.C., an assistant recorder, given on 31 January 1989 at
Kingson-upon-Thames County Court, entering judgment for the plaintiff
for £3,500 damages with £1,400 interest and costs and dismissing the
defendants' counterclaim.

B

The facts

The plaintiff is a carpenter. The defendants are building contractors
who in September 1985 had entered into a contract with Shepherds
Bush Housing Association Ltd. to refurbish a block of flats called
Twynholm Mansions, Lillie Road, London S.W. 6. The defendants were
the main contractors for the works. There are 28 flats in Twynholm   C
Mansions, but the work of refurbishment was to be carried out in 27 of
the flats.

The defendants engaged the plaintiff to carry out the carpentry work
in the refurbishment of the 27 flats, including work to the structure of
the roof. Originally the plaintiff was engaged on three separate sub-
contracts, but these were all superseded by a subcontract in writing
made on 21 January 1986 by which the plaintiff undertook to provide   D
the labour for the carpentry work to the roof of the block and for the
first and second fix carpentry work required in each of the 27 flats for a
total price of £20,000.

The judge found that, though there was no express term providing
for payment to be made in stages, the contract of 21 January 1986 was
subject to an implied term that the defendants would make interim   E
payments to the plaintiff, related to the amount of work done, at
reasonable intervals.

The plaintiff and his men began work on 10 October 1985. The
judge found that by 9 April 1986 the plaintiff had completed the work to
the roof, had carried out the first fix to all 27 flats, and had substantially
completed the second fix to nine flats. By this date the defendants had
made interim payments totalling £16,200.   F

It is common ground that by the end of March 1986 the plaintiff was
in financial difficulty. The judge found that there were two reasons for
this, namely: (i) that the agreed price of £20,000 was too low to enable
the plaintiff to operate satisfactorily and at a profit; Mr. Cotterell, a
surveyor employed by the defendants said in evidence that a reasonable
price for the works would have been £23,783; and (ii) that the plaintiff   G
failed to supervise his workmen adequately.

The defendants, as they made clear, were concerned lest the plaintiff
did not complete the carpentry work on time. The main contract contained
a penalty clause. The judge found that on 9 April 1986 the defendants
promised to pay the plaintiff the further sum of £10,300, in addition to the
£20,000, to be paid at the rate of £575 for each flat in which the carpentry
work was completed. The plaintiff and his men continued work on the flats   H
until the end of May 1986. By that date the defendants, after their promise
on 9 April 1986, had made only one further payment of £1,500. At the end
of May the plaintiff ceased work on the flats. I will describe later the work
which, according to the judge's findings, then remained to be done. Suffice
it to say that the defendants engaged other carpenters to complete the
work, but in the result incurred one week's time penalty in their contract
with the building owners.

The Weekly Law Reports 11 May 1990

1157

2 W.L.R.   **Williams v. Roffey Bros. Ltd. (C.A.)**   Glidewell L.J.

A   *The action*

The plaintiff commenced this action by specially indorsed writ on 10 March 1987. He originally claimed the sum· of £32,708.70. In a re-amended statement of claim served on 3 March 1988 his claim was reduced to £10,847.07. It was, I think, at about this time that the matter was transferred to the county court.

B   It is not necessary to refer to the statement of claim. On every important issue on which the plaintiff's case differed from that of the defendants, the judge found that the ·plaintiff was mistaken, and preferred the evidence of the defendants. In particular, the plaintiff denied the defendants' promise of 9 April 1986 to pay him an additional £10,300, instead alleging an earlier and different agreement which the judge found had not been made.

C   In the amended defence the defendants' promise to pay an additional £10,300 was pleaded as part of paragraph 5 in the following terms:

"In or about the month of May 1986 at a meeting at the offices of the defendants between Mr. Hooper and the plaintiff on the one hand and Mr. Cottrell and· Mr. Roffey on the other hand it was agreed that the defendants would pay the plaintiff an extra £10,300

D   over and above the contract sum of £20,000. Nine flats had been first and second fixed completely at the date of this meeting and there were 18 flats left that had been first fixed but on which the second fixing had not been completed. The sum of £10,300 was to be paid at a rate of £575 per flat to be paid on the completion of each flat."

E   The defence then alleged that neither the balance of the original contract sum nor the £10,300 addition was payable until the work was completed, that the plaintiff did not complete the work before he left the site, and thus that no further sum was due to him. By their amended counterclaim the defendants claimed that the plaintiff was in breach of contract in ceasing work at the end of May 1986, as a result of which

F   they had suffered damage to the extent of £18,121.46.

The judge's·conclusions

The judge found that the defendants' promise to pay an additional £10,300. at the rate of £575 per completed flat, was part of an oral agreement made between the plaintiff and the defendants on 9 April

G   1986, by way of variation to the original contract.

The judge also found that before the plaintiff ceased work at the end of May 1986 the carpentry in 17 flats had been substantially (but not ·totally) completed. This means that between the making of the agreement on 9 April 1986 and the date when the plaintiff ceased work, eight further flats were substantially completed.

The judge calculated that this entitled the plaintiff to receive £4,600 (8 × £575) "less some small deduction for defective and incomplete items." He held that the plaintiff was also entitled to a reasonable proportion of the £2,200 which was outstanding from the original contract sum. I believe this figure should be £2,300, but this makes no practical difference. Adding these two amounts, he decided that the plaintiff was entitled to further payments totalling £5,000 against which he had only received £1.500, and that the defendants were therefore in breach of contract, entitling the plaintiff to cease work.

The Weekly Law Reports 11 May 1990

1158

Glidewell L.J.   Williams v. Roffey Bros. Ltd. (C.A.)   [1990]

The issues
A

Before us Mr. Evans for the defendants advances two arguments. His principal submission is that the defendants' admitted promise to pay an additional £10,300, at the rate of £575 per completed flat, is unenforceable since there was no consideration for it. This issue was not raised in the defence, but we are told that the argument was advanced at the trial without objection, and that there was equally no objection to it being argued before us.
B

Mr. Evans' secondary argument is that the additional payment was only payable as each flat was completed. On the judge's findings, eight further flats had been "substantially" completed. Substantial completion was something less than completion. Thus none of the eight flats had been completed, and no further payment was yet due from the defendants. I will deal with this subsidiary argument first.
C

Does substantial completion entitle the plaintiff to payment?

The agreement which the judge found was made between the parties on 9 April 1986 provided for payment as follows: "The sum of £10,300 was to be paid at the rate of £575 per flat to be paid on the completion of each flat." Mr. Evans argues that the agreement provided for payment
D
on completion, not on substantial completion, of each flat. Since the judge did not find that the work in any additional flat was completed after 9 April 1986, the defendants were under no obligation to pay any part of the £10,300 before the plaintiff ceased work at the end of May.

In his judgment the judge does not explain why in his view substantial completion entitled the plaintiff to payment. In support of the judgment on this issue, however, Mr. Makey for the plaintiff, refers us to the
E
decision of this court in *Hoenig v. Isaacs* [1952] 2 All E.R. 176. In that case the plaintiff was engaged to decorate and furnish the defendant's flat for £750, to be paid "net cash, as the work proceeds, and balance on completion." The defendant paid £400. moved into the flat and used the new furniture, but refused to pay the balance on the ground that some of the work was defective. The official referee found that there were
F
some defects, but that the contract had been substantially performed. The Court of Appeal held that accordingly the plaintiff was entitled to be paid the balance due, less only a deduction for the cost of making good the defects or omissions. Somervell L.J. said, at p. 179:

> "The learned official referee regarded *H. Dakin & Co. Ltd. v. Lee* [1916] 1 K.B. 566 as laying down that the price must be paid
> G
> subject to set-off or counterclaim if there was a substantial compliance with the contract. I think on the facts of this case where the work was finished ' in the ordinary sense. though in part defective. this is right. It expresses in a convenient epithet what is put from another angle in the Sale of Goods Act 1893. The buyer cannot reject if he proves only the breach of a term collateral to the main purpose. I have, therefore, come to the conclusion that the
> H
> first point of counsel for the defendant fails."

Denning L.J. said, at pp. 180–181:

> "In determining this issue the first question is whether. on the true construction of the contract. entire performance was a condition precedent to payment. It was a lump sum contract, but that does not mean that entire performance was a condition precedent to

The Weekly Law Reports 11 May 1990

1159

2 W.L.R.   **Williams v. Roffey Bros. Ltd. (C.A.)**   Glidewell L.J.

A   payment. When a contract provides for a specific sum to be paid on completion of specified work, the courts lean against a construction of the contract which would deprive the contractor of any payment at all simply because there are some defects or omissions. The promise to complete the work is, therefore, construed as a term of the contract, but not as a condition. It is not every breach of that term which absolves the employer from his promise to pay the

B   price, but only a breach which goes to the root of the contract, such as an abandonment of the work when it is only half done. Unless the breach does go to the root of the matter, the employer cannot resist payment of the price. He must pay it and bring a cross-claim for the defects and omissions, or, alternatively, set them up in diminution of the price. The measure is the amount which the work

C   is worth less by reason of the defects and omissions, and is usually calculated by the cost of making them good: see *Mondel v. Steel* (1841) 8 M. & W. 858; *H. Dakin & Co. Ltd. v. Lee* [1916] 1 K.B. 566; and the notes to *Cutter v. Powell* (1795) 6 Term Rep. 320 in *Smith's Leading Cases*, 13th ed. (1929), vol. 2, pp. 19–21. It is, of course, always open to the parties by express words to make entire performance a condition precedent. A familiar instance is when the

D   contract provides for progress payments to be made as the work proceeds, but for retention money to be held until completion. Then entire performance is usually a condition precedent to payment of the retention money, but not, of course, to the progress payments. The contractor is entitled to payment pro rata as the work proceeds, less a deduction for retention money. But he is not

E   entitled to the retention money until the work is entirely finished, without defects or omissions. In the present case the contract provided for 'net cash, as the work proceeds; the balance on completion.' If the balance could be regarded as retention money, then it might well be that the contractor ought to have done all the work correctly, without defects or omissions, in order to be entitled to the balance. But I do not think the balance should be regarded

F   as retention money. Retention money is usually only 10 per cent., or 15 per cent., whereas this balance was more than 50 per cent. I think this contract should be regarded as an ordinary lump sum contract. It was substantially performed. The contractor is entitled, therefore, to the contract price, less a deduction for the defects."

Romer L.J. said, at pp. 182–183:

G   "The defendant's only attack on the plaintiff's performance of his obligations was in relation to certain articles of furniture which the plaintiff supplied and which the defendant says were faulty and defective in various important respects. The finding of the learned official referee on this was 'that the furniture supplied constituted a substantial compliance with the contract so far as the supply of

H   furniture was concerned.' That is a finding of fact, and whether or not another mind might have taken a different view it appears to me impossible to say that there was no sufficient evidence on which the finding could be based. This, then, being a lump sum contract for the supply of furniture (and the carrying out of certain minor work) which was substantially complied with by the plaintiff, the question is whether the official referee was wrong in law in applying the principle of *H. Dakin & Co. Ltd. v. Lee* [1916] 1 K.B. 566 and

The Weekly Law Reports 11 May 1990

1160

Glidewell L.J.   **Williams v. Roffey Bros. Ltd. (C.A.)**   [1990]

rejecting the defendant's submissions that the plaintiff had failed to   A
perform a condition on the fulfilment of which his right to sue
depended. In my judgment, he was quite right in applying the *H.
Dakin & Co. Ltd. v. Lee* principle to the facts of the present case. I
can see no reason why that principle should be approached with
wariness and applied with caution. In certain cases it is right that
the rigid rule for which the defendant contends should be applied,
for example, if a man tells a contractor to build a ten foot wall for   B
him in his garden and agrees to pay £x for it, it would not be right
that he should be held liable for any part of the contract price if the
contractor builds the wall to two feet and then renounces further
performance of the contract, or builds the wall of a totally different
material from that which was ordered, or builds it at the wrong end
of the garden. The work contracted for has not been done and the   C
corresponding obligation to pay consequently never arises. But
when a man fully performs his contract in the sense that he supplies
all that he agreed to supply but what he supplies is subject to
defects of so minor a character that he can be said to have
substantially performed his promise, it is, in my judgment, far more
equitable to apply the *H. Dakin & Co. Ltd. v. Lee* principle than to
deprive him wholly of his contractual rights and relegate him to   D
such remedy (if any) as he may have on a quantum meruit, nor, in
my judgment, are we compelled to a contrary view (having regard
to the nature and terms of the agreement and the official referee's
finding) by any of the cases in the books."

In my view this authority entirely supports the judge's decision on
this issue.   E

*Was there consideration for the defendants' promise made on 9 April
1986 to pay an additional price at the rate of £575 per completed flat?*

The judge made the following findings of fact which are relevant on
this issue. (i) The subcontract price agreed was too low to enable the
plaintiff to operate satisfactorily and at a profit. Mr. Cottrell, the
defendants' surveyor, agreed that this was so. (ii) Mr. Roffey (managing   F
director of the defendants) was persuaded by Mr. Cottrell that the
defendants should pay a bonus to the plaintiff. The figure agreed at the
meeting on 9 April 1986 was £10,300.

The judge quoted and accepted the evidence of Mr. Cottrell to the
effect that a main contractor who agrees too low a price with a
subcontractor is acting contrary to his own interests. He will never get   G
the job finished without paying more money. The judge therefore
concluded:

> "In my view where the original subcontract price is too low, and the
> parties subsequently agree that additional moneys shall be paid to
> the subcontractor, this agreement is in the interests of both parties.
> This is what happened in the present case, and in my opinion the   H
> agreement of 9 April 1986 does not fail for lack of consideration."

In his address to us, Mr. Evans outlined the benefits to his clients, the
defendants, which arose from their agreement to pay the additional
£10,300 as: (i) seeking to ensure that the plaintiff continued work and
did not stop in breach of the subcontract; (ii) avoiding the penalty for
delay; and (iii) avoiding the trouble and expense of engaging other
people to complete the carpentry work.

The Weekly Law Reports 11 May 1990

1161

2 W.L.R.   **Williams v. Roffey Bros. Ltd. (C.A.)**   Glidewell L.J.

A   However, Mr. Evans submits that, though his clients may have derived, or hoped to derive, practical benefits from their agreement to pay the "bonus," they derived no benefit in law, since the plaintiff was promising to do no more than he was already bound to do by his subcontract, i.e., continue with the carpentry work and complete it on time. Thus there was no consideration for the agreement. Mr. Evans relies on the principle of law which, traditionally, is based on the

B   decision in *Stilk v. Myrick* (1809) 2 Camp. 317. That was a decision at first instance of Lord Ellenborough C.J. On a voyage to the Baltic, two seamen deserted. The captain agreed with the rest of the crew that if they worked the ship back to London without the two seamen being replaced, he would divide between them the pay which would have been due to the two deserters. On arrival at London this extra pay was

C   refused, and the plaintiff's action to recover his extra pay was dismissed. Counsel for the defendant argued that such an agreement was contrary to public policy, but Lord Ellenborough C.J.'s judgment was based on lack of consideration. It reads, at pp. 318–319:

"I think *Harris v. Watson* (1791) Peake 102 was rightly decided; but I doubt whether the ground of public policy, upon which Lord Kenyon is stated to have proceeded, be the true principle on which

D   the decision is to be supported. Here, I say the agreement is void for want of consideration. There was no consideration for the ulterior pay promised to the mariners who remained with the ship. Before they sailed from London they had undertaken to do all they could under all the emergencies of the voyage. They had sold all their services till the voyage should be completed. If they had been

E   at liberty to quit the vessel at Cronstadt, the case would have been quite different; or if the captain had capriciously discharged the two men who were wanting, the others might not have been compellable to take the whole duty upon themselves, and their agreeing to do so might have been a sufficient consideration for the promise of an advance of wages. But the desertion of a part of the crew is to be considered an emergency of the voyage as much as their death; and

F   those who remain are bound by the terms of their original contract to exert themselves to the utmost to bring the ship in safety to her destined port. Therefore, without looking to the policy of this agreement, I think it is void for want of consideration, and that the plaintiff can only recover at the rate of £5 a month."

G   In *North Ocean Shipping Co. Ltd. v. Hyundai Construction Co. Ltd.* [1979] Q.B. 705, Mocatta J. regarded the general principle of the decision in *Stilk v. Myrick*, 2 Camp. 317 as still being good law. He referred to two earlier decision of this court, dealing with wholly diferent subjects, in which Denning L.J. sought to escape from the confines of the rule, but was not accompanied in his attempt by the other members of the court. In *Ward v. Byham* [1956] 1 W.L.R. 496 the plaintiff and

H   the defendant lived together unmarried for five years, during which time the plaintiff bore their child. After the parties ended their relationship, the defendant promised to pay the plaintiff £1 per week to maintain the child, provided that she was well looked after and happy. The defendant paid this sum for some months, but ceased to pay when the plaintiff married another man. On her suing for the amount due at £1 per week, he pleaded that there was no consideration for his agreement to pay for the plaintiff to maintain her child, since she was obliged by law to do so:

The Weekly Law Reports 11 May 1990

1162

Glidewell L.J.   **Williams v. Roffey Bros. Ltd. (C.A.)**   [1990]

see section 42 of the National Assistance Act 1948. The county court   A
judge upheld the plaintiff mother's claim, and this court dismissed the
defendant's appeal. Denning L.J. said, at p. 498:

> "I approach the case, therefore, on the footing that the mother, in
> looking after the child, is only doing what she is legally bound to do.
> Even so, I think that there was sufficient consideration to support the
> promise. I have always thought that a promise to perform an existing   B
> duty, or the performance of it, should be regarded as good
> consideration, because it is a benefit to the person to whom it is given.
> Take this very case. It is as much a benefit for the father to have the
> child looked after by the mother as by a neighbour. If he gets the
> benefit for which he stipulated, he ought to honour his promise; and
> he ought not to avoid it by saying that the mother was herself under a
> duty to maintain the child. I regard the father's promise in this case as   C
> what is sometimes called a unilateral contract, a promise in return for
> an act, a promise by the father to pay £1 a week in return for the
> mother's looking after the child. Once the mother embarked on the
> task of looking after the child, there was a binding contract. So long
> as she looked after the child, she would be entitled to £1 a week. The
> case seems to me to be within the decision of *Hicks v. Gregory* (1849)
> 8 C.B. 378 on which the judge relied. I would dismiss the appeal."   D

However, Morris L.J. put it rather differently. He said, at pp. 498–
499:

> "Mr. Lane submits that there was a duty on the mother to support
> the child; that no affiliation proceedings were in prospect or were
> contemplated; and that the effect of the arrangement that followed   E
> the letter was that the father was merely agreeing to pay a bounty
> to the mother. It seems to me that the terms of the letter negative
> those submissions, for the husband says 'providing you can prove
> that she'—that is Carol —'will be well looked after and happy and
> also that she is allowed to decide for herself whether or not she
> wishes to come and live with you.' The father goes on to say that
> Carol is then well and happy and looking much stronger than ever   F
> before. 'If you decide what to do let me know as soon as possible.'
> It seems to me, therefore, that the father was saying, in effect:
> Irrespective of what may be the strict legal position, what I am
> asking is that you shall prove that Carol will be well looked after
> and happy, and also that you must agree that Carol is to be allowed
> to decide for herself whether or not she wishes to come and live   G
> with you. If those conditions were fulfilled the father was agreeable
> to pay. Upon those terms, which in fact became operative, the
> father agreed to pay £1 a week. In my judgment, there was ample
> consideration there to be found for his promise, which I think was
> binding."

Parker L.J. agreed. As I read the judgment of Morris L.J., he and   H
Parker L.J. held that, though in maintaining the child the plaintiff was
doing no more than she was obliged to do by law, nevertheless her
promise that the child would be well looked after and happy was a
practical benefit to the father which amounted to consideration for his
promise.

In *Williams v. Williams* [1957] 1 W.L.R. 148, a wife left her husband,
and he promised to make her a weekly payment for her maintenance.

The Weekly Law Reports 11 May 1990

1163

2 W.L.R.   **Williams v. Roffey Bros. Ltd. (C.A.)**   **Glidewell L.J.**

A   On his failing to honour his promise, the wife claimed the arrears of payment, but her husband pleaded that, since the wife was guilty of desertion she was bound to maintain herself, and thus there was no consideration for his promise. Denning L.J., at p. 151, reiterated his view that:

B   "a promise to perform an existing duty is, I think, sufficient consideration to support a promise, so long as there is nothing in the transaction which is contrary to the public interest."

However, the other members of the court (Hodson and Morris L.JJ.) declined to agree with this expression of view, though agreeing with Denning L.J. in finding that there was consideration because the wife's desertion might not have been permanent, and thus there was a benefit to the husband.

C   It was suggested to us in argument that, since the development of the doctrine of promissory estoppel, it may well be possible for a person to whom a promise has been made, on which he has relied, to make an additional payment for services which he is in any event bound to render under an existing contract or by operation of law, to show that the promisor is estopped from claiming that there was no consideration for

D   his promise. However, the application of the doctrine of promissory estoppel to facts such as those of the present case has not yet been fully developed: see e.g. the judgment of Lloyd J. in *Syros Shipping Co. S.A v. Elaghill Trading Co.* [1980] 2 Lloyd's Rep. 390, 392. Moreover, this point was not argued in the court below, nor was it more than adumbrated before us. Interesting though it is, no reliance can in my view be placed on this concept in the present case.

E   There is, however, another legal concept of relatively recent development which is relevant, namely, that of economic duress. Clearly if a subcontractor has agreed to undertake work at a fixed price, and before he has completed the work declines to continue with it unless the contractor agrees to pay an increased price, the subcontractor may be held guilty of securing the contractor's promise by taking unfair

F   advantage of the difficulties he will cause if he does not complete the work. In such a case an agreement to pay an increased price may well be voidable because it was entered into under duress. Thus this concept may provide another answer in law to the question of policy which has troubled the courts since before *Stilk v. Myrick.* 2 Camp. 317, and no doubt led at the date of that decision to a rigid adherence to the doctrine of consideration.

G   This possible application of the concept of economic duress was referred to by Lord Scarman, delivering the judgment of the Judicial Committee of the Privy Council in *Pao On v. Lau Yiu Long* [1980] A.C. 614. He said, at p. 632:

"Their Lordships do not doubt that a promise to perform, or the performance of, a pre-existing contractual obligation to a third party

H   can be valid consideration. In *New Zealand Shipping Co. Ltd. v. A.M. Satterthwaite & Co. Ltd. (The Eurymedon)* [1975] A.C. 154, 168 the rule and the reason for the rule were stated: 'An agreement to do an act which the promisor is under an existing obligation to a third party to do, may quite well amount to valid consideration . . . the promisee obtains the benefit of a direct obligation. . . . This proposition is illustrated and supported by *Scotson v. Pegg* (1861) 6 H. & N. 295 which their Lordships consider to be good law.'

The Weekly Law Reports 11 May 1990

1164

Unless, therefore, the guarantee was void as having been made for   **A**
an illegal consideration or voidable on the ground of economic
duress, the extrinsic evidence establishes that it was supported by
valid consideration. Mr. Leggatt for the defendants submits that the
consideration is illegal as being against public policy. He submits
that to secure a party's promise by a threat of repudiation of a pre-
existing contractual obligation owed to another can be, and in the
circumstances of this case was, an abuse of a dominant bargaining   **B**
position and so contrary to public policy. . . . This submission found
favour with the majority in the Court of Appeal. Their Lordships,
however, considered it misconceived."

Lord Scarman then referred to *Stilk v. Myrick*, 2 Camp. 317, and its
predecessor *Harris v. Watson* (1791) Peake 102, and to *Williams v.*
Williams [1957] 1 W.L.R. 148, before turning to the development of this   **C**
branch of the law in the United States of America. He then said, at
pp. 634–635:

"Their Lordships' knowledge of this developing branch of American
law is necessarily limited. In their judgment it would be carrying
audacity to the point of foolhardiness for them to attempt to extract
from the American case law a principle to provide an answer to the   **D**
question now under consideration. That question, their Lordships
repeat, is whether, in a case where duress is not established, public
policy may nevertheless invalidate the consideration if there has
been a threat to repudiate a pre-existing contractual obligation or
an unfair use of a dominating bargaining position. Their Lordships'
conclusion is that where businessmen are negotiating at arm's length   **E**
it is unnecessary for the achievement of justice, and unhelpful in the
development of the law, to invoke such a rule of public policy. It
would also create unacceptable anomaly. It is unnecessary because
justice requires that men, who have negotiated at arm's length, be
held to their bargains unless it can be shown that their consent was
vitiated by fraud, mistake or duress. If a promise is induced by
coercion of a man's will, the doctrine of duress suffices to do   **F**
justice. The party coerced, if he chooses and acts in time, can avoid
the contract. If there is no coercion, there can be no reason for
avoiding the contract where there is shown to be a real consideration
which is otherwise legal. Such a rule of public policy as is now being
considered would be unhelpful because it would render the law
uncertain. It would become a question of fact and degree to   **G**
determine in each case whether there had been, short of duress, an
unfair use of a strong bargaining position. It would create anomaly
because, if public policy invalidates the consideration, the effect is
to make the contract void. But unless the facts are such as to
support a plea of 'non est factum,' which is not suggested in this
case, duress does no more than confer upon the victim the
opportunity, if taken in time, to avoid the contract. It would be   **H**
strange if conduct less than duress could render a contract void,
whereas duress does no more than render a contract voidable.
Indeed, it is the defendants' case in this appeal that such an
anomaly is the correct result. Their case is that the plaintiffs, having
lost by cancellation the safeguard of the subsidiary agreement, are
without the safeguard of the guarantee because its consideration is
contrary to public policy, and that they are debarred from restoration

The Weekly Law Reports 11 May 1990

1165

2 W.L.R.   **Williams v. Roffey Bros. Ltd. (C.A.)**   Glidewell L.J.

A   to their position under the subsidiary agreement because the guarantee is void, not voidable. The logical consequence of Mr. Leggatt's submission is that the safeguard which all were at all times agreed the plaintiffs should have—the safeguard against fall in value of the shares—has been lost by the application of a rule of public policy. The law is not, in their Lordships' judgment, reduced to countenancing such stark injustice: nor is it necessary, when one

B   bears in mind the protection offered otherwise by the law to one who contracts in ignorance of what he is doing or under duress. Accordingly, the submission that the additional consideration established by the extrinsic evidence is invalid on the ground of public policy is rejected."

C   It is true that *Pao On* is a case of a tripartite relationship that is, a promise by A to perform a pre-existing contractual obligation owed to B, in return for a promise of payment by C. But Lord Scarman's words at pp. 634–635 seem to me to be of general application, equally applicable to a promise made by one of the original two parties to a contract.

Accordingly, following the view of the majority in *Ward v. Byham*

D   [1956] 1 W.L.R. 496 and of the whole court in *Williams v. Williams* [1957] 1 W.L.R. 148 and that of the Privy Council in *Pao On* [1980] A.C. 614 the present state of the law on this subject can be expressed in the following proposition: (i) if A has entered into a contract with B to do work for, or to supply goods or services to, B in return for payment by B; and (ii) at some stage before A has completely performed his obligations under the contract B has reason to doubt whether A will, or

E   will be able to, complete his side of the bargain; and (iii) B thereupon promises A an additional payment in return for A's promise to perform his contractual obligations on time; and (iv) as a result of giving his promise, B obtains in practice a benefit, or obviates a disbenefit; and (v) B's promise is not given as a result of economic duress or fraud on the part of A; then (vi) the benefit to B is capable of being consideration for

F   B's promise, so that the promise will be legally binding.

As I have said, Mr. Evans accepts that in the present case by promising to pay the extra £10,300 his client secured benefits. There is no finding, and no suggestion, that in this case the promise was given as a result of fraud or duress. If it be objected that the propositions above contravene the principle in *Stilk v. Myrick*, 2 Camp. 317, I answer that in my view they do not; they refine, and limit the application of that

G   principle, but they leave the principle unscathed e.g. where B secures no benefit by his promise. It is not in my view surprising that a principle enunciated in relation to the rigours of seafaring life during the Napoleonic wars should be subjected during the succeeding 180 years to a process of refinement and limitation in its application in the present day. It is therefore my opinion that on his findings of fact in the present case, the judge was entitled to hold, as he did, that the defendants'

H   promise to pay the extra £10,300 was supported by valuable consideration, and thus constituted an enforceable agreement.

As a subsidiary argument, Mr. Evans submits that on the facts of the present case the consideration, even if otherwise good, did not "move from the promisee." This submission is based on the principle illustrated in the decision in *Tweddle v. Atkinson* (1861) 1 B. & S. 393. My understanding of the meaning of the requirement that "consideration

The Weekly Law Reports 11 May 1990

1166

Glidewell L.J.   Williams v. Roffey etc. Ltd. (C.A.)   [1990]

must move from the promisee" is that such consideration must be   A
provided by the promisee, or arise out of his contractual relationship
with the promisor. It is consideration provided by somebody else, not a
party to the contract, which does not "move from the promisee." This
was the situation in *Tweddle v. Atkinson,* but it is, of course, not the
situation in the present case. Here the benefits to the defendants arose
out of their agreement of 9 April 1986 with the plaintiff, the promisee.
In this respect I would adopt the following passage from *Chitty on*   B
Contracts, 26th ed. (1989), p. 126 para. 183, and refer to the authorities
there cited:

> "The requirement that consideration must move from the promisee
> is most generally satisfied where some detriment is suffered by him
> e.g. where he parts with money or goods, or renders services, in
> exchange for the promise. But the requirement may equally well be   C
> satisfied where the promisee confers a benefit on the promisor
> without in fact suffering any detriment."

That is the situation in this case. I repeat, therefore, my opinion that the
judge was, as a matter of law, entitled to hold that there was valid
consideration to support the agreement under which the defendants
promised to pay an additional £10,300 at the rate of £575 per flat. For   D
these reasons I would dismiss this appeal.

RUSSELL L.J.   I agree with and have nothing to add to the judgment
of Glidewell L.J. in so far as it relates to the defendants' submission that
the plaintiff was not entitled to any part of the £10,300 because none of
the eight flats had been completed. The judge found that there had been   E
substantial completion and made a small deduction for defective and
incomplete items. He did not identify those items nor define the extent
of his deductions but no complaint is made about that. For the reasons
appearing in the judgment of Glidewell L.J., supported as they are by
Hoenig v. Isaacs [1952] 2 All E.R. 176. I have no doubt that the judge
was right upon what Mr. Evans, on behalf of the defendants, referred to
as his secondary point.   F
I find his primary argument relating to consideration much more
difficult. It is worth rehearsing some of the facts. The judge found that
the parties made an agreement on 9 April 1986. Subject to the date,
which was inaccurately pleaded, it was the defendants who pleaded the
agreement in paragraph 5 of their amended defence. The relevant
passage reads: G

> "In or about the month of May 1986 at a meeting at the offices of
> the defendants between Mr. Hooper and the plaintiff on the one
> hand and Mr. Cottrell and Mr. Roffey on the other hand it was
> agreed that the defendants would pay the plaintiff an extra £10,300
> over and above the contract sum of £20,000. Nine flats had been
> first and second fixed completely at the date of this meeting and
> there were 18 flats left that had been first fixed but on which the   H
> second fixing had not been completed. The sum of £10,300 was to
> be paid at a rate of £575 per flat to be paid on the completion of
> each flat."

There is no hint in that pleading that the defendants were subjected
to any duress to make the agreement or that their promise to pay the
extra £10,300 lacked consideration. As the judge found, the plaintiff

The Weekly Law Reports 11 May 1990

1167

2 W.L.R.   **Williams v. Roffey etc. Ltd. (C.A.)**   Russell L.J.

A   must have continued work in the belief that he would be paid £575 as he finished each of the 18 uncompleted flats (although the arithmetic is not precisely accurate). For their part the defendants recorded the new terms in their ledger. Can the defendants now escape liability on the ground that the plaintiff undertook to do no more than he had originally contracted to do although, quite clearly, the defendants, on 9 April 1986, were prepared to make the payment and only declined to do so at

B   a later stage. It would certainly be unconscionable if this were to be their legal entitlement.

The submissions advanced on both sides before this court ranged over a wide field. They went far beyond the pleadings, and indeed it is worth noticing that the absence of consideration was never pleaded, although argued before Mr. Assistant Recorder Rupert Jackson Q.C.

C   Speaking for myself—and I notice it is touched upon in the judgment of Glidewell L.J.—I would have welcomed the development of argument, if it could have been properly raised in this court, on the basis that there was here an estoppel and that the defendants, in the circumstances prevailing, were precluded from raising the defence that their undertaking to pay the extra £10,300 was not binding. For example, in *Amalgamated Investment & Property Co. Ltd. v. Texas Commerce International Bank*

D   *Ltd.* [1982] Q.B. 84 Robert Goff J. said, at p. 105:

> "it is in my judgment not of itself a bar to an estoppel that its effect may be to enable a party to enforce a cause of action which, without the estoppel, would not exist. It is sometimes said that an estoppel cannot create a cause of action, or that an estoppel can only act as a shield, not as a sword. In a sense this is true—in the

E   > sense that estoppel is not, as a contract is, a source of legal obligation. But as Lord Denning M.R. pointed out in *Crabb v. Arun District Council* [1976] Ch. 179, 187, an estoppel may have the effect that a party can enforce a cause of action which, without the estoppel, he would not be able to do."

F   When the case came to the Court of Appeal Lord Denning M.R. said, at p. 122:

> "The doctrine of estoppel is one of the most flexible and useful in the armoury of the law. But it has become overloaded with cases. That is why I have not gone through them all in this judgment. It has evolved during the last 150 years in a sequence of separate developments: proprietary estoppel, estoppel by representation of

G   > fact, estoppel by acquiescence, and promissory estoppel. At the same time it has been sought to be limited by a series of maxims: estoppel is only a rule of evidence, estoppel cannot give rise to a cause of action, estoppel cannot do away with the need for consideration, and so forth. All these can now be seen to merge into one general principle shorn of limitations. When the parties to a transaction proceed on the basis of an underlying assumption—

H   > either of fact or of law—whether due to misrepresentation or mistake makes no difference—on which they have conducted the dealings between them—neither of them will be allowed to go back on that assumption when it would be unfair or unjust to allow him to do so. If one of them does seek to go back on it, the courts will give the other such remedy as the equity of the case demands."

Brandon L.J. said, at pp. 131–132:

The Weekly Law Reports 11 May 1990

1168

Russell L.J.   Williams v. Roffey etc. Ltd. (C.A.)   [1990]

"while a party cannot in terms found a cause of action on an   A
estoppel, he may, as a result of being able to rely on an estoppel,
succeed on a cause of action on which, without being able to rely
on that estoppel, he would necessarily have failed."

These citations demonstrate that whilst consideration remains a
fundamental requirement before a contract not under seal can be
enforced, the policy of the law in its search to do justice between the   B
parties has developed considerably since the early 19th century when
Stilk v. Myrick, 2 Camp. 317 was decided by Lord Ellenborough C.J. In
the late 20th century I do not believe that the rigid approach to the
concept of consideration to be found in *Stilk v. Myrick* is either
necessary or desirable. Consideration there must still be but, in my
judgment, the courts nowadays should be more ready to find its existence   C
so as to reflect the intention of the parties to the contract where the
bargaining powers are not unequal and where the finding of consideration
reflect the true intention of the parties.

What was the true intention of the parties when they arrived at the
agreement pleaded by the defendants in paragraph 5 of the amended
defence? The plaintiff had got into financial difficulties. The defendants,
through their employee Mr. Cottrell, recognised the price that had been   D
agreed originally with the plaintiff was less than what Mr. Cottrell
himself regarded as a reasonable price. There was a desire on Mr.
Cottrell's part to retain the services of the plaintiff so that the work
could be completed without the need to employ another subcontractor.
There was further a need to replace what had hitherto been a haphazard
method of payment by a more formalised scheme involving the payment
of a specified sum on the completion of each flat. These were all   E
advantages accruing to the defendants which can fairly be said to have
been in consideration of their undertaking to pay the additional £10,300.
True it was that the plaintiff did not undertake to do any work
additional to that which he had originally undertaken to do but the
terms upon which he was to carry out the work were varied and, in my
judgment, that variation was supported by consideration which a   F
pragmatic approach to the true relationship between the parties readily
demonstrates.

For my part I wish to make it plain that I do not base my judgment
upon any reservation as to the correctness of the law long ago enunciated
in *Stilk v. Myrick*. A gratuitous promise, pure and simple, remains
unenforceable unless given under seal. But where, as in this case, a
party undertakes to make a payment because by so doing it will gain an   G
advantage arising out of the continuing relationship with the promisee
the new bargain will not fail for want of consideration. As I read the
judgment of the assistant recorder this was his true ratio upon that part
of the case wherein the absence of consideration was raised in argument.
For the reasons that I have endeavoured to outline, I think that the
assistant recorder came to a correct conclusion and I too would dismiss   H
this appeal.

PURCHAS L.J. The history and circumstances under which this
appeal comes before the court have been set out in the judgment of
Glidewell L.J. whose exposition I gratefully adopt. I repeat here only
for ease of reference the significant features of the factual matrix against
which the parties came together on 9 April 1986.

The Weekly Law Reports 11 May 1990

1169

2 W.L.R.   **Williams v. Roffey etc. Ltd. (C.A.)**   Purchas L.J.

A   Evidence given by Mr. Cottrell, the defendants' surveyor, established that, to their knowledge, the original contract price was too low to enable the plaintiff to operate satisfactorily and at a profit by something a little over £3,780. It was also known that the plantiff was falling short in the supervision of his own labour force with the result that productivity fell and his financial difficulties had been aggravated. A further difficulty, which the judge found had arisen by the time of the meeting in April,

B   was that the plaintiff had been paid for more than 80 per cent. of the work but had not completed anything like this percentage. These facts were all obviously known to the plaintiff as well as the defendants. Also known to the defendants through Mr. Cottrell, and probably also appreciated by the plaintiff, was that the carpentry work to be executed by the plaintiff was on what was known as "the critical path of the

C   defendants' global operations." Failure to complete this work by the plaintiff, in accordance with the contract, would seriously prejudice the defendants as main contractors vis-à-vis the owners for whom they were working.

   In these circumstances there were clearly incentives to both parties to make a further arrangement in order to relieve the plaintiff of his financial difficulties and also to ensure that the plaintiff was in a

D   position, or alternatively was willing, to continue with the subcontract works to a reasonable and timely completion. Against this context the judge found that on 9 April 1986 a meeting took place between the plaintiff and a man called Hooper, on the one hand, and Mr. Cottrell and Mr. Roffey on the other hand. The arrangement was that the defendants would pay the plaintiff an extra £10,300 by way of increasing the lump sum for the total work. It was further agreed that the sum of

E   £10,300 was to be paid at the rate of £575 per flat on the completion of each flat. This arrangement was beneficial to both sides. By completing one flat at a time rather than half completing all the flats the plaintiff was able to receive moneys on account and the defendants were able to direct their other trades to do work in the completed flats which otherwise would have been held up until the plaintiff had completed his work.

F   The point of some difficulty which arises on this appeal is whether the judge was correct in his conclusion that the agreement reached on 9 April did not fail for lack of consideration because the principle established by the old cases of *Stilk v. Myrick*, 2 Camp. 317 approving *Harris v. Watson*, Peake 102 did not apply. Mr. Makey, who appeared for the plaintiff, was bold enough to submit that *Harris v. Watson*, albeit

G   a decision of Lord Kenyon, was a case tried at the Guildhall at nisi prius in the Court of King's Bench and that *Stilk v. Myrick* was a decision also at nisi prius albeit a judgment of no less a judge than Lord Ellenborough C.J. and that, therefore, this court was bound by neither authority. I feel I must say at once that, for my part, I would not be prepared to overrule two cases of such veneration involving judgments

H   of judges of such distinction except on the strongest possible grounds since they form a pillar stone of the law of contract which has been observed over the years and is still recognised in principle in recent authority: see the decision of *Stilk v. Myrick* to be found in *North Ocean Shipping Co. Ltd. v. Hyundai Construction Co. Ltd.* [1979] Q.B. 705, 712 *per* Mocatta J. With respect, I agree with his view of the two judgments by Denning L.J. in *Ward v. Byham* [1956] 1 W.L.R. 496 and *Williams v. Williams* [1957] 1 W.L.R. 148 in concluding that these

The Weekly Law Reports 11 May 1990

1170

Purchas L.J.   Williams v. Roffey etc. Ltd. (C.A.)   [1990]

judgments do not provide a sound basis for avoiding the rule in *Stilk v. Myrick*, 2 Camp. 317. Although this rule has been the subject of some criticism it is still clearly recognised in current textbooks of authority: see *Chitty on Contracts*, 28th ed. (1989) and *Cheshire, Fifoot and Furmston's Law of Contract*, 11th ed. (1986). By the same token I find myself unable to accept the attractive invitation offered by Mr. Makey to follow the decision of the Supreme Court of New Hampshire in *Watkins and Sons Inc. v. Carrig* (1941) 21 A. 2d 591.

In my judgment, therefore, the rule in *Stilk v. Myrick*, 2 Camp. 317 remains valid as a matter of principle, namely that a contract not under seal must be supported by consideration. Thus, where the agreement upon which reliance is placed provides that an extra payment is to be made for work to be done by the payee which he is already obliged to perform then unless some other consideration is detected to support the agreement to pay the extra sum that agreement will not be enforceable. The two cases, *Harris v. Watson*, Peake 102 and *Stilk v. Myrick*, 2 Camp. 317 involved circumstances of a very special nature, namely the extraordinary conditions existing at the turn of the 18th century under which seamen had to serve their contracts of employment on the high seas. There were strong public policy grounds at that time to protect the master and owners of a ship from being held to ransom by disaffected crews. Thus, the decision that the promise to pay extra wages even in the circumstances established in those cases, was not supported by consideration is readily understandable. Of course, conditions today on the high seas have changed dramatically and it is at least questionable, as Mr. Makey submitted, whether these cases might not well have been decided differently if they were tried today. The modern cases tend to depend more upon the defence of duress in a commercial context rather than lack of consideration for the second agreement. In the present case the question of duress does not arise. The initiative in coming to the agreement of 9 April came from Mr. Cottrell and not from the plaintiff. It would not, therefore, lie in the defendants' mouth to assert a defence of duress. Nevertheless, the court is more ready in the presence of this defence being available in the commercial context to look for mutual advantages which would amount to sufficient consideration to support the second agreement under which the extra money is paid. Although the passage cited below from the speech of Lord Hailsham of St. Marylebone L.C. in *Woodhouse A.C. Israel Cocoa Ltd. S.A. v. Nigerian Produce Marketing Co. Ltd.* [1972] A.C. 741 was strictly obiter dicta I respectfully adopt it as an indication of the approach to be made in modern times. The case involved an agreement to vary the currency in which the buyer's obligation should be met which was subsequently affected by a depreciation in the currency involved. The case was decided on an issue of estoppel but Lord Hailsham of St. Marylebone L.C. commented on the other issue, namely the variation of the original contract in the following terms, at pp. 757–758:

> "If the exchange of letters was not variation, I believe it was nothing. The buyers asked for a variation in the mode of discharge of a contract of sale. If the proposal meant what they claimed, and was accepted and acted upon, I venture to think that the vendors would have been bound by their acceptance at least until they gave reasonable notice to terminate, and I imagine that a modern court would have found no difficulty in discovering consideration for such

The Weekly Law Reports 11 May 1990

1171
2 W.L.R.   **Williams v. Roffey etc. Ltd. (C.A.)**   Purchas L.J.

A   a promise. Business men know their own business best even when they appear to grant an indulgence, and in the present case I do not think that there would have been insuperable difficulty in spelling out consideration from the earlier correspondence."

In the light of those authorities the question now must be addressed: Was there evidence upon which the judge was entitled to find that there
B   was sufficient consideration to support the agreement of 9 April, as set out in the passage from his judgment already set out in the judgment of Glidewell L.J.? The references to this problem in *Chitty on Contracts* 26th ed. (1989), are not wholly without some conflict amongst themselves. In paragraph 1601 the editors turn to the question of consideration to support an agreement to vary an existing contract:

C   "In many cases, consideration can be found in the mutual abandonment of existing rights or the conferment of new benefits by each party on the other."

Reference is made to the *Woodhouse* case to which I have already referred:

D   "For example, an alteration of the money of account in a contract proposed or made by one party and accepted by the other is binding on both parties, since either may benefit from the variation. . . . However, an agreement whereby one party undertakes an additional obligation, but the other party is merely bound to perform his existing obligations, or an agreement whereby one party undertakes an additional obligation, but for the benefit of that party
E   alone, will not be effective to vary the contract as no consideration is present."

These statements are based upon *Stilk v. Myrick*, 2 Camp. 317 and *Syros Shipping Co. S.A. v. Elaghill Trading Co.* [1980] Lloyd's Rep. 390. Reference is also made to paragraph 197 earlier in the textbook where *Stilk v. Myrick* is considered at some length. On the other hand, at paragraph 183 the editors make this proposition:
F
         "The requirement that consideration must move from the promisee is most generally satisfied where some detriment is suffered by him: e.g. where he parts with money or goods, or renders services, in exchange for the promise. But the requirement may equally well be satisfied where the promisee confers a benefit on the promisor without in *fact* suffering any detriment. For example, in *De la Bere*
G   *v. Pearson Ltd.* [1908] 1 K.B. 280 the defendants owned a newspaper and invited readers to apply for financial advice on the terms that the defendants should be entitled to publish the readers' letters and their own replies."

This is an accurate recital of the facts in *De la Bere v. Pearson Ltd.* [1908] 1 K.B. 280 but when the argument and judgments are read the
H   case turned on issues other than consideration, namely remoteness of damage, etc. So the case is doubtful support for the proposition made in this paragraph.

The question must be posed: what consideration has moved from the plaintiff to support the promise to pay the extra £10,300 added to the lump sum provision? In the particular circumstances which I have outlined above, there was clearly a commercial advantage to both sides from a pragmatic point of view in reaching the agreement of 9 April.

The Weekly Law Reports 11 May 1990

1172

Purchas L.J.   **Williams v. Roffey etc. Ltd. (C.A.)**   **[1990]**

The defendants were on risk that as a result of the bargain they had   A
struck the plaintiff would not or indeed possibly could not comply with
his existing obligations without further finance. As a result of the
agreement the defendants secured their position commercially. There
was, however, no obligation added to the contractual duties imposed
upon the plaintiff under the original contract. Prima facie this would
appear to be a classic *Stilk v. Myrick* case. It was, however, open to the
plaintiff to be in deliberate breach of the contract in order to "cut his   B
losses" commercially. In normal circumstances the suggestion that a
contracting party can rely upon his own breach to establish consideration
is distinctly unattractive. In many cases it obviously would be and if
there was any element of duress brought upon the other contracting
party under the modern development of this branch of the law the
proposed breaker of the contract would not benefit. With some hesitation   C
and comforted by the passage from the speech of Lord Hailsham of St.
Marylebone L.C. in *Woodhouse A.C. Israel Cocoa Ltd. S.A. v. Nigerian
Produce Marketing Co. Ltd.* [1972] A.C. 741, 757–758, to which I have
referred. I consider that the modern approach to the question of
consideration would be that where there were benefits derived by each
party to a contract of variation even though one party did not suffer a
detriment this would not be fatal to the establishing of sufficient   D
consideration to support the agreement. If both parties benefit from an
agreement it is not necessary that each also suffers a detriment. In my
judgment, on the facts as found by the judge, he was entitled to reach
the conclusion that consideration existed and in those circumstances I
would not disturb that finding. This is sufficient to determine the appeal.
The judge found as a fact that the flats were 'substantially completed'   E
and that payment was due to the plaintiff in respect of the number of
flats substantially completed which left an outstanding amount due from
the defendants to the plaintiff in the absence of the payment of which
the plaintiff was entitled to remove from the site. For these reasons and
for the reasons which have already been given by Glidewell L.J. I would
dismiss this appeal.

F

Appeal dismissed with costs.
Leave to appeal.

Solicitors: John Pearson, New Malden; Terence W. Lynch & Co.

M. F.   G

——————

H

Appendix B
Davis v *Johnson* [1978] 2 WLR 553

The Weekly Law Reports, March 31, 1978

553

2 W.L.R.

A

[HOUSE OF LORDS]

DAVIS . . . . RESPONDENT

AND

JOHNSON . . . . APPELLANT

B

1978 Jan. 16, 17;   Lord Diplock, Viscount Dilhorne,
     March 9   Lord Kilbrandon, Lord Salmon
                            and Lord Scarman

Injunction—Domestic violence—Exclusion from matrimonial home
—Man and woman " living with each other in the same house-
C *hold "—Joint tenants of council flat—Woman leaving home*
with child because of man's violent behaviour—Whether sub-
stantive right of property limiting jurisdiction of county court
to order exclusion of violent party for indefinite period—
Domestic Violence and Matrimonial Proceedings Act 1976
(c. 50), ss. 1 (1) (c) (2), 2 (1) (2)
Judicial Precedent—Court of Appeal decision—How far binding—
Construction of statute—Two Court of Appeal decisions that
D *new Act procedural only—Whether majority decision of Court*
of Appeal of five members able to overrule previous decisions
where satisfied that they are wrong—Whether class of excep-
tions to general rule of stare decisis closed—Domestic Violence
and Matrimonial Proceedings Act 1976, s. 1 (1)

The respondent, a young unmarried mother, who had a
joint tenancy of a council flat with the appellant, the father
E of her child, left the home with the child because of his
violent behaviour to her. She applied to the county court for
injunctions under section 1 (1) *(a) (b)* and *(c)* of the Domestic
Violence and Matrimonial Proceedings Act 1976 [1] to restrain
him from molesting her or the child and to exclude him
from the home. By section 1 (2), subsection (1) applied to
" a man and a woman who are living with each other in the
same household as husband and wife as it applies to the
F parties to a marriage and any reference to the matrimonial
home shall be construed accordingly." A deputy circuit judge
on October 18 granted the injunctions asked for. The appellant went out of the flat and the woman and child returned
to it.
    On October 13, 1977, a division of the Court of Appeal
in *B.* v. *B.* [1978] 2 W.L.R. 160 construed section 1 of the
Act as procedural only, enabling the county courts to grant
G injunctions of the kinds specified in subsection (1) where that
was the only relief sought and held that the section did not
give the county court jurisdiction to make orders excluding
from the home a person, whether married or unmarried, who,

[1] Domestic Violence and Matrimonial Proceedings Act 1976, s. 1 : " (1) Without
prejudice to the jurisdiction of the High Court, on an application by a party to a
marriage a county court shall have jurisdiction to grant an injunction containing one
H or more of the following provisions, namely.—*(a)* a provision restraining the other
party to the marriage from molesting the applicant; *(b)* a provision restraining the
other party from molesting a child living with the applicant; *(c)* a provision excluding the other party from the matrimonial home or a part of the matrimonial home
or from a specified area in which the matrimonial home is included; *(d)* a provision
requiring the other party to permit the applicant to enter and remain in the matrimonial home or a part of the matrimonial home; whether or not any other relief is
sought in the proceedings. (2) Subsection (1) above shall apply to a man and a
woman who are living with each other in the same household as husband and wife
as it applies to the parties to a marriage and any reference to the matrimonial home
shall be construed accordingly."

554

The Weekly Law Reports, March 31, 1978

Davis v. Johnson (H.L.(E.))   [1978]

A
though behaving with violence, had any right of property in
the home; and the court discharged an excluding injunction
against a man who was sole tenant of a house. On October
20 another division of the Court of Appeal, in *Cantliff* v.
Jenkins [1978] 2 W.L.R. 177, followed *B.* v. *B.* and discharged a county court injunction excluding a man from the
home of which he and the woman with whom he had been
living were joint tenants.

B
After those decisions the judge in the county court in the
instant case rescinded that part of the order of the deputy
judge which excluded the appellant from the home: he went
back to the flat; and the respondent and the child returned
to an overcrowded home for battered wives.

On the respondent's appeal, pursuant to leave granted by
the judge, to a Court of Appeal of five judges, the court, by
a majority, declined to follow the earlier decisions and allowed
the appeal. On the appellant's appeal:—   C

Held, dismissing the appeal, (*per* Viscount Dilhorne, Lord
Kilbrandon, Lord Salmon and Lord Scarman), that on its
true construction section 1, in the context of an Act concerned with the evil of domestic violence, gave jurisdiction to
all county courts to grant an injunction under subsection (1)
(*c*) and subsection (2) to exclude the violent person from the
home which the parties, whether married or living together
unmarried, had shared, irrespective of any right of property   D
vested in the person excluded, whether as owner, tenant or
joint tenant; that such an injunction could in theory last for
an indefinite time but in practice would be "until further
order" and in most cases temporary or short-term; that the
two earlier decisions, by importing into section 1 the concept
of non-interference with the enjoyment of property rights, had
so construed the section as virtually to deprive the unmarried
woman, who scarcely ever had any right of property in a   E
shared home, of any remedy under an Act expressly intended
for her protection; and that those decisions were wrong (post,
pp. 568B–H, 569D–F, 572F, 573B–C, 574B–D, 575A–C, 576A–C,
581F—582C).

B. v. *B.* (*Domestic Violence: Jurisdiction*) [1978] 2 W.L.R.
160, C.A. and *Cantliff* v. *Jenkins* (*Note*) [1978] 2 W.L.R. 177,
C.A. overruled.
F
Per Lord Diplock. I cannot accept that subsection (2), in
contrast to subsection (1), was intended to change the substantive law by authorising judges in county courts to make
drastic inroads upon the respective legal rights of parties to
an illicit union to occupy the premises in which they have
been living together as man and wife. Nevertheless under the
existing substantive law a mistress is entitled to protection
from the tort of assault, and if, as in the instant case, she is   G
joint tenant with her paramour of the premises in which
she has been living with him, she has a legal right to
continue in peaceful occupation of them. Where the judge
is satisfied that there is grave danger that if the mistress
returns to the premises her paramour will assault her or her
child then, as ancillary to an injunction against threatened
violence, the judge has jurisdiction to make an order under
section 1 (1) (*c*) excluding him from the premises; but such   H
an order could properly continue only so long as there was
danger that if permitted to return he would assault his mistress
or her child (post, pp. 564G—565A).

Per curiam (i). The House of Lords should take the
occasion to reaffirm that the rule laid down in *Young* v.
Bristol Aeroplane Co. Ltd. on stare decisis is still binding on
the Court of Appeal (post, pp. 562E, 569H—570A, 573E, 576
G–H, 577A–C, 582D).

Practice Statement (*Judicial Precedent*) [1966] 1 W.L.R.

The Weekly Law Reports, March 31, 1978

555

2 W.L.R.   **Davis v. Johnson (H.L.(E.))**

A   1234, H.L.(E.) and *Young* v. *Bristol Aeroplane Co. Ltd.* [1944]
    K.B. 718, C.A. considered.
        (ii) It has always been a well established and salutary rule
    that Hansard can never be referred to by counsel in court
    and therefore can never be relied on by the court in con-
    struing a statute or for any other purpose. So long as this
    rule is maintained by Parliament it must be wrong for a
    judge to make any judicial use of proceedings in Parliament
B   for the purpose of interpreting statutes (post, pp. 563E, 570E,
    571A–B, 573E, 578A–B, 582D).
        Decision of the Court of Appeal [1978] 2 W.L.R. 183;
    [1978] 1 All E.R. 841 affirmed.

    The following cases are referred to in their Lordships' opinions:

    B. v. *B. (Domestic Violence: Jurisdiction)* [1978] 2 W.L.R. 160; [1978]
C   1 All E.R. 821, C.A.
    Beswick v. *Beswick* [1968] A.C. 58; [1967] 3 W.L.R. 932; [1967] 2 All
        E.R. 1197, H.L.(E.).
    Binions v. *Evans* [1972] Ch. 359; [1972] 2 W.L.R. 729; [1972] 2 All E.R.
        70, C.A.
    Black-Clawson International Ltd. v. *Papierwerke Waldhof-Aschaffenburg
        A.G.* [1975] A.C. 591; [1975] 2 W.L.R. 513; [1975] 1 All E.R. 810,
        H.L.(E.).
D   *Bonsor* v. *Musicians' Union* [1956] A.C. 104; [1955] 3 W.L.R. 788; [1955]
        3 All E.R. 518, H.L.(E.).
    Broome v. *Cassell & Co. Ltd.* [1971] 2 Q.B. 354; [1971] 2 W.L.R. 853;
        [1971] 2 All E.R. 187, C.A.
    Cantliff v. *Jenkins (Note)* [1978] 2 W.L.R. 177; [1978] 1 All E.R. 836,
        C.A.
    Farrell v. *Alexander* [1976] Q.B. 345; [1975] 3 W.L.R. 642; [1976] 1 All
E   E.R. 129, C.A.; [1977] A.C. 59; [1976] 3 W.L.R. 145; [1976] 2 All
        E.R. 721, H.L.(E.).
    Inland Revenue Commissioners v. *Ayrshire Employers Mutual Insurance
        Association Ltd.* [1946] 1 All E.R. 637, H.L.(Sc.).
    Miliangos v. *George Frank (Textiles) Ltd.* [1975] Q.B. 487; [1975] 2
        W.L.R. 555; [1975] 1 All E.R. 1076, Bristow J. and C.A.
    Morelle Ltd. v. *Wakeling* [1955] 2 Q.B. 379; [1955] 2 W.L.R. 672; [1955]
F   1 All E.R. 708, C.A.
    Perrin v. *Morgan* [1943] A.C. 399; [1943] 1 All E.R. 187, H.L.(E.).
    Practice Statement (Judicial Precedent) [1966] 1 W.L.R. 1234; [1966] 3
        All E.R. 77, H.L.(E.).
    Schorsch Meier G.m.b.H. v. *Hennin* [1975] Q.B. 416; [1974] 3 W.L.R.
        823; [1975] 1 All E.R. 152, C.A.
    Tanner v. *Tanner* [1975] 1 W.L.R. 1346; [1975] 3 All E.R. 776, C.A.
G   *Tarr* v. *Tarr* [1973] A.C. 254; [1972] 2 W.L.R. 1068; [1972] 2 All E.R.
        295, H.L.(E.).
    Tiverton Estates Ltd. v. *Wearwell Ltd.* [1975] Ch. 146; [1974] 2 W.L.R.
        176; [1974] 1 All E.R. 209, C.A.
    United Railways of Havana and Regla Warehouses Ltd., In re [1961]
        A.C. 1007; [1960] 2 W.L.R. 969; [1960] 2 All E.R. 332, H.L.(E.).
    Winter Garden Theatre (London) Ltd. v. *Millennium Productions Ltd.*
H   [1948] A.C. 173; [1947] 2 All E.R. 331, H.L.(E.).
    Young v. *Bristol Aeroplane Co. Ltd.* [1944] K.B. 718; [1944] 2 All E.R.
        293, C.A.; [1946] A.C. 163; [1946] 1 All E.R. 98, H.L.(E.).

    The following additional cases were cited in argument:

    Bassett v. *Bassett* [1975] Fam. 76; [1975] 2 W.L.R. 270; [1975] 1 All E.R.
        513, C.A.
    Bull v. *Bull* [1955] 1 Q.B. 234; [1955] 2 W.L.R. 78; [1955] 1 All E.R.
        253, C.A.

The Weekly Law Reports, March 31, 1978

556

Davis v. Johnson (H.L.(E.))   [1978]

Campbell v. *Campbell* [1976] Fam. 347; [1976] 3 W.L.R. 572; [1977] 1   A
    All E.R. 1.
Hall v. *Hall* [1971] 1 W.L.R. 404; [1971] 1 All E.R. 762, C.A.
National Provincial Bank Ltd. v. *Hastings Car Mart Ltd.* [1965] A.C.
    1175; [1965] 3 W.L.R. 1; [1965] 2 All E.R. 472, H.L.(E.).
Rex v. *Cheshire County Court Judge and United Society of Boiler-
    makers, ex p. Malone* [1921] 2 K.B. 694.
Smith (Colin) Music Ltd. v. *Ridge* [1975] 1 W.L.R. 463; [1975] 1 All   B
    E.R. 290, C.A.

APPEAL from the Court of Appeal.
    This was an appeal by the appellant, Nehemiah Johnson, from an
order dated November 28, 1977, of the Court of Appeal (Lord Denning
M.R., Sir George Baker P. and Shaw L.J.; Goff and Cumming-Bruce
L.JJ., dissenting) allowing an appeal by the respondent, Jennifer Therese   C
Davis, from an order dated October 26, 1977, made by Judge Bernard
Lewis sitting at Brentford County Court who had ordered that that part
of an order dated October 18, 1977, made by Mr. Jan G. Paulusz, sitting
as a deputy circuit judge at the county court which ordered the respondent
to vacate certain premises in Hackney, London E9, forthwith and not to
return thereto be rescinded.   D
    The respondent applied on October 18, 1977, to the Brentford County
Court under the Domestic Violence and Matrimonial Proceedings Act
1976 for orders to restrain the appellant with whom she had lived and
by whom she had a child (i) from assaulting, threatening or molesting or
otherwise interfering with her or the child and (ii) that he should vacate
the council flat of which they were joint tenants and not return thereto.
    Mr. Jan G. Paulusz sitting as a deputy circuit judge at the county court   E
accepted the respondent's affidavit evidence as truthful in her allegations
of violence against the appellant, took into account the uncomfortable
conditions in which she and the child were having to live and ordered (1)
that the appellant be restrained from molesting, assaulting or otherwise
interfering with the respondent or the child and (2) that he should vacate
the premises at 13 Nisbet House, Homerton High Road, Hackney, forth-   F
with and not return thereto. The judge also ordered that a copy of the
order be served on the chief police officer at Hackney Police Station.
    On October 24, 1977, following two Court of Appeal decisions,
B. v. *B.* on October 13 and *Cantliff* v. *Jenkins* on October 20, the appellant gave notice that he would apply to the county court on October 26
to ask that that part of the injunction excluding him from the flat should
be suspended, and he be permitted re-entry. Judge Bernard Lewis   G
ordered that that part of the deputy judge's order of October 18 should
be rescinded but granted the respondent leave to appeal. The appellant
went back to the flat and the respondent and her child returned to the
refuge hostel.
    The Court of Appeal (by a majority) (a) allowed the respondent's
appeal; (b) dismissed the appeal of the appellant from so much of the   H
order made by the deputy circuit judge dated October 1977 as ordered
that the appellant should vacate the above-named premises forthwith
and not return thereto; (c) ordered that a copy of the order of the Court
of Appeal be served on the chief police officer at Hackney Police Station.

Joseph Jackson Q.C. and *David McIntyre* for the appellant.
Lionel Swift Q.C. and *Judith Parker* for the respondent.

The Weekly Law Reports, March 31, 1978

557

2 W.L.R.   **Davis v. Johnson (H.L.(E.))**

A   Their Lordships took time for consideration.

March 9, 1978. LORD DIPLOCK. My Lords, this appeal is from a
judgment of the Court of Appeal which, by a majority of three out of
five members who sat (Lord Denning M.R., Sir George Baker P. and
Shaw L.J.; Goff and Cumming-Bruce L.JJ. dissenting) purported to overrule two recent previous decisions of its own as to the meaning of a
B   statute.

Put in a nutshell, the basic question of statutory construction that has
given rise to so acute a conflict of judicial opinion is whether section 1
of the Domestic Violence and Matrimonial Proceedings Act 1976 does
no more than provide additional, expeditious and more easily available
remedies to prevent threatened invasions of existing legal rights originating
C   from other sources, whether statutory or at common law, or whether it
also, of itself, creates new legal rights as well as new remedies for
threatened invasion of them. The former I will call the " narrower," the
latter the " broader " meaning. In *B. v. B. (Domestic Violence: Jurisdiction*) [1978] 2 W.L.R. 160 on October 13, 1977, the Court of Appeal
consisting of Megaw, Bridge, and Waller L.JJ. decided unanimously that
D   it bore the narrower meaning: it gave additional remedies but created no
new legal rights. In *Cantliff* v. *Jenkins (Note)* [1978] 2 W.L.R. 177 on
October 20, 1977, the Court of Appeal then consisting of Stamp, Orr, and
Ormrod L.JJ., while holding itself to be bound by the decision in *B. v. B.*
since it regarded that case as indistinguishable, took occasion, again
unanimously, to express its concurrence with the reasoning of Bridge L.J.
in *B. v. B.* and added, for good measure, an additional reason in support
E   of the narrower meaning placed upon the section in that previous judgment. For my part, I think that *Cantliff* v. *Jenkins* was distinguishable
from *B. v. B.* but it is conceded that the facts in the instant case are
indistinguishable from those held by the Court of Appeal in *Cantliff* v.
Jenkins to be relevant to its decision in that case. So, when the instant
case came before the Court of Appeal, there was a preliminary question
F   which fell to be determined; and that was whether the court was bound
by its previous decisions in *B. v. B.* and *Cantliff* v. *Jenkins.* The view of
a majority of three was that it was not so bound, though their individual
reasons for so holding were not identical. This opened the way to a
fresh consideration of the meaning of the statute by all five members. On
this question they were divided four to one. Cumming-Bruce L.J. sided
with the six Lords Justices who in the two previous cases had adopted
G   the narrower meaning of section 1; the remainder were of opinion that it
bore the wider meaning and did create new legal rights as well as new
remedies for threatened violation of them. So, of the members of the
Court of Appeal who sit regularly in civil matters (of whom there are
now 17) there were seven who had adopted the narrower meaning of the
section, three who, together with the President of the Family Division,
H   had preferred the wider meaning, and a silent minority of seven regular
members of the Court of Appeal whose views had not been expressed by
the conclusion of the hearing of the instant case in the Court of Appeal.

I draw attention to this arithmetic because if the view expressed by
Lord Denning M.R., Sir George Baker P. and Shaw L.J. that the Court of
Appeal was not bound by its own previous decisions is correct, this would
apply to its decision in the instant case; and had there been no appeal to
your Lordships' House to cut the Gordian knot, it would have been open

The Weekly Law Reports, March 31, 1978

558

Lord Diplock   **Davis v. Johnson (H.L.(E.))**   **[1978]**

to the Court of Appeal in any subsequent cases to give effect to the wider   A
or the narrower construction of section 1 of the Domestic Violence and
Matrimonial Proceedings Act 1976 according to the preference of the
majority of the members who happened to be selected to sit on that
particular appeal.

My Lords, the difference of judicial opinion as to the true construction
of the section has spilled over into this House; for although I agree that   B
on the facts of this case it may be that the order of the Court of Appeal
could be upheld, and that the actual decision in *Cantliff* v. *Jenkins* was
wrong, I nevertheless find myself regretfully compelled to part company
with the rest of your Lordships and to align myself with the seven Lords
Justices who have expressed their preference for the narrower meaning.
This cannot affect the disposition of the instant appeal nor will it affect
the application of the Act in subsequent cases; for the section means what   C
a majority of this House declares it means.   But it does make the score
of appellate opinions in favour of the broader and the narrower meanings
eight all.

Although on the question of the construction of section 1 of the
Domestic Violence and Matrimonial Proceedings Act 1976 this House has
not been able to reach unanimity, nevertheless on what in the instant case   D
was the first question for the Court of Appeal, viz. whether it was bound
by its own previous decisions, I understand us to be unanimous, so I too
will deal with it first.

So far as civil matters are concerned the law upon this question is now
clear and unassailable.   It has been so for more than 30 years.   I do not
find it necessary to trace the origin and development of the doctrine of
stare decisis before the present structure of the courts was created in 1875.   E
In that structure the Court of Appeal in civil actions has always played,
save in a few exceptional matters, an intermediate and not a final appellate
role.   The application of the doctrine of stare decisis to decisions of the
Court of Appeal was the subject of close examination by a Court of
Appeal composed of six of its eight regular members in *Young* v. *Bristol
Aeroplane Co. Ltd.* [1944] K.B. 718.   The judgment of the court was   F
delivered by Lord Greene M.R.   Its effect is summarised accurately in the
headnote as being that:

> " The Court of Appeal is bound to follow its own decisions and those
> of courts of co-ordinate jurisdiction, and the 'full' court is in the
> same position in this respect as a division of the court consisting of
> three members.   The only exceptions to this rule are:— (1) The   G
> court is entitled and bound to decide which of two conflicting deci-
> sions of its own it will follow; (2) the court is bound to refuse to
> follow a decision of its own which, though not expressly overruled,
> cannot, in its opinion, stand with a decision of the House of Lords;
> (3) the court is not bound to follow a decision of its own if it is
> satisfied that the decision was given per incuriam, e.g., where a statute   H
> or a rule having statutory effect which would have affected the deci-
> sion was not brought to the attention of the earlier court."

The rule as expounded in the *Bristol Aeroplane* case was not new in
1944.   It had been acted upon on numerous occasions and had, as recently
as the previous year, received the express confirmation of this House of
Viscount Simon L.C. with whose speech Lord Atkin agreed: see *Perrin*
v. *Morgan* [1943] A.C. 399, 405.   Although prior to 1944 there had been

The Weekly Law Reports, March 31, 1978

559

2 W.L.R.   **Davis v. Johnson (H.L.(E.))**   **Lord Diplock**

A   an occasional deviation from the rule, which was why a court of six was brought together to consider it, there has been none since. It has been uniformly acted upon by the Court of Appeal and re-affirmed, notably in a judgment of a Court of Appeal of five, of which Lord Denning as Denning L.J. was a member, in *Morelle Ltd.* v. *Wakeling* [1955] 2 Q.B. 379. This judgment emphasised the limited scope of the per incuriam
B   exception to the general rule that the Court of Appeal is bound by its own previous decisions. The rule has also been uniformly accepted by this House as being correct. Because until recently it has never been questioned, the acceptance of the rule has generally been tacit in the course of recounting the circumstances which have rendered necessary an appeal to your Lordships' House; but occasionally the rule has been expressly referred to, as by Viscount Simon L.C. in the *Bristol Aeroplane* case
C   itself [1946] A.C. 163, 169 and by Lord Morton of Henryton and Lord Porter in *Bonsor* v. *Musicians' Union* [1956] A.C. 104, 120, 128.

Furthermore, the provisions of the Administration of Justice Act 1969 which authorise "leap-frog" appeals in civil cases direct from the High Court to this House are based on the tacit assumption that the rule as stated in the *Bristol Aeroplane* case is correct. One of the two grounds on which a High Court judge may authorise a "leap frog" appeal is if
D   he is satisfied that a point of law of general importance involved in his decision:

"is one in respect of which the judge is bound by a decision of the Court of Appeal or of the House of Lords in previous proceedings, and was fully considered in the judgments given by the Court of Appeal or the House of Lords (as the case may be) in those previous
E   proceedings": section 12 (3) (*b*).

The justification for by-passing the Court of Appeal when the decision by which the judge is bound is one given by the Court of Appeal itself in previous proceedings is because that court also is bound by the decision, if the point of law was fully considered and not passed over per incuriam.

So the rule as it had been laid down in the *Bristol Aeroplane* case
F   [1944] K.B. 718 had never been questioned thereafter until, following upon the announcement by Lord Gardiner L.C. in 1966 [*Practice Statement (Judicial Precedent)* [1966] 1 W.L.R. 1234] that the House of Lords would feel free in exceptional cases to depart from a previous decision of its own, Lord Denning M.R. conducted what may be described, I hope without offence, as a one-man crusade with the object of freeing the
G   Court of Appeal from the shackles which the doctrine of stare decisis imposed upon its liberty of decision by the application of the rule laid down in the *Bristol Aeroplane* case to its own previous decisions; or, for that matter, by any decisions of this House itself of which the Court of Appeal disapproved: see *Broome* v. *Cassell & Co. Ltd.* [1971] 2 Q.B. 354 and *Schorsch Meier G.m.b.H.* v. *Hennin* [1975] Q.B. 416. In his judgment in the instant appeal, Lord Denning M.R. refers to a number of cases after
H   1966 in which he suggests that the Court of Appeal has either refused to apply the rule as laid down in the *Bristol Aeroplane* case or has added so many other exceptions to the three that were stated by Lord Greene M.R. that it no longer operates as a curb on the power of the Court of Appeal to disregard any previous decision of its own which the majority of those members who happen to be selected to sit on a particular appeal think is wrong. Such, however, has not been the view of the other two members of the Court of Appeal who were sitting with the Master of the Rolls in

The Weekly Law Reports, March 31, 1978

560

Lord Diplock   **Davis v. Johnson (H.L.(E.))**   **[1978]**

any of those cases to which he refers. Where they felt able to disregard   **A**
a previous decision of the Court of Appeal this was only because, in their
opinion, it fell within the first or second exception stated in the *Bristol
Aeroplane* case.

When *Miliangos* v. *George Frank (Textiles) Ltd.* [1975] Q.B. 487 was
before the Court of Appeal Lord Denning M.R. appears to have reluctantly
recanted. That was a case in which Bristow J. had held that he was bound
by a decision of this House in *In re United Railways of Havana and*   **B**
Regla Warehouses Ltd. [1961] A.C. 1007, despite the fact that the Court
of Appeal had purported to overrule it in the *Schorsch Meier* case. On
appeal from his decision Lord Denning M.R. disposed of the case by
holding that the Court of Appeal was bound by its own previous decision
in the *Schorsch Meier* case. He added, at p. 503:

> "I have myself often said that this court is not absolutely bound   **C**
> by its own decisions and may depart from them just as the House of
> Lords from theirs: but my colleagues have not gone so far. So that
> I am duty bound to defer to their view."

The reasons why his colleagues had not agreed to follow him are plain
enough. In an appellate court of last resort a balance must be struck
between the need on the one side for the legal certainty resulting from the   **D**
binding effort of previous decisions, and, on the other side the avoidance
of undue restriction on the proper development of the law. In the case
of an intermediate appellate court, however, the second desideratum can
be taken care of by appeal to a superior appellate court, if reasonable means
of access to it are available; while the risk to the first desideratum, legal
certainty, if the court is not bound by its own previous decisions grows   **E**
ever greater with increasing membership and the number of three-judge
divisions in which it sits—as the arithmetic which I have earlier mentioned
shows. So the balance does not lie in the same place as in the case of a
court of last resort. That is why the Lord Chancellor's announcement
about the future attitude towards precedent of the House of Lords in its
judicial capacity concluded with the words: "This announcement is not   **F**
intended to affect the use of precedent elsewhere than in this House."

Much has been said in the instant case about the delay and expense
which would have been involved if the Court of Appeal had treated itself
as bound by its previous decision in *B.* v. *B.* [1978] 2 W.L.R. 160 and
Cantliff v. *Jenkins* [1978] 2 W.L.R. 177, so as to make it necessary for the
respondent to come to this House to argue that those decisions should be   **G**
overruled. But a similar reasoning could also be used to justify any High
Court or county court judge in refusing to follow a decision of the
Court of Appeal which he thought was wrong. It is true that since the
appeal in the instant case was from the county court, not the High Court,
the "leap-frog" procedure was not available, but since it was conceded
that the instant case was indistinguishable from *Cantliff* v. *Jenkins*, there
was no need for anything but the briefest of hearings in the Court of   **H**
Appeal. The appeal to this House could in that event have been heard
before Christmas instead of in January: and at less cost. The decision
could have been announced at once and the reasons given later.

Of the various ways in which Lord Denning M.R.'s colleagues had
expressed the reasons for continuing to regard the rule laid down in the
Bristol Aeroplane case [1944] K.B. 718 as salutary in the interest of the
administration of justice, I select those given by Scarman L.J. in *Tiverton*

The Weekly Law Reports, March 31, 1978

561

A *Estates Ltd.* v. *Wearwell Ltd.* [1975] Ch. 146, 172–173, in the Court of
Appeal.

"The Court of Appeal occupies a central, but, save for a few exceptions, an intermediate position in our legal system.   To a large extent,
the consistency and certainty of the law depend upon it.   It sits almost
always in divisions of three: more judges can sit to hear a case, but
B their decision enjoys no greater authority than a court composed of
three.   If, therefore, throwing aside the restraints of *Young* v. *Bristol
Aeroplane Co. Ltd.*, one division of the court should refuse to follow
another because it believed the other's decision to be wrong, there
would be a risk of confusion and doubt arising where there should
be consistency and certainty.   The appropriate forum for the correction of the Court of Appeal's errors is the House of Lords, where the
C decision will at least have the merit of being final and binding—
subject only to the House's power to review its own decisions.   The
House of Lords, as the court of last resort, needs this power of review:
it does not follow that an intermediate appellate court needs it and,
for the reasons I have given, I believe the Court of Appeal is better
without it, save in the exceptional circumstances specified in *Young*
D v. *Bristol Aeroplane Co. Ltd.*"

My own reason for selecting this passage out of many is because in the
following year in *Farrell* v. *Alexander* [1976] Q.B. 345 Scarman L.J.
again referred to it in dissociating himself from the view, to which Lord
Denning M.R. had by then once again reverted, that the Court of Appeal
was not bound by any previous decision of its own that it was satisfied
E was wrong.   What Scarman L.J: there said, at p. 371, was:

"... I have immense sympathy with the approach of Lord Denning
M.R.   I decline to accept his lead only because I think it damaging to
the law in the long term—though it would undoubtedly do justice in
the present case.   To some it will appear that justice is being denied
by a timid, conservative, adherence to judicial precedent.   They would
be wrong.   Consistency is necessary to certainty—one of the great
F objectives of law.   The Court of Appeal—at the very centre of our
legal system—is responsible for its stability, its consistency, and its
predictability: see my comments in *Tiverton Estates Ltd.* v. *Wearwell
Ltd.* [1975] Ch. 146, 172.   The task of law reform, which calls for
wide-ranging techniques of consultation and discussion that cannot be
compressed into the forensic medium, is for others.   The courts are
G not to be blamed in a case such as this.   If there be blame, it rests
elsewhere."

When *Farrell* v. *Alexander* ([1977] A.C. 59) reached this House
Scarman L.J.'s way of putting it was expressly approved by my noble and
learned friends Viscount Dilhorne, at p. 81, and Lord Simon of Glaisdale
at p. 92, while the other member of this House who adverted to the
H question of stare decisis, Lord Russell of Killowen, at p. 105, expressed his
"unreserved disapproval" of that part of Lord Denning M.R.'s judgment
in which he persisted in his heterodox views on the subject.

In the instant case Lord Denning M.R. in effect reiterated his opinion
that the Court of Appeal in relation to its own previous decisions should
adopt the same rule as that which the House of Lords since the announcement in 1966 has applied in relation to its previous decisions. Sir George
Baker P., on the other hand, preferred to deal with the problem of stare

The Weekly Law Reports, March 31, 1978

562

Lord Diplock   Davis v. Johnson (H.L.(E.))   [1978]

decisis by adding a new exception to the rule in the *Bristol Aeroplane* case   **A**
[1944] K.B. 718, which he formulated as follows [1978] 2 W.L.R. 183,
205:

> " The court is not bound to follow a previous decision of its own
> if satisfied that that decision was clearly wrong and cannot stand in
> the face of the will and intention of Parliament expressed in simple
> language in a recent statute passed to remedy a serious mischief or   **B**
> abuse, and further adherence to the previous decision must lead to
> injustice in the particular case and unduly restrict proper development
> of the law with injustice to others."

Shaw L.J. phrased the exception rather differently.   He said, at pp.
221–222:

> " It would be in some such terms as that the principle of stare decisis   **C**
> should be relaxed where its application would have the effect of
> depriving actual and potential victims of violence of a vital protection
> which an Act of Parliament was plainly designed to afford to them,
> especially where, as in the context of domestic violence, that depriva-
> tion must inevitably give rise to an irremediable detriment to such
> victims and create in regard to them an injustice irreversible by a   **D**
> later decision of the House of Lords."

My Lords, the exception as stated by Sir George Baker P. would seem
wide enough to cover any previous decision on the construction of a
statute which the majority of the court thought was wrong and would have
consequences that were regrettable, at any rate if they felt sufficiently
strongly about it.   As stated by Shaw L.J. the exception would appear to   **E**
be what might be termed a " one-off " exception.   It is difficult to think of
any other statute to which it would apply.

In my opinion, this House should take this occasion to re-affirm
expressly, unequivocally and unanimously that the rule laid down in the
Bristol Aeroplane case [1944] K.B. 718 as to stare decisis is still binding
on the Court of Appeal.

I come now to the construction of section 1 of the Domestic Violence   **F**
and Matrimonial Proceedings Act 1976 under which the applicant, Miss
Davis, sought an injunction against the respondent, Mr. Johnson, to
exclude him from the council flat in Hackney of which they were joint
tenants.

The relevant facts can be stated briefly.   The parties who were unmarried had been living together there as man and wife for about three   **G**
years, together with a child of their illicit union, now aged three.   He
treated her with appalling violence: she was in fear of her life and fled
the premises on September 18, 1977, with the child.   She found asylum
at a refuge for women in her predicament.   It was grossly overcrowded,
insanitary and uncomfortable.   On October 11 she applied to the Brentford
County Court under section 1 of the Act for injunctions restraining the
respondent from using violence towards her and ordering him to vacate   **H**
the flat and not to return to it.   These she was granted initially but after
the decision in *Cantliff* v. *Jenkins* [1978] 2 W.L.R. 177 the injunction
excluding the respondent from the flat was withdrawn.   Against its withdrawal the instant appeal to the Court of Appeal was brought, it being
conceded that the applicant was entitled to the injunctions against violence.

The section under which Miss Davis's application was made reads as
follows:

The Weekly Law Reports, March 31, 1978

563

2 W.L.R. **Davis v. Johnson (H.L.(E.))** **Lord Diplock**

A   " 1. (1) Without prejudice to the jurisdiction of the High Court, on an application by a party to a marriage a county court shall have jurisdiction to grant an injunction containing one or more of the following provisions, namely,—(*a*) a provision restraining the other party to the marriage from molesting the applicant; (*b*) a provision restraining the other party from molesting a child living with the applicant; (*c*) a provision excluding the other party from the matri-

B   monial home or a part of the matrimonial home or from a specified area in which the matrimonial home is included; (*d*) a provision requiring the other party to permit the applicant to enter and remain in the matrimonial home or a part of the matrimonial home; whether or not any other relief is sought in the proceedings. (2) Subsection (1) above shall apply to a man and a woman who are living with

C   each other in the same household as husband and wife as it applies to the parties to a marriage and any reference to the matrimonial home shall be construed accordingly."

I am in agreement with your Lordships that upon the facts that I have summarised the county court judge had jurisdiction to grant an injunction excluding Mr. Johnson temporarily from the flat of which he

D   and Miss Davis were joint tenants. I reach this conclusion notwithstanding that, in disagreement with your Lordships, I remain unpersuaded that section 1 (2) bears the broader meaning rather than the narrower one. As my opinion that the narrower meaning is to be preferred will not prevail I shall resist the temptation to add to or elaborate upon the reasons given by Bridge L.J. in *B.* v. *B.* [1978] 2 W.L.R. 160 for that

E   preference. There are, however, two initial matters of more general application to the interpretation of statutes that arise out of the judgment of the Court of Appeal. Upon these I wish to comment.

I have had the advantage of reading what my noble and learned friends Viscount Dilhorne and Lord Scarman have to say about the use of Hansard as an aid to the construction of a statute. I agree with them entirely and would add a word of warning against drawing too facile an analogy

F   between proceedings in the Parliament of the United Kingdom and those travaux préparatoires which may be looked at by the courts of some of our fellow member states of the European Economic Community to resolve doubts as to the interpretation of national legislation or by the European Court of Justice, and consequently by English courts themselves, to resolve doubts as to the interpretation of Community legislation. Com-

G   munity legislation viz. Regulations and Directives, are required by the Treaty of Rome to state reasons on which they are based, and when submitted to the Council in the form of a proposal by the Commission the practice is for them to be accompanied by an explanatory memorandum by the Commission expanding the reasons which appear in more summary form in the draft Regulation or Directive itself. The explanatory memoranda are published in the Official Journal together with the proposed

H   Regulations or Directives to which they relate. These are true travaux préparatoires; they are of a very different character from what is said in the passion or lethargy of parliamentary debate; yet a survey of the judgments of the European Court of Justice will show how rarely that court refers even to these explanatory memoranda for the purpose of interpreting Community legislation.

A closer analogy with travaux préparatoires is to be found in reports of such bodies as the Law Commissions and committees or commissions

The Weekly Law Reports, March 31, 1978

564

Lord Diplock   Davis v. Johnson (H.L.(E.))   [1978]

appointed by government or by either House of Parliament to consider   A
reforming particular branches of the law.   Where legislation follows upon
a published report of this kind the report may be used as an aid to identify
the mischief which the legislation is intended to remedy; but not for the
purpose of construing the enacting words in such a way as to conform
with recommendations made in the report as to the form the remedy
should take: *Black-Clawson International Ltd.* v. *Papierwerke Waldhof-
Aschaffenburg A.G.* [1975] A.C. 591.   This does not mean, of course,   B
that one must shut one's eyes to the recommendations, for a suggestion as
to a remedy may throw light on what the mischief itself is thought to be;
but it does not follow that Parliament when it legislates to remedy the
mischief has adopted in their entirety or, indeed, at all the remedies
recommended in the report.

This is well illustrated in the instant case.   The report on which the   C
Domestic Violence and Matrimonial Proceedings Act 1976 was undoubtedly
based is the Report of the Select Committee of the House of Commons on
Violence in Marriage published in July 1975 (H.C. 553/1).   It deals
almost exclusively with the plight of married women exposed to violence
by their husbands and resulting homelessness for themselves and their
children.   In the single paragraph referring to unmarried couples described
(regrettably I think) as " co-habitees," the members of the committee dis-   D
claim any particular knowledge of the problem, on which they had not
taken evidence.   Nevertheless they recommended that so far as the grant of
injunctions against violence by their paramours was concerned mistresses
should have the same procedural rights as married women.   As regards
homelessness of mistresses, however, all the committee recommended was
that the Guardianship of Minors Acts should be amended to provide that   E
where there was a child of the illicit union of which paternity could be
proved, the court should have power to make orders giving the mistress
while she was caring for the children during their minority sole right of
occupation of the premises which had been occupied by the unmarried
couple as their home.   Whatever section 1 (2) of the Act may do it does
not do that.

I conclude by explaining briefly my own reasons for dismissing this   F
appeal.   I understand your Lordships to agree in holding, as I myself
would hold, that subsection (1) leaves the substantive law relating to husbands and wives unchanged.   All that it does is to provide them with a
simpler, speedier, more widely available and more effective remedy for
threatened violation of legal rights either already existing when the Act
was passed or newly-created sections 3 and 4.   What I cannot accept is   G
that subsection (2), in contrast to subsection (1), was intended to change
the substantive law by authorising county court judges to make drastic
inroads upon the respective legal rights of parties to an illicit union to
occupy the premises in which they have been living together as man and
wife; yet without any statement in the subsection of the limits, if any, that
are imposed upon those inroads.   Nevertheless under the existing sub-   H
stantive law a mistress is entitled to protection against the tort of assault,
and if, as in the instant case, she is joint tenant with her paramour of the
premises in which she has been living with him, she has a legal right to
continue in peaceful occupation of them.   This latter right of hers is one
that he has no right to disturb, and his own corresponding right of occupation is one that can be lawfully exercised only in a manner that does not
interfere with it.   Where the county court judge is satisfied that there is

The Weekly Law Reports, March 31, 1978

2 W.L.R.   **Davis v. Johnson (H.L.(E.))**   **Lord Diplock**

A grave danger that if the mistress returns to the premises her paramour will assault her or her child then, as ancillary to an injunction against threatened violence, the judge would, in my view, have jurisdiction to make an order under section 1 (1) (c) excluding him from the premises; but such an order could properly continue only so long as there was danger that if permitted to return he would assault his mistress or her child.

B It is the mistress's legal right under a joint tenancy to continue in occupation of the premises that distinguishes the instant case from *B.* v. *B.* [1978] 2 W.L.R. 160. The same distinction could have been drawn in *Cantliff* v. *Jenkins* [1978] 2 W.L.R. 177, which, for this reason, I think was wrongly decided.

For these reasons I too would dismiss this appeal.

C VISCOUNT DILHORNE. My Lords, the result of this appeal depends on the meaning and effect of section 1 of the Domestic Violence and Matrimonial Proceedings Act 1976. Its terms must be considered against the background of the Matrimonial Homes Act 1967, which conferred on a spouse not entitled to occupy a dwelling house by virtue of any estate or interest or contract or enactment, the right, if in occupation, not to be

D evicted or excluded from it by the other spouse except with the leave of the court, and the right, if not in occupation, with the leave of the court to enter into and occupy it. Section 1 (2) of that Act provided that so long as one spouse had rights of occupation, either of the spouses might apply to the court for an order " declaring, enforcing, restricting or terminating those rights or regulating the exercise by either spouse of the right to occupy the dwelling house " and section 1 (3) provided that on an

E application under the section the court might make such order as it thought just and reasonable having regard to the conduct of the spouses toward each other, to their financial resources and the needs of the children.

In *Tarr* v. *Tarr* [1973] A.C. 254 it was held that this section did not give the court power to prohibit, though it gave power to regulate, the occupation of the matrimonial home by a spouse legally entitled to occupy

F it. Lord Pearson in the course of his opinion, with which the other members of the House agreed, pointed out that if the Act enabled a court to prohibit the occupation by a tenant of his house, it made "a very drastic inroad into the common law rights of the property-owning spouse." He said, at p. 264:

    " According to a well-established principle of construction, an inter-
G   pretation which has this effect ought not to be adopted unless the
    enactment plainly bears that meaning. That principle has to be set
    against the possible practical advantages of a liberal interpretation
    which may support its claims to be the reasonable interpretation. In
    the end one has to read the enactment in its context and come to a
    conclusion as to what it means."

H That drastic inroad into the common law rights of property has now been made by the amendment of section 1 (2) of that Act by section 3 of the Domestic Violence and Matrimonial Proceedings Act 1976, which came into force in June 1977. Since then, as a result of the amendments made, a spouse can get an order excluding the other spouse from the matrimonial home even though that spouse is the owner or the tenant of it, and an order requiring that spouse to permit the spouse applying for the order, to enter and to remain in the home.

The Weekly Law Reports, March 31, 1978

566

Viscount Dilhorne   Davis v. Johnson (H.L.(E.))   [1978]

Section 1 of the Domestic Violence and Matrimonial Proceedings Act   A
has the marginal note " Matrimonial injunctions in the county court " and
subsection (1) begins with the words " Without prejudice to the jurisdiction
of the High Court " so the jurisdiction of the High Court is not affected.
Bridge L.J. in *B.* v. *B.* [1978] 2 W.L.R. 160 thought that if the section
altered the substantive law affecting parties' rights to occupy premises, it
would produce the astonishing result that the substantive law in the county
court was different from that to be applied in the High Court.   So far as   B
spouses are concerned, I do not think that the section in any way extends
the substantive law as now, since the amendment of the Act of 1967,
applied in the High Court.

It provides that a county court has jurisdiction to grant an injunction
containing the following provisions:

" (*a*) a provision restraining the other party to the marriage from   C
molesting the applicant; (*b*) a provision restraining the other party
from molesting a child living with the applicant; (*c*) a provision
excluding the other party from the matrimonial home or a part of
the matrimonial home or from a specified area in which the matrimonial home is included; (*d*) a provision requiring the other party to
permit the applicant to enter and remain in the matrimonial home or
a part of the matrimonial home; whether or not any other relief is   D
sought in the proceedings."

Injunctions restraining one spouse from molesting the other are and
were obtainable in the Family Division of the High Court and in the
county courts designated for divorce work; and, since this Act came into
force, there is power under the Matrimonial Homes Act 1967 to grant in
the High Court an injunction containing the provisions set out in (*c*) and   E
(*d*) above against a spouse who is the owner or tenant of the home.

So far as spouses are concerned, the changes made by section 1 are
that injunctions containing these provisions are made obtainable in any
county court: the requirement in the Family Division that proceedings
for divorce or judicial separation must be pending or an undertaking
given to start them is dispensed with; and, in relation to applications   F
for injunctions under the section, the requirement in the county court
that in addition to a claim for an injunction, there must be a claim for
some other relief is also dispensed with.

Subsection (2) of section 1 provides that subsection (1) shall apply to
a man and woman who are living with each other in the same household
as husband and wife as it applies to the parties to a marriage; and that
any reference to the matrimonial home shall be construed accordingly.   G
Their home, despite the fact that they are unmarried, is to be treated as
the matrimonial home.

It is in relation to the application of subsection (2) to subsection (1)
that difficulty has arisen.   Since June 1977, when the Act of 1976 came
into force, there have been three decisions of the Court of Appeal on it.
In the first of them *B.* v. *B.* [1978] 2 W.L.R. 160 Megaw, Bridge and   H
Waller L.JJ. held that subsection (1) did not give a county court power to
exclude from a council house a man who was the tenant of it at the
instance of the woman with whom he had been living.   In the second
Cantliff v. *Jenkins* [1978] 2 W.L.R. 177 Stamp, Orr and Ormrod L.JJ.
rightly held that they were bound by the decision in *B.* v. *B.* but made it
clear that if they had not been bound by it they would have reached the
same conclusion.

The Weekly Law Reports, March 31, 1978

567

2 W.L.R.   **Davis v. Johnson (H.L.(E.))**   **Viscount Dilhorne**

A   To hear the appeal in the present case a court of five was convened, a court described by Lord Denning M.R. as " a court of all the talents." Its members were Lord Denning M.R., Sir George Baker P., Goff, Shaw and Cumming-Bruce L.JJ. Lord Denning, the President and Shaw L.J. did not regard themselves as bound by the previous decisions of the court. They held that an injunction could be granted to an unmarried applicant excluding the man with whom she had been living from the occupation

B   of the premises of which he was with her a joint tenant. Goff L.J. would have joined with them had he not felt bound by the previous decisions; Cumming-Bruce L.J. agreed with the decisions in the earlier cases.

So seven eminent Lords Justices have come to one conclusion and Lord Denning M.R., Sir George Baker P. and two Lords Justices take the opposite view; and there is a division of opinion in the House. Few, if

C   any, sections of a modern Act can have given rise to so much litigation in so short a time and to such a difference of opinion. A few more words in the Act would have avoided all this litigation and I regard it as surprising, in view of the issue raised in *Tarr* v. *Tarr* [1973] A.C. 254, that it was not made clear beyond doubt whether or not a county court was to be enabled by subsection (1) of the Act to grant an injunction excluding a man at the instance of the woman with whom he had been living as if

D   she was his wife from the occupation of a house which he had a legal right to occupy or compelling him to allow her to enter into and remain in the house which he had and she had not a legal right to occupy. The Act of 1976 gives the same rights to an unmarried man as it does to an unmarried woman living in the same household as husband and wife, but as in the majority of cases it will be the woman who invokes the Act, I

E   propose to refer to her only.

It was held in *B.* v. *B.* [1978] 2 W.L.R. 160 that section 1 made no change in the substantive law. So far as spouses are concerned, as I have said, I agree that is the case. Not having changed the substantive law, it was held that it conferred no rights on an unmarried person coming within subsection (2): so an unmarried woman could only obtain an injunction

F   under subsection (1) (*c*) or (*d*) (excluding the man from the home or requiring him to permit her to enter and remain in it) to support a legal right she had apart from the section. In that case Mr. B., the tenant, had an indefeasible right as against Mrs. B. to continue in occupation by virtue of his tenancy and she had no legal right to occupy. In *Cantliff* v. *Jenkins* [1978] 2 W.L.R. 177, where, as in this case, the unmarried man and woman were joint tenants, Stamp L.J. said, at p. 181, that " Put in lay-

G   men's language, what it " (the section) " does is to confer a remedy to protect a right."

Violence is a form of molestation but molestation may take place without the threat or use of violence and still be serious and inimical to mental and physical health. Where, as here, violence was used, it was not disputed that an injunction restraining it could be granted. Where other

H   forms of molestation occur, it is probable that if it is of such a character that the court would be disposed to grant an injunction in respect of it, there would be a right of action for nuisance.

If, however, the views expressed in *B.* v. *B.*, in *Cantliff* v. *Jenkins* and by Cumming-Bruce L.J. in the present case are right, it means that an unmarried woman, no matter the degree of violence or other molestation threatened or used, will not be entitled to obtain an injunction excluding a man from what has been their home or one requiring him to allow her

The Weekly Law Reports, March 31, 1978

568

Viscount Dilhorne   Davis v. Johnson (H.L.(E.))   [1978]

to enter and remain in it if he is the owner or tenant and she has no legal **A**
right to be there. A battered wife can get such injunctions; a battered
mistress to whom subsection (2) applies will not be able to do so unless
she has a legal right to be in the home. The vast majority of women to
whom subsection (2) is intended to apply will have no such rights and so
to interpret the section means that an unmarried woman is not given the
same rights as a married one.

An injunction to exclude the man from the premises may be necessary **B**
to protect the woman from violence and molestation but I do not see how
an injunction requiring him to permit her to enter and remain in the
house can be linked with protection from violence or molestation.

Our task is to give effect to the intention of Parliament if that can be
seen from the language of the statute. Here the language is clear and
unambiguous and Parliament's intention apparent. Unmarried persons **C**
living together in the same household as husband and wife are for the
purposes of section 1 (1) to be treated as if they were married. The
unmarried woman to whom subsection (2) applies is to have the same
rights as a married woman. A county court judge in the exercise of his
discretion can grant an injunction excluding a husband from the home or
requiring him to permit her to enter and remain there whether or not she **D**
has been subjected to or threatened with violence or molestation. In my
opinion subsection (2) entitles him to grant one to an unmarried woman
if he would grant it were she married, if the circumstances warrant it and
whether or not she has been threatened or molested. Just as a married
woman can be protected from eviction from the matrimonial home, so
can an unmarried woman coming within subsection (2) be protected from
eviction from what has been her home, it may be for a long time. A man **E**
who has been living with a woman as his wife in the same household may
suddenly tell her to leave and she without violence or molestation may
leave and become homeless. He may not say anything but just change
the locks on the house when she is out and refuse to admit her. In such
cases I do not doubt that it was Parliament's intention to protect her and
in my opinion a county court judge now has power to do so. **F**

To hold that protection can only be given if she has property rights is
to differentiate between married women and unmarried women to whom
subsection (1) is intended to apply and would in my opinion frustrate
the intention of Parliament. Subsection (1) is not concerned with property
rights. Injunctions granted under it can interfere with the enjoyment of
such rights, as I have said. In this case and in *Cantliff* v. *Jenkins* [1978]
2 W.L.R. 177 the man and woman were joint tenants but the fact that the **G**
woman is a joint tenant in my opinion makes no difference to and does
not affect her rights under the subsection. It was not intended to provide
a means for the enforcement of property rights but to give protection from
domestic violence and from eviction. Reliance should not be placed on it
for the enforcement of property rights. If an injunction has been granted
under subsection (1) (c) or (d), it is, I think, inconceivable that an order **H**
for possession should be made in favour of the man if he is the owner or
tenant who has been living with her in the premises as his wife while the
injunction is in force.

I recognise that to give effect to that intention, means that an unmarried
woman may get an injunction in a county court unobtainable by her in the
High Court, an injunction excluding the man from premises of which he is
the tenant or owner and to which she has no legal right, and an injunction

The Weekly Law Reports, March 31, 1978

2 W.L.R.   Davis v. Johnson (H.L.(E.))   Viscount Dilhorne

A   entitling her to enter into and remain in premises which, if such an injunction is not granted, he or she would have no right to occupy. But it is within the competence of Parliament so to provide and in my opinion Parliament has done so, in clear and unmistakable language. By amending the Matrimonial Homes Act 1967, it has made a drastic inroad into the common law rights of the property owning spouse. By section 1 it has also made a drastic inroad into the exercise of the common law rights of
B   the owner or tenant of the home who has been living there with another person as husband and wife though unmarried.

In *Cantliff* v. *Jenkins* Stamp L.J. posed the question: How long would such an injunction last? He thought that as a practical matter it would be equivalent to a transfer of property. With great respect I do not agree. Such an injunction will not affect the legal rights to the home. It will, or
C   may, interfere with the enjoyment of those rights.

As I see it the main purpose of section 1 was to facilitate applications by those for whose benefit it was enacted, for the speedy grant of orders protecting them from molestation and from being immediately evicted from the home in which, it may be, they had lived for many years. In *B.* v. *B.* [1978] 2 W.L.R. 160 the parties had been living together for 10 years. Its purpose was the provision of immediate relief not permanent resolution
D   of the situation arising on the break-up of a marriage or an association where the parties though unmarried had been living as if they were.

It will be within the discretion of the county court judge to decide whether an injunction should be granted and to decide how long it shall operate. It would obviously be terminated should spouses be reconciled. In the case of spouses it might be followed by an application under the
E   Matrimonial Homes Act 1967 and it may be that a county court judge in the exercise of his discretion would grant an injunction till further order and would make it clear that it would lapse if no application was made under that Act and if such an application was made, only continued until an order had been made under it.

In the case of unmarried persons where the injunction excludes the
F   party who has property rights from his home or permits the party with no property rights to occupy it, a county court judge might think it right to make it clear that the injunction is to be of a temporary character to enable both parties to regulate their affairs. It appears that in this case the council granted the tenancy of the flat on account of the respondent's and her child's housing needs, and that she and the appellant became joint tenants of it at his instance and after she and the child had been living there
G   without him for some three months. If this be so, then the council might have been willing to grant her the tenancy alone and, in view of what has happened, may now be disposed to terminate the joint tenancy and give her the sole tenancy; and the county court judge may think that the injunction should only continue until the council has dealt with the matter.

Were it not for what my noble and learned friend Lord Diplock has said
H   with regard to the departure from precedent made by the majority of the Court of Appeal in the present case, I would have felt it necessary to write at some length on the question whether the Court of Appeal is entitled not to follow an earlier decision of that court which is not distinguishable. My noble and learned friend has dealt so fully with that, and I am in such complete agreement with what he has said that it is not necessary for me to do so.

That question was conclusively, and one would have hoped finally,

The Weekly Law Reports, March 31, 1978

570

Viscount Dilhorne   Davis v. Johnson (H.L.(E.))   [1978]

settled by the decision in *Young* v. *Bristol Aeroplane Co. Ltd.* [1944] K.B.   **A**
718, a court indeed of all the talents consisting as it did of Lord Greene
M.R., Scott, MacKinnon, Luxmore, Goddard and du Parcq L.JJ.

Since then one new factor has arisen and I wish to add a few observations with regard to that.   Prior to 1966 this House treated earlier decisions
made by it which were not distinguishable as binding.   It was left to
Parliament to amend the law laid down by the earlier decisions if in the
light of modern conditions it was felt that that decision should no longer   **B**
be followed.   Owing to pressure on Parliamentary time this sometimes led
to no action being taken or on its being taken only after long delay.

In 1966 consideration was given to whether as a matter of law this
House was bound to follow its earlier decision.   After considerable discussion it was agreed that it was not, and so the announcement to which
my noble and learned friend refers was made.   " If the House of Lords is   **C**
not bound by its previous decision, why should we be? " so the argument
runs, an argument that could be advanced in every court of record in the
land, but an argument which ignores the unique character of the House
of Lords sitting judicially.   It is a character not possessed by any other
court and herein lies the fallacy in the argument.   This House is not bound
by any previous decision to which it may have come.   It can, if it wishes,
reach a contrary conclusion.   This is so whether or not the House is sitting   **D**
to discharge its judicial functions.   That is the ground on which those who
were parties to the announcement made in 1966 felt, I think, that it could
be made without impropriety.   It is not a ground available to any other
court and the fact that this House made that announcement is consequently
no argument which can properly be advanced to support the view that the
Court of Appeal or any other court has similar liberty of action.   **E**

There is one other matter to which I must refer.   It is a well and long
established rule that counsel cannot refer to Hansard as an aid to the
construction of statute.   What is said by a Minister or by a member
sponsoring a Bill is not a legitimate aid to the interpretation of an Act:
see *Craies on Statute Law*, 7th ed. (1971), pp. 128–129.   As Lord Reid
said in *Beswick* v. *Beswick* [1968] A.C. 58, 73–74:   **F**

" In construing any Act of Parliament we are seeking the intention
of Parliament and it is quite true that we must deduce that intention
from the words of the Act. . . .   For purely practical reasons we do
not permit debates in either House to be cited: it would add greatly
to the time and expense involved in preparing cases involving the
construction of a statute if counsel were expected to read all the debates   **G**
in Hansard, and it would often be impracticable for counsel to get
access to at least the older reports of debates in Select Committees
of the House of Commons; moreover, in a very large proportion of
cases such a search, even if practicable, would throw no light on the
question before the court."

If it was permissible to refer to Hansard, in every case concerning the   **H**
construction of a statute counsel might regard it as necessary to search
through the Hansards of all the proceedings in each House to see if in
the course of them anything relevant to the construction had been said.
If it was thought that a particular Hansard had anything relevant in it
and the attention of the court was drawn to it, the court might also think
it desirable to look at the other Hansards.   The result might be that
attention was devoted to the interpretation of ministerial and other state-

The Weekly Law Reports, March 31, 1978

2 W.L.R.   **Davis v. Johnson (H.L.(E.))**   **Viscount Dilhorne**

A ments in Parliament at the expense of consideration of the language in which Parliament had thought to express its intention.

   While, of course, anyone can look at Hansard, I venture to think that it would be improper for a judge to do so before arriving at his decision and before this case I have never known that done. It cannot be right that a judicial decision should be affected by matter which a judge has seen but to which counsel could not refer on which counsel
B had no opportunity to comment.

   For the reasons I have stated I would dismiss this appeal.

   LORD KILBRANDON. My Lords, it is a sad paradox that human brutality should be disclosed so plainly in domestic relationships into which a man and a woman have voluntarily entered. Recently some
C enterprising journalist has christened the problem " battered wives," as if he had uncovered a modern tendency, a recent development in wickedness and indeed Lord Denning M.R. [1978] 2 W.L.R. 182, 187, says that the phrase " was invented to call the attention of the public to an evil. Few were aware of it." In many more humble circles the practice was only too familiar, and to anyone who has sat as a divorce judge, at any rate, none of the stories told in the public press can have come as a
D surprise. They are instances of what had long been matter of common knowledge. In 1975 the House of Commons set up a Select Committee to consider, inter alia, " the extent, nature and causes of the problems of families where there is violence between the partners or where children suffer non-accidental injury." These words, it is hardly necessary to point out, are wide enough to include families in which the parties are un-
E married and the children illegitimate. I did not intend to refer to the Report of the Select Committee further than to say that I agree with the opinion of my noble and learned friend Lord Diplock as to the notice which may in general be taken of such reports in judicial proceedings.

   In the following Session a Bill, which became the Domestic Violence and Matrimonial Proceedings Act 1976, was introduced by a private
F member into the House of Commons. It may be, I do not know, that the matters it dealt with were deemed to be of such urgency that the usual researches, necessary to anticipate and deal with all contingencies likely to attend reform of a complicated branch of the law, were omitted or abridged. However that may be, in the short life-time of the Act the problem now before your Lordships arising out of one of its provisions has had to be considered by 16 Lords Justices and Lords of Appeal, of
G whom 8 have taken one view of the meaning of the Act and 8 an opposite view.

   As regards married couples and their families, sections 3 and 4 make certain provisions amending and clarifying the Matrimonial Homes Act 1967, and need not be further referred to. By sections 1 and 2 the scope of the rights of married persons, on behalf of themselves or their children,
H to obtain the protection of the court in the event of molestation, violence, or unlawful denial of the right of a spouse, arising from status, to access to and occupation of the matrimonial home, is enlarged. Besides exercising these rights in a matrimonial suit, or on an undertaking that a matrimonial suit is in preparation, a summary application may be made to *any* county court for an injunction containing one or more of the provisions set out in section 1, and in certain circumstances the court may, under section 2, buttress that injunction by attaching a power to

The Weekly Law Reports, March 31, 1978

572

Lord Kilbrandon   **Davis v. Johnson (H.L.(E.))**   **[1978]**

arrest the party complained of. Such an application may be made, A
contrary to the general rule of practice, " whether or not any other relief
is sought in the proceedings." So far no difficulty arises.

It is, however, notorious, as the terms of reference of the Select Committee indicate, that the problems of violence, molestation and denial of
proper accommodation are by no means confined to families in which the
parties are married. Unmarried women and illegitimate children are just
as much at risk. It is in my opinion quite plain that the intention of B
Parliament was to give them some protection. For that purpose section
1 (2) provided that the subsection conferring power on the county court
to grant injunctions in the case of married persons:

> " shall apply to a man and a woman who are living with each other
> in the same household as husband and wife as it applies to the
> parties to a marriage and any reference to the matrimonial home C
> shall be construed accordingly."

It is unfortunate that this has been described, in popular language, as an
attempt to protect " battered mistresses." The English language is poor
in this context. " Mistress," having lost its respectable if not reverential
significance, came to mean a woman installed, in a clandestine way, by
someone of substance, normally married, for his intermittent sexual D
enjoyment. This class of woman, if indeed she still exists, is not dealt
with by the Act of 1976 at all. The subsection was included for the
protection of families—households in which a man and a woman either
do or do not bring up children—the man and the woman being, for
whatever reason, unmarried. The Act says in so many words that in
such a case the woman is to have a " matrimonial home " in so far as E
the provisions of sections 1 and 2 of the Act are concerned, and as
regards her home she is to have the same protections, and the same power
to apply to the county court for them, including an order for arrest, as
has her married sister. I do not know a single English word which will
accurately describe the unmarried housewife, but that is what Parliament
is talking about.

Coming to the interpretation of the Act as it applies to the facts of the F
instant case, I will begin by saying that I have read in draft the speeches
prepared by my noble and learned friends Lord Salmon and Lord Scarman,
and that I entirely agree with them. The difficulty which has given rise
to so much difference of judicial opinion is this. It is plain, as I have
tried to point out, that married persons get nothing out of sections 1 and
2 of the Act except, first, access to the summary powers of any county G
court, second, the relaxation of the rule as to " any other relief," and,
third, the supplementary weapon of arrest. No legal rights are conferred,
in the sense of causes of action giving rise to judicial remedies. The
benefits are described, quite fairly, as procedural. If, then, it is said on
behalf of the appellant, no causes of action are made available to married
persons, neither are they to the unmarried. Since unmarried persons did
not have the relevant statutory protection equivalent to that enjoyed by H
married persons, namely the right of one to restrain the other from entering the matrimonial home, even when that other is joint or sole tenant,
and they cannot be said to have acquired it in virtue merely of an
enlargement of available procedures, this application should have been
dismissed, since the statute provides the respondent with no means of
overriding the property right of the other joint tenant. The supposed
protection of unmarried women under this Act accordingly turns out to

The Weekly Law Reports, March 31, 1978

A   be largely illusory since it amounts to no more than procedural advantages available to a woman who has the sole right of occupation, whether as owner or tenant, of what the statute calls her "matrimonial home." This, in the social conditions with which we are all familiar, must be a rare bird indeed.

I can readily appreciate the intellectual force of the appellant's argument. On the other hand I must decline to hold that Parliament decreed

B   a trifling and illusory remedy for a known disgraceful mischief, and to hold it in the interest of the conceptual purity of the law. Leaving that interest aside, the plain fact is that the Act of 1976 has authorised county courts to give one married person an injunction excluding from the matrimonial home the other, saying nothing about the property rights of either, and that that authority applies to a household where the parties are not

C   married to one another "as it applies" to one where they are. That is sufficient for the disposal of this case.

In *Inland Revenue Commissioners* v. *Ayrshire Employers Mutual Insurance Association Ltd.* [1946] 1 All E.R. 637 it was given as an adequate ground of decision that "The legislature has plainly missed fire": *per* Lord Macmillan at p. 641. Whether that metaphor leads to a rational interpretation of statutes may nowadays be doubted, but certainly

D   it would be an inevitable commentary on a decision in favour of the appellant. The intention of the legislature is plain from the language used. The fact that that language also leads to legal difficulties, and that the intention could well have been expressed in language which did not, should not affect the result.

My Lords, I do not find it necessary to add anything to what has been

E   said by my noble and learned friends on the subjects of the handling of precedents by the Court of Appeal, and of judicial reference to the Parliamentary debates. I entirely agree with their opinions.

I would dismiss this appeal.

LORD SALMON. My Lords, the Domestic Violence and Matrimonial

F   Proceedings Act 1976 appears to have been hurried through Parliament to provide urgently needed first aid for "battered wives," about whom there had been a great deal of publicity. They included a lawfully wedded woman living with her husband in their home and also an unmarried woman, commonly but not very appropriately referred to as a "common law wife," living with her paramour in the equivalent of a matrimonial home. I do not consider that there is any ambiguity about the Act and I

G   have no doubt that it will afford much needed first aid to many married and unmarried women. I regret that the Act omits a clause regulating the duration of the aid it affords in relation to the occupancy of the matrimonial home by an unmarried woman. Such a clause could easily have removed the difficulties which I think may well arise under the Act in its present form and to which I shall return later. Section 1 of the

H   Act reads as follows:

"1. (1) Without prejudice to the jurisdiction of the High Court, on an application by a party to a marriage a county court shall have jurisdiction to grant an injunction containing one or more of the following provisions, namely, (*a*) a provision restraining the other party to the marriage from molesting the applicant; (*b*) a provision restraining the other party from molesting a child living with the applicant; (*c*) a provision excluding the other party from the matrimonial home

The Weekly Law Reports, March 31, 1978

574

Lord Salmon   **Davis v. Johnson (H.L.(E.))**   [1978]

or a part of the matrimonial home or from a specified area in which   A
the matrimonial home is included; (*d*) a provision requiring the other
party to permit the applicant to enter and remain in the matrimonial
home or a part of the matrimonial home; whether or not any other
relief is sought in the proceedings. (2) Subsection (1) above shall
apply to a man and a woman who are living with each other in the
same household as husband and wife as it applies to the parties to a
marriage and any reference to the matrimonial home shall be   B
construed accordingly."

I have no doubt that the opening words of section 1 (1) "Without
prejudice to the jurisdiction of the High Court" refer to two things:
first to the jurisdiction of the High Court to grant injunctions restraining
violence. The word "molesting" in section 1 (1) (*a*) and (*b*) certainly
includes acts and threats of violence. They no doubt cover a multitude   C
of other things which I will not attempt to enumerate. When an injunction is granted under (*a*) or (*b*), it will, I think almost invariably be in
respect of acts or threats of violence or possibly sometimes in respect of
nuisance. In any event, I cannot think of anything in respect of which
the county court would grant an injunction under (*a*) or (*b*) which the
High Court would not also have jurisdiction to grant.   D

Secondly, the opening words of section 1 (1) in my view, also refer to
the jurisdiction of the High Court under section 1 (2) of the Matrimonial
Homes Act 1967 (as amended by sections 3 and 4 of the Act of 1976) (*a*)
to prohibit, suspend or restrict the exercise by either spouse of the right
to occupy the matrimonial home or (*b*) to require either spouse to permit
the exercise by the other of that right. A similar jurisdiction is conferred
on the county courts by section 1 (1) (*c*) and (*d*) of the Act of 1976. It   E
follows therefore that section 1 (1) effected no change in the substantive
law relating to husbands and wives. All it did was to enable them to
obtain the same kind of redress from the county court as they could have
obtained from the High Court and (having regard to the closing words
of section 1 (1)) to obtain it without seeking any other relief. If the
Family Division makes an order under section 1 (2) of the Act of 1967   F
(as amended) or the county court makes an order under section 1 (1) (*c*)
or (*d*) of the Act of 1976 prohibiting a spouse, say the husband or paramour, who is the freeholder or tenant of the matrimonial home from
occupying it and permitting his wife or mistress to do so, that order whilst
it remains in force would be a complete answer to an action in the Queen's
Bench Division by the freeholder or tenant to enforce his proprietary
rights by ejecting his wife so that he may re-enter into possession himself.   G

In my opinion, it by no means follows that because section 1 (1)
involves no alteration in substantive law, section 1 (2) does not. The
latter subsection is very short and equally clear. It has been said that its
meaning is as plain as a pikestaff. I agree. If one were in any doubt
about it, it would only be necessary to strike out of section 1 (1) the words
"on an application by a party to a marriage" and substitute the words   H
"on an application by a man or a woman who are living with each other
in the same household as husband and wife": and perhaps in order to
tidy up the section also to strike out the words "to the marriage" in
paragraph (*a*) of section 1 (1).

The whole purpose of the Act was to afford some protection to
"battered wives," married or unmarried. And to the unmarried ones in
particular. The married already had the very full protection afforded by

The Weekly Law Reports, March 31, 1978

A the Act of 1967. The unmarried did not. The married gained little from
the Act of 1976 save a quicker and cheaper method of obtaining protection and also the power of arrest attached to an injunction granted under
section 2 of the Act. To my mind, the principal object of section 1 (1)
(c) and (d) combined with section 1 (2) was to allow the battered so called
" common law wife " safely to occupy the " matrimonial home " for a
fairly short period in which to find other accommodation for herself and
B her children if she had any. I do not think that a county court judge
could properly exclude the paramour from his home or its environs under
section 1 (1) (c) unless he had been guilty of serious molestation likely to
expose the so called " common law wife or her children " to serious danger
or intolerable conditions whilst he remained there. Nor do I think that the
county court would or could properly make an order under section 1 (1)
C (d) unless it was satisfied that the common law wife had been driven from
the home by serious molestation or locked out of the home without reasonable justification. It also seems unlikely to me that the county court judge
would, save in exceptional cases, make an order under section 1 (1) (d)
without also making an order under section 1 (1) (c).

In my view, Parliament in passing this Act, was not concerned with the
preservation of proprietary rights but with affording protection to " battered
D wives " by giving them the chance of finding fresh accommodation in
safety when the husband or paramour had made life in the matrimonial
home intolerable, impossible or dangerous.

More often than not, the man is the tenant or owner of the home. If in
the case of an unmarried couple he is immune under section 1 (2) from the
provisions of section 1 (1) (c) and (d) and under section 2 (2) from the
E provisions of section 2 (1) (c), what I regard as being the chief purpose of
the Act will be defeated. This is why I do not think that Parliament
intended any wider construction than that which I have already postulated
to be put upon the opening words of section 1 (1). The wider construction
of the opening words of section 1 postulates that they are intended to
include a power of the High Court to eject a man's wife or so called
" common law wife " from the matrimonial home, if the husband or para-
F mour is the owner or tenant of the premises. I reject that construction
because as I have already indicated it would defeat the obvious purpose of
the Act. Ample scope, in my view, is given to the opening words of
section 1 if they are confined to the meanings I have suggested.

The proposition initiated by Bridge L.J. in *B.* v. *B.* [1978] 2 W.L.R.
160 and adopted by many other eminent judges that the wider construction
G should be put upon those opening words because in cases in which the so
called common law wife is the tenant or the owner of the home, she will
still have the benefit of section 1 (1) (c) and (d) and of section 2 (1) (c)
does not appeal to me—firstly because I think that there are very few
women in cases of this kind who are the tenants or owners of the matrimonial home, and secondly because when they are, they have no need to
H rely on the Act of 1976 for protection. They would be entitled to bring
an action for ejectment against the paramour to which there could be no
defence.

To return to the case where the paramour is the tenant or owner of the
home. I am certain that the Act of 1976 was not intended to deprive him
of his proprietary rights in his flat or house but only to interfere for a
fairly short period with his occupation of his home whilst his former
mistress had an opportunity to look for other accommodation. In *Cantliff*

The Weekly Law Reports, March 31, 1978

576

Lord Salmon   **Davis v. Johnson (H.L.(E.))**   [1978]

v. *Jenkins* [1978] 2 W.L.R. 177, Stamp L.J. asked the very pertinent   A
question "For how long?" It is a pity that the Act did not regulate the
period in which he could be deprived of occupation and his former mistress
allowed to enjoy it. I could hope that Parliament may consider amending
the Act by specifying such a period or, perhaps better still, laying down
principles upon which its duration may be calculated. In the meantime
the period is entirely in the discretion of a multitude of county court
judges and there being nothing in the statute to guide them in the exercise   B
of that discretion, it might be exercised with a considerable amount of
discrepancy. I am sure, however, that those exercising the discretion will
understand that to make a final order for a maximum period would probably convert it into a minimum period. I would hesitantly express the view
that the best course would be to make an order for say a month with liberty
for both parties to apply. Much depends on the circumstances of each   C
case, but I find it difficult to believe that it could ever be fair, save in most
exceptional circumstances, to keep a man out of his own flat or house for
more than a few months. It must also be remembered that under the Act
the former mistress acquires no proprietary right in the premises in question
and there is nothing to prevent the man from selling or letting his own
property whenever he likes. But this would take a little while and would
accordingly prevent the former mistress from being thrown out without   D
giving her any breathing space in which to look for suitable accommodation. And this, I believe, is the major object which the Act sought to
achieve—first aid but not intensive care for "battered wives."

I would add a word about cases in which, as here, the premises in
question are held in common. There is no doubt that under the Act a
violent man may be excluded for a limited period from the "matrimonial   E
home." I cannot however agree that this exclusion can properly be made
to continue for as long as there is a danger that if he returns he will assault
his former mistress. This might well be for ever. I do not think that
the purpose of the Act is to punish the violent. Property held in common
need not be lived in by both owners: one could buy the other out or the
property could be sold and the proceeds divided between them. In the   F
absence of agreement the matter could be referred to the courts for decision.
In the present case, however, the flat is a council flat and I do not suppose
there is anything to sell. I expect that probably the council may bring
the joint tenancy to an end to decide to whom the flat shall be let. Having
regard to the learned county court judge's finding that the appellant who
was twice the respondent's age beat her frequently, on two occasions "used
violence of a horrifying nature," threatened to kill her and dump her in   G
the river and alternatively to chop her up with a chopper he kept under
the bed and then put her remains in the deep freeze, I should not be sur-
prised if the council after terminating the joint tenancy allowed the
respondent to remain in the flat as its sole tenant.

I entirely agree with your Lordships that in appeals in civil cases, the
Court of Appeal is bound by its own previous decisions subject to the   H
three exceptions laid down in *Young* v. *Bristol Aeroplane Co.* [1944]
K.B. 718. Although the balance of authority prior to 1944 supported that
rule, there had been a number of dicta and decisions of the Court of Appeal
(alluded to by Lord Denning M.R.) which had rejected it. That is why
the appeal in the *Bristol Aeroplane Co.* case was heard by Lord Greene
M.R. and five out of the eight Lords Justices who then sat regularly in
that court.

The Weekly Law Reports, March 31, 1978

2 W.L.R.   Davis v. Johnson (H.L.(E.))   Lord Salmon

A   Ever since 1944, this rule has been applied by the Court of Appeal except in the instant case. Your Lordships' House on a number of occasions (once before and three times after 1944) has confirmed the application of the rule to decisions of the Court of Appeal, and has thereby greatly strengthened the rule. In the nature of things however, the point could never come before your Lordships' House for decision or form part of its ratio decidendi. This House decides every case that comes before it
B   according to the law. If, as in the instant case, the Court of Appeal decides an appeal contrary to one of its previous decisions, this House, much as it may deprecate the Court of Appeal's departure from the rule, will nevertheless dismiss the appeal if it comes to the conclusion that the decision appealed against was right in law.

    I am afraid that I disagree with Lord Denning M.R. when he says that
C   the Court of Appeal is not absolutely bound by its own decisions and may depart from them just as your Lordships may depart from yours. As my noble and learned friend Lord Diplock has pointed out, the announcement made in 1966 by Lord Gardiner L.C. about the future attitudes of this House towards precedent ended with the words: "This announcement is not intended to affect the use of precedent elsewhere than in this House."
D   I would also point out that that announcement was made with the un-animous approval of all the Law Lords: and that, by contrast, the over-whelming majority of the present Lords Justices have expressed the view that the principle of stare decisis still prevails and should continue to prevail in the Court of Appeal. I do not understand how, in these circumstances, it is even arguable that it does not.

    I sympathise with the views expressed on this topic by Lord Denning
E   M.R., but until such time, if ever, as all his colleagues in the Court of Appeal agree with those views, stare decisis must still hold the field. I think that this may be no bad thing. There are now as many as 17 Lords Justices in the Court of Appeal, and I fear that if stare decisis disappears from that court there is a real risk that there might be a plethora of conflicting decisions which would create a state of irremediable confusion
F   and uncertainty in the law. This would do far more harm than the occasional unjust result which stare decisis sometimes produces but which can be remedied by an appeal to your Lordships' House. I recognise, as Cumming-Bruce L.J. points out, that only those who qualify for legal aid or the very rich can afford to bring such an appeal. This difficulty could however be surmounted if when the Court of Appeal gave leave to
G   appeal from a decision it has felt bound to make by an authority with which it disagreed, it had a power conferred on it by Parliament to order the appellants' and/or the respondents' costs of the appeal to be paid out of public funds. This would be a very rare occurrence and the consequent expenditure of public funds would be minimal.

    I do not agree with the reasons given by Sir George Baker P. for departing from the rule in the *Bristol Aeroplane* case [1944] K.B. 718.
H   A high proportion of the decisions of the Court of Appeal turns upon the construction of statutes. The fact that the decision concerns a recent statute, is to my mind, irrelevant. Shaw L.J.'s decision however is based on the ground that the most exceptional and appalling facts of the present case were never in the contemplation of the Court of Appeal in the *Bristol Aeroplane* case; and I confess that I find the reasons on which he founded his decision very persuasive. I need not however express any opinion upon that judgment for I agree with my noble and learned

The Weekly Law Reports, March 31, 1978

578

Lord Salmon   Davis v. Johnson (H.L.(E.))   **[1978]**

friend Lord Diplock that the exception formulated by Shaw L.J. is what   A
may be termed a "one off" exception and that it is difficult to think of
any other statute to which it could apply. I therefore entirely agree with
your Lordships that the rule laid down in the *Bristol Aeroplane* case
binds the Court of Appeal.

I also agree that it has always been a well established and salutary rule
that Hansard can never be referred to by counsel in court and therefore
can never be relied on by the court in construing a statute or for any other   B
purpose. The reasons for this rule have been lucidly expressed by Lord
Reid in *Beswick* v. *Beswick* [1968] A.C. 58, 73, and also by my noble
and learned friend Lord Dilhorne in his speech in this appeal.

It is now well settled that when legislation follows upon the report
of a Select Committee, as e.g. the Act of 1976 followed upon the report
published in 1975 of the Select Committee of the House of Commons on   C
Violence in Marriage, it is permissible for the courts, when necessary, to
refer to the report as a guide to the mischief at which the Act was aimed.
Even for this purpose, however, such reports are sometimes uncertain
guides. They do not by any means always reveal the full mischief
which the Act is intended to remedy. In the present case for example,
the Select Committee devoted only one paragraph to unmarried couples.
They stated they had no real knowledge of this problem and had taken   D
no evidence about it. This is of little consequence because, in my view,
the Act itself makes the mischief at which it was aimed abundantly plain.
It seems to me that either before or as the Bill passed through Parliament,
it became clear to our legislators that the battered so called "common
law wives" were in dire need of legislative protection. I consider that
sections 1 and 2 of the Act unambiguously gave them this protection to   E
the extent I have described earlier in this speech; and clearly the meaning
of these sections cannot be altered by the report of the Select Committee.

My Lords, for the reasons I have stated, I would overrule *B.* v. *B.*
[1978] 2 W.L.R. 160 and *Cantliff* v. *Jenkins* [1978] 2 W.L.R. 177 and
dismiss the appeal.

LORD SCARMAN. My Lords, the central question in this appeal is as   F
to the construction of section 1 of the Domestic Violence and Matrimonial
Proceedings Act 1976. The section is as follows:

"1. (1) Without prejudice to the jurisdiction of the High Court, on
an application by a party to a marriage a county court shall have
jurisdiction to grant an injunction containing one or more of the
following provisions, namely,—(*a*) a provision restraining the other   G
party to the marriage from molesting the applicant; (*b*) a provision
restraining the other party from molesting a child living with the
applicant; (*c*) a provision excluding the other party from the matrimonial home or a part of the matrimonial home or from a specified
area in which the matrimonial home is included; (*d*) a provision
requiring the other party to permit the applicant to enter and remain   H
in the matrimonial home or a part of the matrimonial home; whether
or not any other relief is sought in the proceedings. (2) Subsection
(1) above shall apply to a man and a woman who are living with
each other in the same household as husband and wife as it applies
to the parties to a marriage and any reference to the matrimonial
home shall be construed accordingly."

A layman could be forgiven for thinking that the section was tailor-

The Weekly Law Reports, March 31, 1978

579

2 W.L.R.   Davis v. Johnson (H.L.(E.))   Lord Scarman

A made to enable a county court judge to make the order that was made in
this case. But in three cases reaching the Court of Appeal in the last few
months seven Lords Justices have taken a different view. They found
the section difficult and obscure. In *B.* v. *B.* [1978] 2 W.L.R. 160 the
court (Megaw, Bridge and Waller L.JJ.) accepted the submission that the
provisions of section 1 of the Act do not alter in any way the substantive
law affecting parties' rights to occupy premises and that, in considering
B the question whether relief can be granted under the section, the court
must consider the respective rights and obligations of the parties un-
affected by the provisions of the section. In the result, the court in
B. v. *B.* held that an unmarried woman could not obtain under the section
an order excluding from the home the man with whom she was living,
unless she could show that she had a right by the law of property to
C exclusive possession of the premises. In other words, while she could
get relief against molestation, as specified in subsection (1) (*a*) and (*b*),
she could not get an order enabling her to occupy the home under (*c*)
or (*d*) of the subsection.
    In *Cantliff* v. *Jenkins* [1978] 2 W.L.R. 177 another division in the
Court of Appeal followed this decision.
    In the present case a specially constituted five-judge bench of the
D Court of Appeal has by a majority (4 to 1) rejected the interpretation
put upon the section by the court in *B.* v. *B.* and has held that the full
range of relief set out in subsection (1), i.e., orders containing all or any
of the relief set out in (*a*), (*b*), (*c*) and (*d*) of the subsection, is available
to an unmarried woman, who can bring herself within subsection (2).
    For reasons which I shall briefly outline, I have reached the conclusion
E that the case of *B.* v. *B.* was wrongly decided. In my view the relief
specified in (*a*), (*b*), (*c*) and (*d*) of the subsection is available to an unmarried family partner. I would, therefore, dismiss the appeal.
    Jennifer Therese Davis, the respondent in this appeal, is 21 years old
and unmarried. She has a daughter who is now nearly 3 years old. The
father of her child is Nehemiah Johnson, the appellant. Miss Davis and the
F appellant lived together in the same household as man and wife for some
years. In 1977 the local council granted them the tenancy of a flat, 13
Nisbet House, Hackney. They were joint tenants. Because of the appellant's violence towards her, Miss Davis left home with her daughter on
September 18, 1977. She went to the Chiswick refuge for battered wives
maintained by Mrs. Pizzey. On October 11 she applied under section 1
of the Act of 1976 to the Brentford County Court for an order restraining
G the appellant from assaulting or molesting her, requiring him to vacate the
flat, and restraining him from entering it or coming within half a mile of
it. On October 18 the deputy circuit judge granted her an injunction
restraining the appellant from assaulting or molesting her or their daughter
and requiring him forthwith to vacate the flat and not to return. The
judge, being satisfied that the appellant had caused Miss Davis actual
bodily harm and being of the opinion that he was likely to do so again,
H attached, pursuant to section 2 of the Act, a power of arrest to the
injunction.
    The judge found that the violence and threats of violence, to which
Miss Davis had been subjected, were of a horrifying nature. He thought
that there was a real risk of further violence in the future and he had
regard to the uncomfortable and overcrowded living conditions at the
refuge to which she had fled when she left the flat.

The Weekly Law Reports, March 31, 1978

580

Lord Scarman   Davis v. Johnson (H.L.(E.))   [1978]

This was an order entirely appropriate to the circumstances of the case. A
More particularly, the exclusion of the appellant from the flat and the
prohibition upon his return were necessary to protect Miss Davis and her
child in their own home. The only question, therefore, is whether the
judge had jurisdiction to include in the injunction provisions excluding
the appellant from the flat and prohibiting his return.

The Act is a short one, its substance being contained in four sections.
Section 1 enables the county court to grant the injunctive relief specified B
in subsection (1), irrespective of whether the applicant is married or
unmarried. Section 2 enables a court which grants an injunction in matrimonial proceedings or under section 1 to add to it in certain circumstances
a power of arrest. Sections 3 and 4 amend the Matrimonial Homes Act
1967 so as to eliminate two weaknesses in that Act revealed by recent
judicial decisions. Section 5 declares the short title, commencement and C
extent of the Act. That is all there is to it.

Section 1 consists of two subsections. Subsection (1) enables a party
to a marriage to make application to a county court. It is without prejudice to the jurisdiction of the High Court and it empowers a county court
(any county court, whether or not invested with divorce jurisdiction) to
grant an injunction " whether or not any other relief is sought." Clearly D
the subsection provides a new remedy additional to, but not in substitution
for, what already exists in the law.

Subsection (2) enables an unmarried woman (or man) who is living
with a man (or woman) in the same household as husband and wife to
apply to the county court under subsection (1) and expressly provides that
reference in subsection (1) to the matrimonial home shall be construed as
a reference to the household in which they are living together. This refer- E
ence indicates to my mind that those provisions of subsection (1), which
make available to married people an injunction excluding the other party
from the matrimonial home and an injunction requiring the other party to
permit the applicant to enter and remain in the matrimonial home, are
intended to be available also to unmarried partners.

The availability of paragraphs (c) and (d) of subsection (1) to un- F
married partners without any express restriction to those who have a
property right in the house has an important bearing on the answer to
the question which I consider to be crucial to a correct understanding
of the scope of the section; i.e. what is the mischief for which Parliament
has provided the remedies specified in subsection (1)? It suggests strongly
that the remedies are intended to protect people, not property: for it is G
highly unlikely that Parliament could have intended by the sidewind of
subsection (2) to have introduced radical changes into the law of property.
Nor is it necessary so to construe the section. The personal rights of an
unmarried woman living with a man in the same household are very real.
She has his licence to be in the home, a right which in appropriate cases
the courts can and will protect: see *Winter Garden Theatre (London) Ltd.*
v. *Millennium Productions Ltd.* [1948] A.C. 173, *per* Viscount Simon at H
pp. 188–191; *Binions* v. *Evans* [1972] Ch. 359 *per* Lord Denning M.R.
at p. 367 and *Tanner* v. *Tanner* [1975] 1 W.L.R. 1346. She has also her
fundamental right to the integrity and safety of her person. And the
children living in the same household enjoy the same rights.

Bearing in mind the existence of these rights and the extent to which
they are endangered in the event of family breakdown, I conclude that
the mischief against which Parliament has legislated by section 1 of the

The Weekly Law Reports, March 31, 1978

581

2 W.L.R.   **Davis v. Johnson (H.L.(E.))**   **Lord Scarman**

A   Act may be described in these terms: —conduct by a family partner which puts at risk the security, or sense of security, of the other partner in the home. Physical violence, or the threat of it, is clearly within the mischief. But there is more to it than that. Homelessness can be as great a threat as physical violence to the security of a woman (or man) and her children. Eviction—actual, attempted or threatened—is, therefore, within the mis-chief: likewise, conduct which makes it impossible or intolerable, as in

B   the present case, for the other partner, or the children, to remain at home.

Where, in my opinion, the seven Lords Justices fell into error, is in their inference that because the section is not intended to give unmarried family partners rights which they do not already enjoy under existing property law it cannot be construed as conferring upon the county court the power to restrict or suspend the right of possession of the partner who

C   does have that right under the property law or to confer for a period a right of occupancy which overrides his right of possession. I find nothing illogical or surprising in Parliament legislating to over-ride a property right, if it be thought to be socially necessary. If in the result a partner with no property right who obtains an injunction under paragraph (c) or (d) thereby obtains for the period of the injunction a right of occupation,

D   so be it. It is no more than the continuance by court order of a right which previously she had by consent: and it will endure only for so long as the county court thinks necessary. Moreover, the restriction or suspen-sion for a time of property rights is a familiar aspect of much of our social legislation: the Rent Acts are a striking example. So far from being sur-prised, I would expect Parliament, when dealing with the mischief of domestic violence, to legislate in such a way that property rights would

E   not be allowed to undermine or diminish the protection being afforded. Accordingly I am unmoved by the arguments which influenced the Court of Appeal in *B.* v. *B.* [1978] 2 W.L.R. 160 and *Cantliff* v. *Jenkins* [1978] 2 W.L.R. 177. Nor do I find it surprising that this jurisdiction was given to the county court but not the High Court. The relief has to be avail-able immediately and cheaply from a local and easily accessible court.

F   Nor am I dismayed by the point that the section, while doing no more for married women than strengthen remedies for existing rights, confers upon an unmarried woman protection in her home including a right of occupation which can for a period over-ride the property rights of her family partner.

For these reasons, my conclusion is that section 1 of the Act is con-cerned to protect not property but human life and limb. But, while the

G   section is not intended to confer, and does not confer upon an unmarried woman property rights in the home, it does enable the county court to suspend or restrict her family partner's property right to possession and to preserve to her a right of occupancy (which owes its origin to her being in the home as his consort and with his consent) for as long as may be thought by the court to be necessary to secure the protection of herself

H   and the children.

How, then does the section fit into the law? First, the purpose of the section is not to create rights but to strengthen remedies. Subsection (2) does, however, confer upon the unmarried woman with no property in the home a new right. Though enjoying no property right to possession of the family home, she can apply to the county court for an order restricting or suspending for a time her family partner's right to possession of the premises and conferring upon her a limited right of occupancy. In most

The Weekly Law Reports, March 31, 1978

582

Lord Scarman   Davis v. Johnson (H.L.(E.))   [1978]

cases the period of suspension or restriction of his right and of her occupancy   **A**
will prove, I expect, to be brief. But in some cases this period may be a
lengthy one. The continuance of the order will, however, be a matter for
the discretion of the county court judge to be decided in the light of the
circumstances of the particular case.

Secondly, the section is concerned to regulate relations between the two
family partners. It does not, for instance, prevent the property owner from
disposing of his property. It does not confer upon an unmarried woman   **B**
any right of occupation of the family home comparable with that which
a married woman has and can protect against all the world under the
Matrimonial Homes Act 1967.

Thirdly, and most importantly, the grant of the order is in the discretion of the county court judge. It is for him to decide whether, and for
how long, it is necessary for the protection of the applicant or her child.   **C**
Normally he will make the order " until further order," each party having
the right to apply to the court for its discharge or modification. The
remedy is available to deal with an emergency; it is, as my noble and
learned friend, Lord Salmon has said, a species of first aid. The order
must be discontinued as soon as it is clear, upon the application of either
or both family partners, that it is no longer needed.   **D**

For these reasons I would dismiss the appeal. I have had the advant-
age of reading in draft the speeches of my noble and learned friends, Lord
Diplock and Viscount Dilhorne. I agree with what my Lord, Lord
Diplock, has said on the principle of stare decisis in the Court of Appeal.
I also agree with what my Lord, Viscount Dilhorne, has said on the use of
Parliamentary material in the interpretation of statutes, and would wish to
add only a few observations of my own.   **E**

There are two good reasons why the courts should refuse to have regard
to what is said in Parliament or by Ministers as aids to the interpretation
of a statute. First, such material is an unreliable guide to the meaning of
what is enacted. It promotes confusion, not clarity. The cut and thrust
of debate and the pressures of executive responsibility, essential features of
open and responsible government, are not always conducive to a clear and   **F**
unbiased explanation of the meaning of statutory language. And the volume
of Parliamentary and ministerial utterances can confuse by its very size.
Secondly, counsel are not permitted to refer to Hansard in argument. So
long as this rule is maintained by Parliament (it is not the creation of the
judges), it must be wrong for the judge to make any judicial use of proceedings in Parliament for the purposes of interpreting statutes.

In *Black-Clawson International Ltd.* v. *Papierwerke Waldhof-Aschaffen-*   **G**
burg A.G. [1975] A.C. 591 this House clarified the law on the use by the
courts of travaux préparatoires. Reports such as are prepared by the
Law Commission, by Royal Commissions, law reform bodies and Select
Committees of either House which lead to legislation may be read by the
courts to identify the mischief, including the weaknesses in the law, which
the legislation is intended to remedy or reduce. The difficulty, however,   **H**
remains that one cannot always be sure, without reference to proceedings
in Parliament which is prohibited, that Parliament has assessed the mischief
or understood the law in the same way as the reporting body. It may be
that, since membership of the European Communities has introduced into
our law a style of legislation (regulations having direct effect) which by
means of the lengthy recital (or preamble) identifies material to which resort
may be had in construing its provisions, Parliament will consider doing

The Weekly Law Reports, March 31, 1978

583

2 W.L.R.   **Davis v. Johnson (H.L.(E.))**   Lord Scarman

A   likewise in statutes where it would be appropriate, e.g. those based on a
report by the Law Commission, a Royal Commission, a departmental
committee, or other law reform body.

Appeal dismissed.

B   Solicitors: *Rose & Birn; Darlington & Parkinson.*

J. A. G.

C

[COURT OF APPEAL]

SHALLOW *v.* SHALLOW

1977   Oct. 6; 20   Stamp, Orr and Ormrod L.JJ.

D
*Husband and Wife — Financial provision — Financial position —
Supplementary benefit scale — Applicability of formula used
by Supplementary Benefits Commission when assessing contribution—Periodical payments order reducing husband below
supplementary benefit scale — Distinction between supplementary benefit scale and subsistence level*

E   The husband who was earning £62·44 net a week was
ordered by the registrar to pay sums totalling £30·50 a
week for the maintenance of his former wife and the two
children of the marriage. On appeal Judge Peck affirmed
the registrar's order holding that although the husband was
left with less than the "supplementary benefit scale," he
could afford the amount ordered by the registrar and the
wife clearly needed that amount.

F   On appeal by the husband:—
        Held, dismissing the appeal, that the supplementary benefit
scale, which was the product of a formula applied by the
Supplementary Benefits Commission in negotiating with liable
relatives the amount of their contributions towards the
support of their dependants, was altogether different from
the subsistence level; that under the formula the liable relative
would be allowed to retain one quarter of his net earnings
G   in addition to the amount of his rent and the amounts that
would be payable to him as supplementary benefit if he had
no other resources; whereas the subsistence level meant
approximately the current amount of supplementary benefit
appropriate to a single man or a man with dependants plus
a rent allowance; that, accordingly, the principle that orders
for maintenance or periodical payments should not reduce a
husband below the subsistence level did not apply to the
H   supplementary benefit scale and that as the result of applying the formula to the husband's earning would be to leave
him with about £15 a week above his subsistence level while
reducing the wife and children to about £2 a week below
theirs, the judge was right to reject that result.
        Smethurst v. *Smethurst* [1977] 3 W.L.R. 472, D.C. and
Ashley v. *Ashley* [1968] P. 582, D.C. considered.

[Reported by EVERARD CORBALLY, ESQ., Barrister-at-Law]

Appendix C
Treasure Act 1996

Treasure Act 1996

CHAPTER 24

ARRANGEMENT OF SECTIONS

ELIZABETH II   c. 24

Treasure Act 1996

1996 CHAPTER 24

An Act to abolish treasure trove and to make fresh provision in relation to treasure. [4th July 1996]

BE IT ENACTED by the Queen's most Excellent Majesty, by and with the advice and consent of the Lords Spiritual and Temporal, and Commons, in this present Parliament assembled, and by the authority of the same, as follows:—

Meaning of "treasure"

1.—(1) Treasure is—

  (a) any object at least 300 years old when found which—

      (i) is not a coin but has metallic content of which at least 10 per cent by weight is precious metal;

      (ii) when found, is one of at least two coins in the same find which are at least 300 years old at that time and have that percentage of precious metal; or

      (iii) when found, is one of at least ten coins in the same find which are at least 300 years old at that time;

  (b) any object at least 200 years old when found which belongs to a class designated under section 2(1);

  (c) any object which would have been treasure trove if found before the commencement of section 4;

  (d) any object which, when found, is part of the same find as—

      (i) an object within paragraph (a), (b) or (c) found at the same time or earlier; or

      (ii) an object found earlier which would be within paragraph (a) or (b) if it had been found at the same time.

(2) Treasure does not include objects which are—

  (a) unworked natural objects, or

  (b) minerals as extracted from a natural deposit,

or which belong to a class designated under section 2(2).

Meaning of "treasure".

2   c. **24**   *Treasure Act 1996*

Power to alter
meaning.

2.—(1) The Secretary of State may by order, for the purposes of section 1(1)(b), designate any class of object which he considers to be of outstanding historical, archaeological or cultural importance.

(2) The Secretary of State may by order, for the purposes of section 1(2), designate any class of object which (apart from the order) would be treasure.

(3) An order under this section shall be made by statutory instrument.

(4) No order is to be made under this section unless a draft of the order has been laid before Parliament and approved by a resolution of each House.

Supplementary.

3.—(1) This section supplements section 1.

(2) "Coin" includes any metal token which was, or can reasonably be assumed to have been, used or intended for use as or instead of money.

(3) "Precious metal" means gold or silver.

(4) When an object is found, it is part of the same find as another object if—

    (a) they are found together,

    (b) the other object was found earlier in the same place where they had been left together,

    (c) the other object was found earlier in a different place, but they had been left together and had become separated before being found.

(5) If the circumstances in which objects are found can reasonably be taken to indicate that they were together at some time before being found, the objects are to be presumed to have been left together, unless shown not to have been.

(6) An object which can reasonably be taken to be at least a particular age is to be presumed to be at least that age, unless shown not to be.

1995 c. 21.

(7) An object is not treasure if it is wreck within the meaning of Part IX of the Merchant Shipping Act 1995.

Ownership of treasure

Ownership of
treasure which is
found.

4.—(1) When treasure is found, it vests, subject to prior interests and rights—

    (a) in the franchisee, if there is one;

    (b) otherwise, in the Crown.

(2) Prior interests and rights are any which, or which derive from any which—

    (a) were held when the treasure was left where it was found, or

    (b) if the treasure had been moved before being found, were held when it was left where it was before being moved.

(3) If the treasure would have been treasure trove if found before the commencement of this section, neither the Crown nor any franchisee has any interest in it or right over it except in accordance with this Act.

(4) This section applies—

    (a) whatever the nature of the place where the treasure was found, and

    (b) whatever the circumstances in which it was left (including being lost or being left with no intention of recovery).

    5.—(1) The franchisee for any treasure is the person who—   Meaning of "franchisee".

    (a) was, immediately before the commencement of section 4, or

    (b) apart from this Act, as successor in title, would have been,

the franchisee of the Crown in right of treasure trove for the place where the treasure was found.

    (2) It is as franchisees in right of treasure trove that Her Majesty and the Duke of Cornwall are to be treated as having enjoyed the rights to treasure trove which belonged respectively to the Duchy of Lancaster and the Duchy of Cornwall immediately before the commencement of section 4.

    6.—(1) Treasure vesting in the Crown under this Act is to be treated as   Treasure vesting part of the hereditary revenues of the Crown to which section 1 of the   in the Crown. Civil List Act 1952 applies (surrender of hereditary revenues to the   1952 c. 37. Exchequer).

    (2) Any such treasure may be transferred, or otherwise disposed of, in accordance with directions given by the Secretary of State.

    (3) The Crown's title to any such treasure may be disclaimed at any time by the Secretary of State.

    (4) If the Crown's title is disclaimed, the treasure—

    (a) is deemed not to have vested in the Crown under this Act, and

    (b) without prejudice to the interests or rights of others, may be delivered to any person in accordance with the code published under section 11.

Coroners' jurisdiction

    7.—(1) The jurisdiction of coroners which is referred to in section 30 of   Jurisdiction of the Coroners Act 1988 (treasure) is exercisable in relation to anything   coroners. which is treasure for the purposes of this Act.   1988 c. 13.

    (2) That jurisdiction is not exercisable for the purposes of the law relating to treasure trove in relation to anything found after the commencement of section 4.

    (3) The Act of 1988 and anything saved by virtue of section 36(5) of that Act (saving for existing law and practice etc.) has effect subject to this section.

    (4) An inquest held by virtue of this section is to be held without a jury, unless the coroner orders otherwise.

    8.—(1) A person who finds an object which he believes or has   Duty of finder to reasonable grounds for believing is treasure must notify the coroner for   notify coroner. the district in which the object was found before the end of the notice period.

    (2) The notice period is fourteen days beginning with—

    (a) the day after the find; or

    (b) if later, the day on which the finder first believes or has reason to believe the object is treasure.

(3) Any person who fails to comply with subsection (1) is guilty of an offence and liable on summary conviction to—

    (a) imprisonment for a term not exceeding three months;

    (b) a fine of an amount not exceeding level 5 on the standard scale; or

    (c) both.

(4) In proceedings for an offence under this section, it is a defence for the defendant to show that he had, and has continued to have, a reasonable excuse for failing to notify the coroner.

(5) If the office of coroner for a district is vacant, the person acting as coroner for that district is the coroner for the purposes of subsection (1).

Procedure for inquests.

    9.—(1) In this section, "inquest" means an inquest held under section 7.

(2) A coroner proposing to conduct an inquest must notify—

    (a) the British Museum, if his district is in England; or

    (b) the National Museum of Wales, if it is in Wales.

(3) Before conducting the inquest, the coroner must take reasonable steps to notify—

    (a) any person who it appears to him may have found the treasure; and

    (b) any person who, at the time the treasure was found, occupied land which it appears to him may be where it was found.

(4) During the inquest the coroner must take reasonable steps to notify any such person not already notified.

(5) Before or during the inquest, the coroner must take reasonable steps—

    (a) to obtain from any person notified under subsection (3) or (4) the names and addresses of interested persons; and

    (b) to notify any interested person whose name and address he obtains.

(6) The coroner must take reasonable steps to give any interested person notified under subsection (3), (4) or (5) an opportunity to examine witnesses at the inquest.

(7) In subsections (5) and (6), "interested person" means a person who appears to the coroner to be likely to be concerned with the inquest—

    (a) as the finder of the treasure or otherwise involved in the find;

    (b) as the occupier, at the time the treasure was found, of the land where it was found, or

    (c) as having had an interest in that land at that time or since.

Rewards, codes of practice and report

10.—(1) This section applies if treasure—   Rewards.

    (a) has vested in the Crown under section 4; and

    (b) is to be transferred to a museum.

(2) The Secretary of State must determine whether a reward is to be paid by the museum before the transfer.

(3) If the Secretary of State determines that a reward is to be paid, he must also determine, in whatever way he thinks fit—

    (a) the treasure's market value;

    (b) the amount of the reward;

    (c) to whom the reward is to be payable; and

    (d) if it is to be payable to more than one person, how much each is to receive.

(4) The total reward must not exceed the treasure's market value.

(5) The reward may be payable to—

    (a) the finder or any other person involved in the find;

    (b) the occupier of the land at the time of the find;

    (c) any person who had an interest in the land at that time, or has had such an interest at any time since then.

(6) Payment of the reward is not enforceable against a museum or the Secretary of State.

(7) In a determination under this section, the Secretary of State must take into account anything relevant in the code of practice issued under section 11.

(8) This section also applies in relation to treasure which has vested in a franchisee under section 4, if the franchisee makes a request to the Secretary of State that it should.

11.—(1) The Secretary of State must—   Codes of practice.

    (a) prepare a code of practice relating to treasure;

    (b) keep the code under review; and

    (c) revise it when appropriate.

(2) The code must, in particular, set out the principles and practice to be followed by the Secretary of State—

    (a) when considering to whom treasure should be offered;

    (b) when making a determination under section 10; and

    (c) where the Crown's title to treasure is disclaimed.

(3) The code may include guidance for—

    (a) those who search for or find treasure; and

    (b) museums and others who exercise functions in relation to treasure.

(4) Before preparing the code or revising it, the Secretary of State must consult such persons appearing to him to be interested as he thinks appropriate.

6   c. **24**   *Treasure Act 1996*

(5) A copy of the code and of any proposed revision of the code shall be laid before Parliament.

(6) Neither the code nor any revision shall come into force until approved by a resolution of each House of Parliament.

(7) The Secretary of State must publish the code in whatever way he considers appropriate for bringing it to the attention of those interested.

(8) If the Secretary of State considers that different provision should be made for—

(a) England and Wales, and

(b) Northern Ireland,

or that different provision should otherwise be made for treasure found in different areas, he may prepare two or more separate codes.

Report on
operation of Act.

12. As soon as reasonably practicable after each anniversary of the coming into force of this section, the Secretary of State shall lay before Parliament a report on the operation of this Act in the preceding year.

Miscellaneous

Application of Act
to Northern
Ireland.

13. In the application of this Act to Northern Ireland—

(a) in section 7—

1959 c. 15 (N.I.).

(i) in subsection (1), for "section 30 of the Coroners Act 1988" substitute "section 33 of the Coroners Act (Northern Ireland) 1959";

(ii) in subsection (3), for the words from "1988" to "practice etc.)" substitute "1959";

(b) in section 9(2), for the words from "British Museum" to the end substitute "Department of the Environment for Northern Ireland".

Consequential
amendments.

14.—(1) In section 33 of the Coroners Act (Northern Ireland) 1959 (inquest on treasure trove), for "treasure trove" substitute "treasure".

1979 c. 46.

(2) In section 54(3) of the Ancient Monuments and Archaeological Areas Act 1979 (saving for rights in relation to treasure trove) for "in relation to treasure trove" substitute "under the Treasure Act 1996".

S.I. 1995/1625
(NI).

(3) In Article 42 of the Historic Monuments and Archaeological Objects (Northern Ireland) Order 1995 (reporting of archaeological objects)—

(a) after paragraph (10) insert—

"(10A) This Article does not apply in relation to an object if the person who found it believes or has reasonable grounds for believing that the object is treasure within the meaning of the Treasure Act 1996.";

(b) in paragraph (11)(a) for "treasure trove" substitute "any treasure within the meaning of the Treasure Act 1996".

(4) Subsections (2) and (3)(b) have effect in relation to any treasure found after the commencement of section 4.

(5) Subsection (3)(a) has effect in relation to any object found after the commencement of section 8.

15.—(1) This Act may be cited as the Treasure Act 1996.

(2) This Act comes into force on such day as the Secretary of State may by order made by statutory instrument appoint; and different days may be appointed for different purposes.

(3) This Act does not extend to Scotland.

Short title, commencement and extent.

PRINTED IN THE UNITED KINGDOM BY MIKE LYNN
Controller and Chief Executive of Her Majesty's Stationery Office
and Queen's Printer of Acts of Parliament

Appendix D
Case 152/84 *Marshall* v *Southampton and South-West Hampshire Area Health Authority (Teaching)* [1986] ECR 723

Case 152/84

M. H. Marshall

v

Southampton and South-West Hampshire
Area Health Authority (Teaching)

(reference for a preliminary ruling
from the Court of Appeal of England and Wales)

(Equality of treatment for men and women —
Conditions governing dismissal)

Summary

1. *Social policy — Men and women workers — Access to employment and working conditions — Equal treatment — Directive No 76/207 — Article 5 (1) — Dismissal — Concept*
(Council Directive No 76/207, Art. 5 (1)).

2. *Social policy — Men and women workers — Access to employment and working conditions — Equal treatment — Exceptions with regard to social security matters — Exception with regard to pensionable age — Strict interpretation*
(Council Directive No 76/207, Art. 1 (2), and Council Directive No 79/7, Art. 7 (1)(a))

3. *Social policy — Men and women workers — Access to employment and working conditions — Equal treatment — Policy linking entitlement to a State retirement pension and dismissal — Different pensionable age for men and women — Discrimination*
(Council Directive No 76/207, Art. 5 (1))

4. *Measures adopted by the institutions — Directives — Direct effect — Conditions*
(EEC Treaty, Art. 189)

723

5. *Measures adopted by the institutions — Directives — Direct effect — Limits — Not possible to rely upon a directive against an individual*
   (EEC Treaty, Art. 189)

6. *Social policy — Men and women workers — Access to employment and working conditions — Equal treatment — Directive No 76/207 — Article 5 (1) — Effect in relations between the State and individual — State acting as employer*
   (Council Directive No 76/207, Art. 5 (1))

1. The term 'dismissal' contained in Article 5 (1) of Directive No 76/207 must be given a wide meaning; an age limit for the compulsory dismissal of workers pursuant to an employer's general policy concerning retirement falls within the term 'dismissal' construed in that manner, even if the dismissal involves the grant of a retirement pension.

2. In view of the fundamental importance of the principle of equality of treatment for men and women, Article 1 (2) of Directive No 76/207 on the implementation of that principle as regards access to employment and working conditions, which excludes social security matters from the scope of the directive, must be interpreted strictly. It follows that the exception to the prohibition of discrimination on grounds of sex provided for in Article 7 (1)(a) of Directive No 79/7 on the progressive implementation of the principle of equal treatment in matters of social security applies only to the determination of pensionable age for the purposes of granting old-age and retirement pensions and the possible consequences thereof for other benefits.

3. Article 5 (1) of Directive No 76/207 must be interpreted as meaning that a general policy concerning dismissal involving the dismissal of a woman solely because she has attained the qualifying age for a State pension, which age is different under national legislation for men and for women, constitutes discrimination on grounds of sex, contrary to that directive.

4. Wherever the provisions of a directive appear, as far as their subject-matter is concerned, to be unconditional and sufficiently precise, those provisions may be relied upon by an individual against the State where that State fails to implement the directive in national law by the end of the period prescribed or where it fails to implement the directive correctly.

It would in fact be incompatible with the binding nature which Article 189 confers on the directive to hold as a matter of principle that the obligation imposed thereby cannot be relied on by those concerned. Consequently, a Member State which has not adopted the implementing measures required by the directive within the prescribed period may not plead, as against individuals, its own failure to perform the obligations which the directive entails. In that respect the capacity in which the State acts, whether as employer or public authority, is irrelevant. In either case it is necessary to prevent the State from taking advantage of its own failure to comply with Community law.

MARSHALL v SOUTHAMPTON AND SOUTH-WEST HAMPSHIRE AREA HEALTH AUTHORITY

5. According to Article 189 of the EEC Treaty the binding nature of a directive, which constitutes the basis for the possibility of relying on the directive before a national court, exists only in relation to 'each Member State to which it is addressed'. It follows that a directive may not of itself impose obligations on an individual and that a provision of a directive may not be relied upon as such against such a person.

6. Article 5 (1) of Council Directive No 76/207, which prohibits any discrimination on grounds of sex with regard to working conditions, including the conditions governing dismissal, may be relied upon as against a State authority acting in its capacity as employer, in order to avoid the application of any national provision which does not conform to Article 5 (1).

OPINION OF ADVOCATE GENERAL
SIR GORDON SLYNN
delivered on 18 September 1985

My Lords,

This case comes to the Court by way of a reference dated 12 March 1984 for a preliminary ruling under Article 177 of the EEC Treaty by the English Court of Appeal in an action proceeding before that court on appeal from the Employment Appeal Tribunal.

Miss Marshall was born on 4 February 1918. The Southampton and South-West Hampshire Area Health Authority (Teaching) (hereinafter 'the Authority') was at all material times constituted under section 8 (1A) (b) of the National Health Service Act 1977. The Court of Appeal states 'it was accordingly an emanation of

the State'. Miss Marshall worked for the Authority from June 1966 and had a contract of employment with them as Senior Dietician from 23 May 1974 until her dismissal. Since about 1975 the Authority has had a written policy that in general their female employees should retire at the age of 60 and their male employees at the age of 65. Paragraph 1 of this policy states: 'The normal retirement age will be the age at which social security pensions become payable.' The policy was an implied term of Miss Marshall's contract of employment. The Authority is prepared to waive the policy partly or wholly in respect of a particular individual in particular circumstances. It waived its policy partly in the case of Miss Marshall who, if the policy had been applied to her without qualification, would have been dismissed on 4 February 1978, but who in fact was employed until 31 March 1980. On that date the Authority dismissed her. The only reason for the dismissal was that Miss Marshall was a woman who had passed the retiring age applicable to women: the Authority would not have dismissed her when it did had she been a man. At the date of this dismissal, Miss Marshall was able and willing to continue in the employment of the Authority and would, if she had been allowed to do so, have continued in its employment until she had reached the age of 65, i.e. until 4 February 1983. Since she could not go on working, Miss Marshall suffered financial loss, i.e. the difference between what she would have earned in employment with the Authority and her pension. She also lost the satisfaction which she derived from her employment.

At the date of her dismissal, pension legislation in the United Kingdom provided that men were eligible to receive State pensions from the age of 65 and that women were eligible to receive State pensions from the age of 60 (section 27 (1) of the Social Security Act 1975). Where an employee continues in employment, that legislation provides for the deferment of the payment of State pensions. Thus when dismissed, Miss Marshall was entitled to a State pension. She would have been so entitled since the age of 60 had she not remained in employment after reaching that age.

Miss Marshall complains that her dismissal at the date and for the reasons established constituted less favourable treatment by the Authority on the grounds of her sex and accordingly that she has been unlawfully discriminated against contrary to the Sex Discrimination Act 1975 and European Community law. As to the latter she relies in particular on Council Directive 76/207 of 9 February 1976 on the implementation of the principle of equal treatment for men and women as regards access to employment, vocational training and promotion, and working conditions (Official Journal 1976, L 39/40). Both the Industrial Tribunal and the Employment Appeal Tribunal dismissed her claim under the Sex Discrimination Act 1975 on the grounds that the Authority's act was not unlawful because section 6 (4) of the Act excluded from the prohibition of discrimination by an employer on the ground of sex 'provision in relation to death or retirement'. Miss Marshall's claim under EEC law was upheld by the Industrial Tribunal on the ground that her dismissal violated the principle of equal treatment set out in Directive 76/207, in particular Articles 1 (1), 2 (1) and 5 (1) thereof; the Employment Appeal Tribunal, however, dismissed this claim also, on the ground that the violation of the Directive could not be relied on in proceedings before a United Kingdom court or tribunal. Miss Marshall appealed against this decision to the Court of Appeal.

The Court of Appeal has referred the following two questions to the Court:

(1) Whether the Authority's dismissal of Miss Marshall after she had passed her 60th birthday pursuant to the Authority's retirement age policy and on the grounds only that she was a woman who had passed the normal retiring age applicable to women, was an act of discrimination prohibited by Directive 76/207.

MARSHALL v SOUTHAMPTON AND SOUTH-WEST HAMPSHIRE AREA HEALTH AUTHORITY

(2) If the answer to (1) above is in the affirmative, whether or not Directive 76/207 can be relied upon by Miss Marshall in the circumstances of the present case in national courts or tribunals notwithstanding the inconsistency (if any) between the Directive and section 6 (4) of the Sex Discrimination Act 1975.

Miss Marshall and the Commission consider that the first question should be answered in the affirmative, i.e. to the effect that a dismissal in circumstances such as those described is contrary to the Directive, in particular to Article 5 thereof. Reliance is placed on Case 149/77 *Defrenne* v *Sabena* [1978] ECR 1365 ('*Defrenne (No 3)*').

The Authority and the United Kingdom Government, on the other hand, submit that the first question should be answered in the negative. They rely on Article 7 (1) of Council Directive 79/7 of 19 December 1978 on the progressive implementation of the principle of equal treatment for men and women in matters of social security (Official Journal 1979, L 6, p. 24) and on the Court's judgment in Case 19/81 *Burton* v *British Railways Board* [1982] ECR 555.

As to the second question, Miss Marshall and the Commission again agree in submitting that the question should be answered in the affirmative. Miss Marshall argues that in the first instance the national court is under an obligation to interpret national law in such a way as to make it conform to the Directive (see the judgment of the Court of 10 April 1984 in Case 14/83

Von Colson and Kamann v *Land Nordrhein-Westfalen* [1984] ECR 1891, particularly paragraph 26 at p. 1909) and it is only in so far as any inconsistency between national law and Community law cannot be removed by such interpretation that a national court is obliged to declare that inconsistent provisions of national law are inapplicable to the case in question. The Commission asserts that section 6 (4) of the Act as it has been interpreted by the English courts is not compatible with Directive 76/207. Both contend that an individual can rely on the Directive in the circumstances of this case, once the date for the implementation of that Directive (12 August 1978) has passed.

The Authority and the United Kingdom Government both submit that the second question should be answered in the negative. The Authority argues, firstly, that the Directive is neither unconditional nor sufficiently clear and precise to produce direct effects. Secondly, it is said that a directive which has not been implemented cannot be relied on by one private individual against another; and that where the State is acting as an employer, it should be treated in the same way as a private employer. The UK Government makes similar submissions.

Before examining the two questions in general terms, rather than in relation to the specific facts of this case, which it is of course for the national court to decide, it is right to recall that the Court has already held that the elimination of discrimination based on sex forms part of the fundamental rights the observance of which the Court has a duty to ensure (*Defrenne (No 3)*, paragraph 27; and more recently paragraph 13 of the decision in Case 165/82 *Commission* v *United Kingdom* [1983] ECR 3431 at p. 3448, and paragraph 16 of the decision in Joined Cases 75 and 117/82 *Razzouk and Beydoun* v *Commission* [1984] ECR 1509 at p. 1530).

The first question

Directive 76/207 recites the Council's Resolution of 21 January 1974 concerning a social action programme (Official Journal 1974, C 13, p. 1) which included as one of its priorities the undertaking of action to achieve equality between men and women as regards access to employment and vocational training and advancement and as regards working conditions, including pay, and adds that 'equal treatment for male and female workers constitutes one of the objectives of the Community, in so far as the harmonization of living and working conditions while maintaining their improvement are *inter alia* to be furthered'.

The relevant provisions are these:

Article 1 (1)

'The purpose of this Directive is to put into effect in the Member States the principle of equal treatment for men and women as regards access to employment, including promotion, and to vocational training and as regards working conditions and, on the conditions referred to in paragraph 2, social security. This principle is hereinafter referred to as "the principle of equal treatment".'

Article 1 (2)

'With a view to ensuring the progressive implementation of the principle of equal treatment in matters of social security, the Council, acting on a proposal from the Commission, will adopt provisions defining its substance, its scope and the arrangements for its application.'

Article 2 (1)

'For the purposes of the following provisions, the principle of equal treatment shall mean that there shall be no discrimination whatsoever on grounds of sex either directly or indirectly by reference in particular to marital or family status.'

Article 5

'1. Application of the principle of equal treatment with regard to working conditions, including the conditions governing dismissal, means that men and women shall be guaranteed the same conditions without discrimination on grounds of sex.

2. To this end, Member States shall take the measures necessary to ensure that:

(a) ... ;

(b) any provisions contrary to the principle of equal treatment which are included in collective agreements, individual contracts of employment, internal rules of undertakings or in rules governing the independent occupations and professions shall be, or may be declared, null and void or may be amended;

(c) ...'

A provision in a person's contract of employment that in general he or she must retire at a certain age is, in my view, part of that person's 'working conditions, including the conditions governing dismissal'. It means in effect that the employer can terminate the employment at that age, in the absence of a

MARSHALL v SOUTHAMPTON AND SOUTH-WEST HAMPSHIRE AREA HEALTH AUTHORITY

decision to prolong the employment or a practice, under which extensions are normally granted, which is substituted for that term of the contract.

If a different age is provided for men, on the one hand, and women on the other, that is on the face of it a failure to guarantee the same conditions without discrimination on grounds of sex within the meaning of Article 5 (1) of the Directive.

In the present case the normal retiring age, in general, for men was 65, for women 60. The Court of Appeal has accepted that the provision as to 60 for Miss Marshall was an implied term of her contract. It is to be assumed that there would be an implied term in a man's contract that he would continue to 65. The Court of Appeal finds that, even after an extension, she was dismissed because she had passed 60 and that she would not have been dismissed if she had been a man.

On those facts there was *prima facie* a failure to comply with Article 5 (1).

To rebut this, reliance is placed firstly on those parts of Article 1 (1) and (2) of Directive 76/207 which deal with social security. This was plainly a matter to be dealt with by further provisions adopted by the Council.

The only such provisions so far adopted are those of Directive 79/7. The ambit of that Directive is defined in Article 3 (1), which provides:

'This Directive shall apply to:

(a) statutory schemes which provide protection against the following risks:

sickness,

invalidity,

old age,

accidents at work and occupational diseases,

unemployment;

(b) social assistance, in so far as it is intended to supplement or replace the schemes referred to in (a).'

Article 7 of Directive 79/7 provides:

'1. This Directive shall be without prejudice to the right of Member States to exclude from its scope:

(a) the determination of pensionable age for the purposes of granting old-age and retirement pensions and the possible consequences thereof for other benefits;

(b) ...

(c) ...

2. Member States shall periodically examine matters excluded under paragraph 1 in order to ascertain, in the light of social developments in the matter concerned, whether there is justification for maintaining the exclusions concerned.'

It is commonplace that people normally cease work when they become entitled to a pension, either under a social security scheme or under arrangements which, so far as age is concerned, are geared to the social security scheme. There is frequently a factual link between the two. It does not, however, follow that rules as to 'working conditions, including the conditions governing dismissal' have to be on the same footing as rules as to social security entitlement or access to it. A person may not necessarily be liable to be dismissed because he has satisfied the conditions for a pension, including that of reaching a certain age.

In my view, shorn of authority of this Court, Directive 76/207 draws a distinction between conditions governing dismissal and matters of social security, and Directive 79/7 deals only with matters of social security.

Article 7 (1) (a) of the latter does not itself exclude from the principle of equal treatment the determination of pensionable age for the purposes and consequences referred to. It enables Member States to make such exclusions subject to their duty under paragraph (2) of the Article, to review from time to time whether such exclusions continue to be justified. Moreover, the discretion is to determine 'pensionable age' (the age at which entitlement to pension arises) and not 'retirement age', which I take to mean the age at which a person must retire or normally retires. There may thus be continued (or *sed quaere* introduced) only differentials between pensionable ages for men and women 'for the purposes of granting old-age and retirement pensions'.

A provision that a person must cease work at 60 or 65 is not the determination of a pensionable age for the purpose of granting such a pension, even if the one age may coincide with the other. Nor is it the determination of pensionable age for 'the possible consequences thereof for other benefits'. That, as I read it, is dealing with other benefits under State schemes which are geared to the pensionable age fixed by the Member States. The right to continue at work, or to retire, and the liability to be

retired are not 'other benefits' for the purposes of Article 7 (1) (a).

Accordingly, in my opinion, the fixing of an age at which a person must cease work is not the determination of pensionable age for the purposes or consequences referred to in Article 7 (1) (a) of Directive 79/7. That Article accordingly does not exempt from the overriding obligation in Article 5 (1) of Directive 76/207 that discrimination on the grounds of sex, in regard to working conditions, including conditions governing dismissal, are to be prohibited. It does permit discrimination as to the age at which old-age and retirement pensions may be taken. Under these Directives the fact that a woman can take a pension earlier does not involve that she can be retired earlier than a man.

It is said, however, that discrimination between men and women as to the age at which they must retire is permitted as a consequence of the Court's decision in *Burton*.

That case was concerned with access to a voluntary redundancy scheme which was made available to men and women, on the same financial basis, within five years of the normal minimum pensionable age for men and women (namely 65 and 60) under national legislation for social security purposes, so that it was available at 60 and 55 respectively. That age was treated as being the retirement age though there is not, according to the Commission and so far as I am aware, any fixed 'retirement age' in United Kingdom legislation. The Court held on the basis of Article 7 of Directive 79/7 that 'the determination of a minimum pensionable age for social security purposes which is not the same for men as for women does not amount to discrimination prohibited by Community law' (paragraph 14). The difference in the scheme adopted by the employers 'stems from the fact that the minimum pensionable age under the national legislation is not the same for men as for women' (paragraph 15). It was accordingly held not to be discriminatory within the meaning of Directive 76/207.

The fact that access at different ages to benefits in the context of social security is in certain circumstances not discrimination, does not mean, and the Court did not say that it did mean, that different retirement ages which prevent a woman from working as long as a man are not discriminatory. In any event in the present case Miss Marshall was not dismissed at the State pensionable age, and in that respect this case is different from *Burton*. I do not read the judgment in that case as deciding the present issue against the applicant.

Accordingly in my opinion the first question should be answered on the following lines:

For an employer to dismiss a woman employee after she has passed her 60th birthday pursuant to a policy of retiring men at the age of 65 and women at the age of 60 and on the grounds only that she is a woman who has passed the said age of 60 is an act of discrimination prohibited by Article 5 (1) of Directive 76/207.

The second question

Directive 76/207 has not been specifically implemented in the United Kingdom, nor, since the date when it should have been implemented, have the measures prescribed by Article 5 (2) (b) thereof been adopted — i.e. those measures necessary to ensure that any provisions contrary to the principle of equal treatment which are included in individual contracts of employment shall be, or may be declared null and void or may be amended.

If the Sex Discrimination Act 1975 achieved the same result there would, of course, be no problem. Section 6 (2) (b) of that Act provides that 'it is unlawful for a person, in the case of a woman employed by him at an establishment in Great Britain to discriminate against her by dismissing her'. On the face of it that seems, in the present context, capable of producing the same effect as Article 5. Section 6 (4) however, provides that section 6 (2) (b), *inter alia*, does 'not apply to provision in relation to death or retirement'. It has been suggested in this case that the reference to retirement can be read as covering a provision only as to pensionable age within the meaning of Article 7 (1) (a) of Directive 79/7 and, therefore, as not excluding section 6 (2) (b) in respect of ages of termination of employment. The Court of Appeal in *Roberts* v *Cleveland Area Health Authority* [1979] 1 WLR 754, however, decided that provision 'in relation to' retirement means provision 'about' retirement. Per Lord Denning MR 'the phrase . . . is very wide'; per Lawton LJ 'to fix a retiring age is to make a provision in relation to retirement'.

On that basis the Sex Discrimination Act 1975 does not produce a result which satisfies Article 5 of Directive 76/207.

It is clearly not for this Court to construe that section of the Act. It is contended, however, that national courts have a duty to construe domestic legislation in such a way as to be consistent with Community legislation and that the Sex Discrimination Act 1975 can be construed in such a way as to satisfy Article 5 of the Directive. It is clear that in *Roberts* v *Cleveland*, the Court of Appeal did not refer to either of the Directives in issue in the present case, and as far as can be seen was not referred to them. In *Garland* v *British Railway Engineering Limited* [1983] 2 AC 751, at p. 771, Lord Diplock, with whom the other members of the House of Lords concurred, said that, 'it is a principle of construction of United Kingdom statutes, now too well established to call for citation of authority, that the words of the statute passed after the Treaty has been signed and dealing with the subject matter of the international obligation of the United Kingdom, are to be construed, if they are reasonably capable of bearing such a meaning, as intended to carry out the obligation, and not to be inconsistent with it. *A fortiori* is this the case where the Treaty obligation arises under one of the Community Treaties to which section 2 of the European Communities Act 1972 applies'. He expressed the view that if Article 119 of the Treaty had been cited, the Court of Appeal would have construed section 6 (4) of the Sex Discrimination Act 1975 so as not to be inconsistent with it.

That, however, does not cover the present case which is concerned with two Directives made *after* the Sex Discrimination Act 1975 was enacted, one of which should have been implemented seven months before the judgment in *Roberts* v *Cleveland* in 1979, the other of which was adopted three months before that judgment, though the period within which it was to be implemented had not then expired. In paragraph 26 of the Court's judgment in Case 14/83, *Von Colson and Kamann* v *Land Nordrhein-Westfalen*, it was said that, 'the Member States' obligation arising from a directive to achieve the result envisaged by the directive and their duty under Article 5 of the Treaty to take all appropriate measures, whether general or particular, to ensure the fulfilment of that obligation, is binding on all the authorities of Member States including, for matters within their jurisdiction, the courts. It follows that, in applying the national law *and in particular the provisions of a national law specifically introduced in order to implement Directive 76/207*, national courts are required to interpret their national law in the light of the wording and the purpose of the directive in order to achieve the result referred to in the third paragraph of Article 189'.

It is said that the use of the words which I have underlined indicates that even national legislation not specifically introduced in order to implement a directive, including prior legislation, must be, if possible, so construed. The operative part of the judgment is, however, more limited. 'It is for the national court to interpret and apply the legislation *adopted for the implementation of (Directive 76/207)* in conformity with the requirements of Community law, in so far as it is given discretion to do so under national law.'

MARSHALL v SOUTHAMPTON AND SOUTH-WEST HAMPSHIRE AREA HEALTH AUTHORITY

It is thus plain that where legislation is adopted to implement a directive, or consequent upon a Treaty obligation, national courts should seek so far as possible to construe the former in such a way as to comply with the latter. To construe a pre-existing statute of 1975 or even 1875 in order to comply with a subsequent directive, which the legislature or executive has not implemented, in breach of its obligation, when it has a discretion as to the form and method to be adopted, is, in my view, wholly different. I am not satisfied that it is a rule of Community law that national courts have a duty to do so — unless it is clear that the legislation was adopted specifically with ; a proposed directive in mind. It seems to me that it is a matter for the national courts, and subject to the limits imposed on them by domestic rules, as to whether section 6 (4) of the Sex Discrimination Act 1975 is to be construed in such a way that it does in fact comply with the Directive — subject of course to the right of any court to refer questions of Community law to this Court under Article 177 of the Treaty (Case 166/73 *Rheinmühlen-Düsseldorf* v *Einfuhr- und Vorratsstelle Getreide* [1974] ECR 33).

I proceed, therefore, on the basis that the Directive has not been implemented and that the English statute has been construed by the Court of Appeal in such a way that it does not achieve the principle set out in Article 5 (1) of Directive 76/207.

The Court has consistently accepted that if the provisions of a directive are unconditional and sufficiently precise they may not be without effect even if in the absence of implementing measures within the prescribed period.

In the present case the time limit for the implementation of Directive 76/207 expired on 12 August 1978 — before the events in question here. In my opinion the obligation to put into effect the principle of equal treatment - that there should be no discrimination whatever on grounds of sex in respect of the matters specified in Article 1 of the Directive and more particularly with regard to working conditions including the conditions governing dismissal as spelled out in Article 5 — is sufficiently precise as to satisfy the Court's test. It is also in my view unconditional. Article 5 (1) — the overriding obligation in the present context — is in no sense made conditional by the specific obligation to adopt measures, which is imposed on Member States under Article 5 (2).

The question then arises as to whether such a directive can be relied on generally by a citizen falling within its provisions.

In Case 8/81 *Becker* v *Finanzamt Münster-Innenstadt* [1982] ECR 53 at pp. 70-71) the Court said in paragraph 23: 'Particularly in cases in which the Community authorities have, by means of a directive, placed Member States under a duty to adopt a certain course of action, the effectiveness of such a measure would be diminished if persons were prevented from relying upon it in proceedings before a court and national courts were prevented from taking it into consideration as an element of Community law.' If that sentence is taken in isolation it can be argued that the principle is of general application. Paragraph 24 of the Court's judgment, however, is more limited; a Member State 'which has not adopted the implementing measures required by the directive within the prescribed period may

733

not plead as against individuals, its own failure to perform the obligations which the directive entails'.

In paragraph 25 it is said that a directive which satisfies the test to which I have referred 'may . . . be relied upon as against any national provision which is incompatible with the directive *or* in so far as the provisions define rights which individuals are able to assert against the State' (the underlining is mine).

The first of these two alternatives may suggest that ·the right is of general application and that the second alternative is the more specific case of a right asserted against a defaulting State.

In my opinion the decision in *Becker* is to be taken as limited to the situation before the Court — where a litigant was held entitled to say that a Member State could not rely on national provisions kept alive by its own failure to adopt a Community directive which would have conferred rights on the litigant. As against the State in default the litigant could assert those rights.

I remain, despite the arguments in this case and in the case of *Roberts*, of the view expressed in my opinion in *Becker* that a directive not addressed to an individual cannot of itself impose obligations on him. It is, in cases like the present, addressed to Member States and not to the individual. The obligations imposed by such a directive are on the Member States. Such a directive does not have to be notified to the individual and it is only published in the *Official Journal* by way of information — in my

view far too tenuous a link with the individual concerned to create a legal obligation.

Despite the general phrases to which I have referred, I read the Court's judgment as saying implicitly, as I said explicitly, that a directive comes into play *only* to enable rights to be claimed by individuals against the State in default. The State cannot rely on its own failure to confer those rights. The citizen may assert them against the State either as a sword or as a shield.

To give what is called 'horizontal effect' to directives would totally blur the distinction between regulations and directives which the Treaty establishes in Articles 189 and 191. I do not read the Court in *Defrenne (No 3)* as saying the opposite. Mr Advocate General Capotorti's Opinion is relied on to the contrary. It does not, however, consider the distinction between the position of the Member State in default and a private person against whom such a right is asserted. If, which I doubt, he is saying that a directive may be relied on generally even though it has not been implemented, his Opinion is, in my view, overtaken by the decision in *Becker*.

Moreover, it does not follow that because a directive has not been implemented, conflicting national legislation is void. The Court has power only to declare that national law is incompatible with Community law, when national courts are under an obligation not to apply conflicting

MARSHALL v SOUTHAMPTON AND SOUTH-WEST HAMPSHIRE AREA HEALTH AUTHORITY

national provisions (Case 106/76 *Amministrazione delle Finanze dello Stato* v *Simmenthal* [1978] ECR 629), and not declare it void. If the Member State is in default it is for the Commission to proceed under Article 169 of the Treaty.

This raises the question whether the Authority in the present case is to be treated as the State for this purpose, so that the provisions of the Directive can be relied upon against it, since if it is not, Miss Marshall cannot rely on it in national proceedings. What constitutes the 'State' in a particular national legal system must be a matter for the national court to decide. However (even if contrary to the trend of decisions in cases involving sovereign immunity where the exercise of *imperium* is distinguished from commercial and similar activities) as a matter of Community law, where the question of an individual relying upon the provisions of a directive as against the State arises, I consider that the 'State' must be taken broadly, as including all the organs of the State. In matters of employment, which is what Directive 76/207 is concerned with, this means all the employees of such organs and not just the central civil service.

I would, thus, reject the argument put to the Court that a distinction should be drawn between the State as employer and the State in some other capacity. For present purposes

the State is to be treated as indivisible, whichever of its activities is envisaged. It was argued that, where the State is acting as an employer, it should be treated in the same way as a private employer, and that it would be unfair to draw a distinction. I reject that argument. The State can legislate but a private employer cannot. It is precisely because the State can legislate that it can remedy its failure to implement the directive concerned. This consideration puts it at the outset in a fundamentally different position from a private employer, and justifies its being treated differently as regards the right of a person to rely upon the provisions of a directive. The Court has already accepted that in the Community's relations with its officials fundamental principles may be relied on which are not necessarily applicable to other employees *(Razzouk)*. I see no reason why Member States in default in implementing Community rules should not be in an analogous position to that of the Community. If this means that employees of private employers are at a disadvantage compared with State employees, it is for the State, as its duty is to do, to remedy the position by conferring the same advantages upon other employees.

In the present case the United Kingdom asserted in its observations that in terms of United Kingdom constitutional law, health authorities are Crown bodies and their employees, including hospital doctors and nurses and administrative staff, are Crown servants: *(Wood* v *Leeds Area Health Authority* [1974] Industrial Cases Reports 535), even if not civil servants and even if excluded from the Employment Protection (Consolidation) Act 1978. Secondly, the Employment Appeal Tribunal in the decision appealed against in the present proceedings, stated that Miss Marshall was employed by the Authority 'who are agents for the Ministry of Health. In effect therefore her employers were the State'. Finally, in the order for reference the Court of Appeal stated that the Authority was 'an emanation of the State'. If the latter two findings are maintained, it seems to me that Miss Marshall can assert the right she claims against the Authority.

The questions referred to this Court by the Court of Appeal should therefore in my opinion be answered as follows:

(1) For an employer to dismiss a woman employee after she has passed her 60th birthday pursuant to its policy of retiring men at the age of 65 and women at the age of 60 and on the grounds only that she is a woman who has passed the said age of 60 is an act of discrimination prohibited by Article 5 (1) of Directive 76/207.

(2) If national legislation, in this case section 6 (4) of the Sex Discrimination Act 1975 is held by national courts to be inconsistent with Directive 76/207, a person who has been dismissed from his or her employment by a Member State which has failed to implement the Directive, and in breach of Article 5 (1) of the Directive, may rely on the terms of that Article as against that Member State.

The costs of the parties to the main action fall to be dealt with by the national court. The costs incurred by the Government of the United Kingdom and the Commission are not recoverable.

JUDGMENT OF THE COURT
26 February 1986 *

In Case 152/84

REFERENCE to the Court under Article 177 of the EEC Treaty by the Court of Appeal of England and Wales for a preliminary ruling in the proceedings pending before that court between

M. H. Marshall

and

Southampton and South-West Hampshire Area Health Authority (Teaching)

on the interpretation of Council Directive No 76/207/EEC of 9 February 1976 on the implementation of the principle of equal treatment for men and women as regards access to employment, vocational training and promotion, and working conditions (Official Journal 1976, L 39, p. 40),

THE COURT

composed of: Lord Mackenzie Stuart, President, U. Everling and K. Bahlmann (Presidents of Chambers), G. Bosco, T. Koopmans, O. Due and T. F. O'Higgins, Judges,

Advocate General: Sir Gordon Slynn
Registrar: D. Louterman, Administrator

after considering the observations submitted on behalf of

the appellant in the main proceedings, by S. Grosz, Solicitor, and M. Beloff, QC during the written procedure and by M. Beloff, QC, during the oral procedure,

the respondent, by C. H. Brown, Solicitor, Winchester, during the written procedure, and by A. Hillier, Barrister-at-law, during the oral procedure,

* Language of the Case: English.

the United Kingdom, by S. J. Hay, of the Treasury Solicitor's Department, acting as Agent, during the written procedure, and by S. J. Hay and P. Goldsmith, Barrister-at-law, during the oral procedure,

the Commission of the European Communities, by its Principal Legal Adviser, A. Toledano Laredo, and J. R. Currall, a member of its Legal Department, acting as Agents,

after hearing the Opinion of the Advocate General delivered at the sitting on 18 September 1985,

gives the following

JUDGMENT

(The account of the facts and issues which is contained in the complete text of the judgment is not reproduced)

Decision

1 By an order of 12 March 1984, which was received at the Court on 19 June 1984, the Court of Appeal of England and Wales referred to the Court for a preliminary ruling under Article 177 of the EEC Treaty two questions on the interpretation of Council Directive No 76/207/EEC of 9 February 1976 on the implementation of the principle of equal treatment for men and women as regards access to employment, vocational training and promotion, and working conditions (Official Journal 1976, L 39, p. 40).

2 The questions were raised in the course of proceedings between Miss M. H. Marshall (hereinafter referred to as 'the appellant') and Southampton and South-West Hampshire Area Health Authority (Teaching) (hereinafter referred to as 'the respondent') concerning the question whether the appellant's dismissal was in accordance with section 6 (4) of the Sex Discrimination Act 1975 and with Community law.

3 The appellant, who was born on 4 February 1918, was employed by the respondent from June 1966 to 31 March 1980. From 23 May 1974 she worked under a contract of employment as Senior Dietician.

MARSHALL v SOUTHAMPTON AND SOUTH-WEST HAMPSHIRE AREA HEALTH AUTHORITY

On 31 March 1980, that is to say approximately four weeks after she had attained the age of 62, the appellant was dismissed, notwithstanding that she had expressed her willingness to continue in the employment until she reached the age of 65, that is to say until 4 February 1983.

According to the order for reference, the sole reason for the dismissal was the fact that the appellant was a woman who had passed 'the retirement age' applied by the respondent to women.

In that respect it appears from the documents before the Court that the respondent has followed a general policy since 1975 that 'the normal retirement age will be the age at which social security pensions become payable'. The Court of Appeal states that, although that policy was not expressly mentioned in the appellant's contract of employment, it none the less constituted an implied term thereof.

Sections 27 (1) and 28 (1) of the Social Security Act 1975, the United Kingdom legislation governing pensions, provide that State pensions are to be granted to men from the age of 65 and to women from the age of 60. However, the legislation does not impose any obligation to retire at the age at which the State pension becomes payable. Where an employee continues in employment after that age, payment of the State pension or of the pension under an occupational pension scheme is deferred.

However, the respondent was prepared, in its absolute discretion, to waive its general retirement policy in respect of a particular individual in particular circumstances and it did in fact waive that policy in respect of the appellant by employing her for a further two years after she had attained the age of 60.

In view of the fact that she suffered financial loss consisting of the difference between her earnings as an employee of the respondent and her pension and since she had lost the satisfaction she derived from her work, the appellant instituted proceedings against the respondent before an Industrial Tribunal. She contended that her dismissal at the date and for the reason indicated by the respondent constituted discriminatory treatment by the respondent on the ground of sex and, accordingly, unlawful discrimination contrary to the Sex Discrimination Act and Community law.

739

10   The Industrial Tribunal dismissed the appellant's claim in so far as it was based on infringement of the Sex Discrimination Act, since section 6 (4) of that Act permits discrimination on the ground of sex where it arises out of 'provision in relation to retirement'; the Industrial Tribunal took the view that the respondent's general policy constituted such provision. However, the claim that the principle of equality of treatment laid down by Directive No 76/207 had been infringed was upheld by the Industrial Tribunal.

11   On appeal to the Employment Appeal Tribunal that decision was confirmed as regards the first point but was set aside as regards the second point on the ground that, although the dismissal violated the principle of equality of treatment laid down in the aforementioned directive, an individual could not rely upon such violation in proceedings before a United Kingdom court or tribunal.

12   The appellant appealed against that decision to the Court of Appeal. Observing that the respondent was constituted under section 8 (1) A (b) of the National Health Service Act 1977 and was therefore an 'emanation of the State', the Court of Appeal referred the following questions to the Court of Justice for a preliminary ruling:

   '(1) Whether the respondent's dismissal of the appellant after she had passed her 60th birthday pursuant to the policy [followed by the respondent] and on the grounds only that she was a woman who had passed the normal retiring age applicable to women was an act of discrimination prohibited by the Equal Treatment Directive.

   (2) If the answer to (1) above is in the affirmative, whether or not the Equal Treatment Directive can be relied upon by the appellant in the circumstances of the present case in national courts or tribunals notwithstanding the inconsistency (if any) between the directive and section 6 (4) of the Sex Discrimination Act.'

Relevant legal provisions

13   Article 1 (1) of Directive No 76/207 provides as follows:

'The purpose of this directive is to put into effect in the Member States the principle of equal treatment for men and women as regards access to employment, including promotion, and to vocational training and as regards working conditions

MARSHALL v SOUTHAMPTON AND SOUTH-WEST HAMPSHIRE AREA HEALTH AUTHORITY

and, on the conditions referred to in paragraph (2), social security. This principle is hereinafter referred to as "the principle of equal treatment".'

14 Article 2 (1) of the directive provides that:

'... the principle of equal treatment shall mean that there shall be no discrimination whatsoever on grounds of sex either directly or indirectly by reference in particular to marital or family status'.

15 Article 5 (1) of the directive provides that:

'Application of the principle of equal treatment with regard to working conditions, including the conditions governing dismissal, means that men and women shall be guaranteed the same conditions without discrimination on grounds of sex.'

Article 5 (2) thereof provides that:

'To this end, Member States shall take the measures necessary to ensure that:

(a) any laws, regulations and administrative provisions contrary to the principle of equal treatment shall be abolished;

(b) any provisions contrary to the principle of equal treatment which are included in collective agreements, individual contracts of employment, internal rules of undertakings or in rules governing the independent occupations and professions shall be, or may be declared, null and void or may be amended;

(c) those laws, regulations and administrative provisions contrary to the principle of equal treatment when the concern for protection which originally inspired them is no longer well founded shall be revised; and that where similar provisions are included in collective agreements labour and management shall be requested to undertake the desired revision.'

741

16   Article 1 (2) of the directive provides that:

'With a view to ensuring the progressive implementation of the principle of equal treatment in matters of social security, the Council, acting on a proposal from the Commission, will adopt provisions defining its substance, its scope and the arrangements for its application.'

17   Pursuant to the last-mentioned provision, the Council adopted Directive No 79/7/EEC of 19 December 1978 on the progressive implementation of the principle of equal treatment for men and women in matters of social security (Official Journal 1979, L 6, p. 24), which the Member States were to transpose into national law, according to Article 8 (1) thereof, within six years of its notification. The directive applies, according to Article 3 (1) thereof, to:

'(a) statutory schemes which provide protection against the following risks:

sickness,

invalidity,

old age,

accidents at work and occupational diseases,

unemployment;

(b) social assistance, in so far as it is intended to supplement or replace the schemes referred to in (a).'

18   According to Article 7 (1) thereof, the directive is to be:

'without prejudice to the right of Member States to exclude from its scope:

(a) the determination of pensionable age for the purposes of granting old-age and retirement pensions and the possible consequences thereof for other benefits'.
. . .'.

19   With regard to occupational social security schemes, Article 3 (3) of the directive provides that with a view to ensuring implementation of the principle of equal

MARSHALL v SOUTHAMPTON AND SOUTH-WEST HAMPSHIRE AREA HEALTH AUTHORITY

treatment in such schemes 'the Council, acting on a proposal from the Commission, will adopt provisions defining its substance, its scope and the arrangements for its application'. On 5 May 1983 the Commission submitted to the Council a proposal for a directive on the implementation of the principle of equal treatment for men and women in occupational social security schemes (Official Journal 1983, C 134, p. 7). The proposed directive would, according to Article 2 (1) thereof, apply to 'benefits intended to supplement the benefits provided by statutory social security schemes or to replace them'. The Council has not yet responded to that proposal.

20 Observations were submitted to the Court by the United Kingdom and the Commission, in addition to the appellant and the respondent.

The first question

21 By the first question the Court of Appeal seeks to ascertain whether or not Article 5 (1) of Directive No 76/207 must be interpreted as meaning that a general policy concerning dismissal, followed by a State authority, involving the dismissal of a woman solely because she has attained or passed the qualifying age for a State pension, which age is different under national legislation for men and for women, constitutes discrimination on grounds of sex, contrary to that directive.

22 The appellant and the Commission consider that the first question must be answered in the affirmative.

23 According to the appellant, the said age limit falls within the term 'working conditions' within the meaning of Articles 1 (1) and 5 (1) of Directive No 76/207. A wide interpretation of that term is, in her opinion, justified in view of the objective of the EEC Treaty to provide for 'the constant improving of the living and working conditions of [the Member States'] peoples' and in view of the wording of the prohibition of discrimination laid down in the above-mentioned articles of Directive No 76/206 and in Article 7 (1) of Regulation No 1612/68 of the Council of 15 october 1968 on freedom of movement of workers within the Community (Official Journal, English Special Edition 1968 (II), p. 475).

24 The appellant argues furthermore, that the elimination of discrimination on grounds of sex forms part of the *corpus* of fundamental human rights and therefore of the general principles of Community law. In accordance with the case-law of

the European Court of Human Rights, those fundamental principles must be given a wide interpretation and, conversely, any exception thereto, such as the reservation provided for in Article 1 (2) of Directive No 76/207 with regard to social security, must be interpreted strictly.

25   In addition, the appellant considers that the exception provided for in Article 7 (1) of Directive No 79/7 with regard to the determination of pensionable age for the purposes of granting old-age and retirement pensions, is not relevant since, unlike Case 19/81 (*Burton* v *British Railways Board* [1982] ECR 555), this case does not relate to the determination of pensionable age. Moreover, in this case there is no link between the contractual retirement age and the qualifying age for a social security pension.

26   The Commission emphasizes that neither the respondent's employment policy nor the State social security scheme makes retirement compulsory upon a person's reaching pensionable age. On the contrary, the provisions of national legislation take into account the case of continued employment beyond the normal pensionable age. In those circumstances, it would be difficult to justify the dismissal of a woman for reasons based on her sex and age.

27   The Commission also refers to the fact that the Court has recognized that equality of treatment for men and women constitutes a fundamental principle of Community law.

28   The respondent maintains, in contrast, that account must be taken, in accordance with the *Burton* case, of the link which it claims exists between the retirement ages imposed by it in the context of its dismissal policy, on the one hand, and the ages at which retirement and old-age pensions become payable under the State social security scheme in the United Kingdom, on the other. The laying down of different ages for the compulsory termination of a contract of employment merely reflects the minimum ages fixed by that scheme, since a male employee is permitted to continue in employment until the age of 65 precisely because he is not protected by the provision of a State pension before that age, whereas a female employee benefits from such protection from the age of 60.

29   The respondent considers that the provision of a State pension constitutes an aspect of social security and therefore falls within the scope not of Directive No 76/207 but of Directive No 79/7, which reserves to the Member States the right to impose different ages for the purpose of determining entitlement to State pensions. Since the situation is therefore the same as that in the *Burton* case, the fixing by the contract of employment of different retirement ages linked to the different minimum pensionable ages for men and women under national legislation does not constitute unlawful discrimination contrary to Community law.

30   The United Kingdom, which also takes that view, maintains, however, that treatment is capable of being discriminatory even in respect of a period after retirement in so far as the treatment in question arises out of employment or employment continues after the normal contractual retirement age.

31   The United Kingdom maintains, however, that in the circumstances of this case there is no discrimination in working conditions since the difference of treatment derives from the normal retirement age, which in turn is linked to the different minimum ages at which a State pension is payable.

32   The Court observes in the first place that the question of interpretation which has been referred to it does not concern access to a statutory or occupational retirement scheme, that is to say the conditions for payment of an old-age or retirement pension, but the fixing of an age limit with regard to the termination of employment pursuant to a general policy concerning dismissal. The question therefore relates to the conditions governing dismissal and falls to be considered under Directive No 76/207.

33   Article 5 (1) of Directive No 76/207 provides that application of the principle of equal treatment with regard to working conditions, including the conditions governing dismissal, means that men and women are to be guaranteed the same conditions without discrimination on grounds of sex.

34   In its judgment in the *Burton* case the Court has already stated that the term 'dismissal' contained in that provision must be given a wide meaning. Consequently, an age limit for the compulsory dismissal of workers pursuant to an

employer's general policy concerning retirement falls within the term 'dismissal' construed in that manner, even if the dismissal involves the grant of a retirement pension.

35   As the Court emphasized in its judgment in the *Burton* case, Article 7 of Directive No 79/7 expressly provides that the directive does not prejudice the right of Member States to exclude from its scope the determination of pensionable age for the purposes of granting old-age and retirement pensions and the possible consequences thereof for other benefits falling within the statutory social security schemes. The Court thus acknowledged that benefits tied to a national scheme which lays down a different minimum pensionable age for men and women may lie outside the ambit of the aforementioned obligation.

36   However, in view of the fundamental importance of the principle of equality of treatment, which the Court has reaffirmed on numerous occasions, Article 1 (2) of Directive No 76/207, which excludes social security matters from the scope of that directive, must be interpreted strictly. Consequently, the exception to the prohibition of discrimination on grounds of sex provided for in Article 7 (1) (a) of Directive No 79/7 applies only to the determination of pensionable age for the purposes of granting old-age and retirement pensions and the possible consequences thereof for other benefits.

37   In that respect it must be emphasized that, whereas the exception contained in Article 7 of Directive No 79/7 concerns the consequences which pensionable age has for social security benefits, this case is concerned with dismissal within the meaning of Article 5 of Directive No 76/207.

38   Consequently, the answer to the first question referred to the Court by the Court of Appeal must be that Article 5 (1) of Dirctive No 76/207 must be interpreted as meaning that a general policy concerning dismissal involving the dismissal of a woman solely because she has attained the qualifying age for a State pension, which age is different under national legislation for men and for women, constitutes discrimination on grounds of sex, contrary to that directive.

746

The second question

39 Since the first question has been answered in the affirmative, it is necessary to consider whether Article 5 (1) of Directive No 76/207 may be relied upon by an individual before national courts and tribunals.

40 The appellant and the Commission consider that that question must be answered in the affirmative. They contend in particular, with regard to Articles 2 (1) and 5 (1) of Directive No 76/207, that those provisions are sufficiently clear to enable national courts to apply them without legislative intervention by the Member States, at least so far as overt discrimination is concerned.

41 In support of that view, the appellant points out that directives are capable of conferring rights on individuals which may be relied upon directly before the courts of the Member States; national courts are obliged by virtue of the binding nature of a directive, in conjunction with Article 5 of the EEC Treaty, to give effect to the provisions of directives where possible, in particular when construing or applying relevant provisions of national law (judgment of 10 April 1984 in Case 14/83 *von Colson and Kamann* v *Land Nordrhein-Westfalen* [1984] ECR 1891). Where there is any inconsistency between national law and Community law which cannot be removed by means of such a construction, the appellant submits that a national court is obliged to declare that the provision of national law which is inconsistent with the directive is inapplicable.

42 The Commission is of the opinion that the provisions of Article 5 (1) of Directive No 76/207 are sufficiently clear and unconditional to be relied upon before a national court. They may therefore be set up against section 6 (4) of the Sex Discrimination Act, which, according to the decisions of the Court of Appeal, has been extended to the question of compulsory retirement and has therefore become ineffective to prevent dismissals based upon the difference in retirement ages for men and for women.

43 The respondent and the United Kingdom propose, conversely, that the second question should be answered in the negative. They admit that a directive may, in certain specific circumstances, have direct effect as against a Member State in so

747

far as the latter may not rely on its failure to perform its obligations under the directive. However, they maintain that a directive can never impose obligations directly on individuals and that it can only have direct effect against a Member State *qua* public authority and not against a Member State *qua* employer. As an employer a State is no different from a private employer. It would not therefore be proper to put persons employed by the State in a better position than those who are employed by a private employer.

44   With regard to the legal position of the respondent's employees the United Kingdom states that they are in the same position as the employees of a private employer. Although according to United Kingdom constitutional law the health authorities, created by the National Health Service Act 1977, as amended by the Health Services Act 1980 and other legislation, are Crown bodies and their employees are Crown servants, nevertheless the administration of the National Health Service by the health authorities is regarded as being separate from the Government's central administration and its employees are not regarded as civil servants.

45   Finally, both the respondent and the United Kingdom take the view that the provisions of Directive No 76/207 are neither unconditional nor sufficiently clear and precise to give rise to direct effect. The directive provides for a number of possible exceptions, the details of which are to be laid down by the Member States. Furthermore, the wording of Article 5 is quite imprecise and requires the adoption of measures for its implementation.

46   It is necessary to recall that, according to a long line of decisions of the Court (in particular its judgment of 19 January 1982 in Case 8/81 *Becker v Finanzamt Münster-Innenstadt* [1982] ECR 53), wherever the provisions of a directive appear, as far as their subject-matter is concerned, to be unconditional and sufficiently precise, those provisions may be relied upon by an individual against the State where that State fails to implement the directive in national law by the end of the period prescribed or where it fails to implement the directive correctly.

47   That view is based on the consideration that it would be incompatible with the binding nature which Article 189 confers on the directive to hold as a matter of principle that the obligation imposed thereby cannot be relied on by those concerned. From that the Court deduced that a Member State which has not

adopted the implementing measures required by the directive within the prescribed period may not plead, as against individuals, its own failure to perform the obligations which the directive entails.

48   With regard to the argument that a directive may not be relied upon against an individual, it must be emphasized that according to Article 189 of the EEC Treaty the binding nature of a directive, which constitutes the basis for the possibility of relying on the directive before a national court, exists only in relation to 'each Member State to which it is addressed'. It follows that a directive may not of itself impose obligations on an individual and that a provision of a directive may not be relied upon as such against such a person. It must therefore be examined whether, in this case, the respondent must be regarded as having acted as an individual.

49   In that respect it must be pointed out that where a person involved in legal proceedings is able to rely on a directive as against the State he may do so regardless of the capacity in which the latter is acting, whether employer or public authority. In either case it is necessary to prevent the State from taking advantage of its own failure to comply with Community law.

50   It is for the national court to apply those considerations to the circumstances of each case; the Court of Appeal has, however, stated in the order for reference that the respondent, Southampton and South West Hampshire Area Health Authority (Teaching), is a public authority.

51   The argument submitted by the United Kingdom that the possibility of relying on provisions of the directive against the respondent *qua* organ of the State would give rise to an arbitrary and unfair distinction between the rights of State employees and those of private employees does not justify any other conclusion. Such a distinction may easily be avoided if the Member State concerned has correctly implemented the directive in national law.

52   Finally, with regard to the question whether the provision contained in Article 5 (1) of Directive No 76/207, which implements the principle of equality of treatment set out in Article 2 (1) of the directive, may be considered, as far as its

contents are concerned, to be unconditional and sufficiently precise to be relied upon by an individual as against the State, it must be stated that the provision, taken by itself, prohibits any discrimination on grounds of sex with regard to working conditions, including the conditions governing dismissal, in a general manner and in unequivocal terms. The provision is therefore sufficiently precise to be relied on by an individual and to be applied by the national courts.

53   It is necessary to consider next whether the prohibition of discrimination laid down by the directive may be regarded as unconditional, in the light of the exceptions contained therein and of the fact that according to Article 5 (2) thereof the Member States are to take the measures necessary to ensure the application of the principle of equality of treatment in the context of national law.

54   With regard, in the first place, to the reservation contained in Article 1 (2) of Directive No 76/207 concerning the application of the principle of equality of treatment in matters of social security, it must be observed that, although the reservation limits the scope of the directive *ratione materiae*, it does not lay down any condition on the application of that principle in its field of operation and in particular in relation to Article 5 of the directive. Similarly, the exceptions to Directive No 76/207 provided for in Article 2 thereof are not relevant to this case.

55   It follows that Article 5 of Directive No 76/207 does not confer on the Member States the right to limit the application of the principle of equality of treatment in its field of operation or to subject it to conditions and that that provision is sufficiently precise and unconditional to be capable of being relied upon by an individual before a national court in order to avoid the application of any national provision which does not conform to Article 5 (1).

56   Consequently, the answer to the second question must be that Article 5 (1) of Council Directive No 76/207 of 9 February 1976, which prohibits any discrimination on grounds of sex with regard to working conditions, including the conditions governing dismissal, may be relied upon as against a State authority acting in its capacity as employer, in order to avoid the application of any national provision which does not conform to Article 5 (1).

MARSHALL v SOUTHAMPTON AND SOUTH-WEST HAMPSHIRE AREA HEALTH AUTHORITY

Costs

57 The costs incurred by the United Kingdom and the Commission of the European Communities, which have submitted observations to the Court, are not recoverable. As these proceedings are, in so far as the parties to the main proceedings are concerned, in the nature of a step in the action before the national court, the decision as to costs is a matter for that court.

On those grounds,

THE COURT,

in answer to the questions referred to it by the Court of Appeal by an order of 12 March 1984, hereby rules:

(1) Article 5 (1) of Directive No 76/207 must be interpreted as meaning that a general policy concerning dismissal involving the dismissal of a woman solely because she has attained or passed the qualifying age for a State pension, which age is different under national legislation for men and for women, constitutes discrimination on grounds of sex, contrary to that directive.

(2) Article 5 (1) of Council Directive No 76/207 of 9 February 1976, which prohibits any discrimination on grounds of sex with regard to working conditions, including the conditions governing dismissal, may be relied upon as against a State authority acting in its capacity as employer, in order to avoid the application of any national provision which does not conform to Article 5 (1).

Mackenzie Stuart	Everling	Bahlmann
Bosco	Koopmans	Due	O'Higgins

Delivered in open court in Luxembourg on 26 February 1986.

P. Heim   A. J. Mackenzie Stuart

Registrar   President

Index

Suggested Solutions to Past Examination Questions 2001–2002

The Suggested Solutions series provides examples of full answers to the questions regularly set by examiners. Each suggested solution has been broken down into three stages: general comment, skeleton solution and suggested solution. The examination questions included within the text are taken from past examination papers set by the London University. The full opinion answers will undoubtedly assist you with your research and further your understanding and appreciation of the subject in question.

Only £6.95 due November 2003

Company Law
ISBN: 1 85836 519 8

Evidence
ISBN: 1 85836 521 X

Employment Law
ISBN: 1 85836 520 1

Family Law
ISBN: 1 85836 525 2

European Union Law
ISBN: 1 85836 524 4

For further information on contents or to place an order, please contact:

Mail Order
Old Bailey Press
at Holborn College
Woolwich Road
Charlton
London
SE7 8LN

Telephone No: 020 8317 6039
Fax No: 020 8317 6004
Website: www.oldbaileypress.co.uk

Old Bailey Press

The Old Bailey Press integrated student law library is tailor-made to help you at every stage of your studies from the preliminaries of each subject through to the final examination. The series of Textbooks, Revision WorkBooks, 150 Leading Cases and Cracknell's Statutes are interrelated to provide you with a comprehensive set of study materials.

You can buy Old Bailey Press books from your University Bookshop, your local Bookshop, direct using this form, or you can order a free catalogue of our titles from the address shown overleaf.

The following subjects each have a Textbook, 150 Leading Cases/Casebook, Revision WorkBook and Cracknell's Statutes unless otherwise stated.

Administrative Law
Commercial Law
Company Law
Conflict of Laws
Constitutional Law
Conveyancing (Textbook and 150 Leading Cases)
Criminal Law
Criminology (Textbook and Sourcebook)
Employment Law (Textbook and Cracknell's Statutes)
English and European Legal Systems
Equity and Trusts
Evidence
Family Law
Jurisprudence: The Philosophy of Law (Textbook, Sourcebook and
    Revision WorkBook)
Land: The Law of Real Property
Law of International Trade
Law of the European Union
Legal Skills and System
    (Textbook)
Obligations: Contract Law
Obligations: The Law of Tort
Public International Law
Revenue Law (Textbook,
    Revision WorkBook and
    Cracknell's Statutes)
Succession

Mail order prices:	
Textbook	£15.95
150 Leading Cases	£11.95
Revision WorkBook	£9.95
Cracknell's Statutes	£11.95
Suggested Solutions 1999–2000	£6.95
Suggested Solutions 2000–2001	£6.95
Suggested Solutions 2001–2002	£6.95
Law Update 2003	£10.95
Law Update 2004	£10.95

Please note details and prices are subject to alteration.

To complete your order, please fill in the form below:

Module	Books required	Quantity	Price	Cost
		Postage		
		TOTAL		

For Europe, add 15% postage and packing (£20 maximum).

For the rest of the world, add 40% for airmail.

ORDERING

By telephone to Mail Order at 020 8317 6039, with your credit card to hand.

By fax to 020 8317 6004 (giving your credit card details).

Website: www.oldbaileypress.co.uk

By post to: Mail Order, Old Bailey Press at Holborn College, Woolwich Road, Charlton, London, SE7 8LN.

When ordering by post, please enclose full payment by cheque or banker's draft, or complete the credit card details below. You may also order a free catalogue of our complete range of titles from this address.

We aim to despatch your books within 3 working days of receiving your order.

Name

Address

Postcode   Telephone

Total value of order, including postage: £

I enclose a cheque/banker's draft for the above sum, or

charge my   ☐ Access/Mastercard   ☐ Visa   ☐ American Express

Card number

☐☐☐☐ ☐☐☐☐ ☐☐☐☐ ☐☐☐☐

Expiry date   ☐☐☐☐

Signature: ....Date: ....